PHILLIMON ZONG

THE GIFT OF OBSTACLES

A Memoir of Grit, Grace and Gratitude

First published in 2022 by Phillimon Zongo
Copyright © 2022 Phillimon Zongo
Th e moral rights of the author have been asserted.

ISBN: 978-0-6453891-1-1 (Paperback)
ISBN: 978-0-6453891-0-4 (Ebook)

Produced by Phillimon Zongo — www.philzongo.com
Cover design by Theo Wasserberg
Chapter illustrations by Ivi Olszewska
Layout and typesett ing by WorkingType Studio

All of the events in this memoir are true to the best of the author's memory. It refl ects the author's present recollections of experiences over time. Some timelines have been condensed and dialogue recreated from memory. Most names and identifying characteristics have been changed to protect the identity of certain parties and to avoid hurting anyone.

NATIONAL LIBRARY OF AUSTRALIA

A catalogue record for this book is available from the National Library of Australia

CONTENTS

PROLOGUE

Savannah Grasslands

The first day I drove my father's cattle into the savannah plains, I was as fragile as a baby gazelle. But the long and exacting savannah days quickly schooled me to be a man. By my early teens, I was already ancient with trials and tougher than the Tasmanian devil. For years, I followed a steady and tedious daily routine. I rose in the predawn darkness to dig out deep-rooted weeds from our cornfields before running to school barefooted or driving twenty head of my father's cattle deep into the savannah grasslands. Herding cattle was a dreary chore, but it was unavoidable as I was the youngest boy.

Those years I steered my father's cattle across the savannah changed me and marked me deeply.

I quickly morphed into a thick-skinned herder, a necessity to survive the frequent fights. Big boys arranged bare-knuckled bouts to entertain themselves or to claim bragging rights when their younger brothers pummelled opponents from other villages. I was never the violent type, but no one was exempt from these vicious brawls.

My last savannah fight was in the summer of 1991, when I was eleven years old, against a boy a year older than me from Chipfuwa village, who bore a striking resemblance to Shrek. People mocked his looks but he was definitely good at something. Nduna was a ferocious hand-to-hand combatant who could relentlessly absorb blows.

Nduna's older brother set off the brawl. Malume was one of the most notorious instigators of savannah bouts. He was short but had the musculature of a boy born to fight. One of his legs had been amputated when he was young but none of the herders knew why or exactly when. Someone else might have given up but Malume beat tremendous odds, refusing to let his physical disability define him. In a valley of young warriors, he was the gutsiest of them all. A pit bull of a youngster, he unquestionably had all his able-bodied peers cowed, and hobbled on his crutches after his herd all day long. I never heard him complain.

'Phidza, word is spreading around the grasslands that you think you can beat Nduna. Show us what you've got, man.'

Malume cut straight to the chase as he struggled to bend over and mould two little sandhills, roughly the same size, next to one another. The sandhill to the left represented Nduna's mother's breast, the one to the right, my mum's. According to a savannah code that predated us all, demolishing an adversary's mum's sand boob was the highest form of insult. It was like saying, *Dude, you are the lame duck that you are because of the skim milk you sucked from your mother's breast.* You only dared take up the challenge if you thought you could kick your adversary's backside. Otherwise, you squeezed your tail between your legs and simply walked away.

Screw that, I thought to myself. My heart pounded faster than a V8 engine but I didn't let it show. I didn't want to shame Lancelot, my older brother, and my allies. Savannah bouts were a long-standing tradition for budding toughs to test their prowess and gain standing as 'real' men. Nduna had built a reputation with these fights that I had set my mind on destroying.

I kicked over the left sand boob. Herders totting *sjamboks,* whips made of cowhide or msasa bark, booed Nduna. Some clapped their hands in awe of me; others whistled. I had crossed the Rubicon. I never instigated fights, but arranged bouts were not new to me. I had recently dismantled a boy called Tinarwo. He was much taller but severely lacking in confidence, so comparing him to Nduna would be stupid. Something like beating Bolton Wanderers at soccer and then deluding yourself that next you can beat Real Madrid. Nduna wasn't Tinarwo: even older boys feared him.

Word had spread that Nduna's father rubbed mangoromera into razor cuts made on his son's wrists, chest and forehead: a potent *muti,* or traditional medicine, supplied by Malawian farm labourers. This was believed to summon magical powers during bouts and a boundless appetite for combat. Nduna was a gifted fighter *anyway* with no known defeats. His bouts were few and far between because no one had the courage to challenge him.

Amid the hysteria, boys from Chimera, a polygamous village across the river, near to my homestead, started chanting. They sided with me and detested Nduna.

'Phidza, Phidza, Phidza-aaaaaaaa!'

If there had been bookmakers in the savannah, my odds of defeating Nduna would have been long — a village version of the

Buster Douglas versus Mike Tyson professional boxing match the previous year.

If I can pull this off, I will leapfrog everyone to become the toughest youngster across the savannah, I naively got ahead of myself.

The jeers were deafening. Nduna saw the destruction of his mum's sand boob and leapt at me, his eyes squinting in rage. I bounced backwards in self-defence, lifting my left arm in anticipation of a right jab. A terrible miscalculation: Nduna was a left-handed monster. He landed a savage hook on my jaw and I lost my balance. I saw stars. As I staggered back, Nduna vaulted high, striking me with an open foot on the chest, a ferocious kick known as a *zhaba*. I fell heavily on my back onto the dust. As Nduna jumped and was about to finish me off, Malume restrained him — ironically, he had become my redeemer.

The spectators were left hungry for more action but I was relieved the fight had ended quickly and got to my feet. But not so fast: the episode had started with fake boobs and would only end with fake boobs. Malume remoulded the little sandhills and gestured to me to dare Nduna again.

In dead silence, the herders moved their eyes slowly between me and the pair of sand boobs. Younger boys, fearing Malume would pick them next, dropped their faces. Nduna stared at me with hate-filled eyes, as if saying, *Now you know, little villain!* He didn't blink. I looked at his clenched fists, thinking he might be wearing a knuckleduster. No, Nduna had smashed me with a bare fist. Forget the finishing *zhaba*, that left hook alone had shattered my confidence.

Mike Tyson was right to say that everyone has a plan until they are hit in the mouth. I also had a solid strategy. I anticipated an orthodox fight that would start slowly and gradually escalate as we sized each other up. During those early, less heated moments, I would break

Nduna's nose with a vicious headbutt, followed by a torrent of upper-cuts. Up to this day, that plan remains just a plan.

I dropped my head slightly and shook it vigorously. From hero to zero in a flash, just like that. The crowd, whistling wildly in my favour a minute ago, booed. Other young toughs, sensing my vulnerability, walked over to my mum's sand boob and ripped into it. Malume hobbled over to Nduna and gave him a pat on the shoulder.

'Good job, Shava Vhuramayi!' he said, praising him using their ancient totem, the mighty eland.

Lancelot couldn't look me in the eye. The shame my brother felt was beyond the world. That stuff they tell you on TV not to try at home, happened to me in less than a minute. Nduna had beaten me decisively. The deeply humiliating experience induced lasting caution in me and a reverence for the famed mangoromera. We never told anyone at home. I nursed my pain for weeks until it eventually subsided on its own. There were no antibiotics, ice blocks, or blenderised foods in the savannah.

As we walked away, I noticed the herders chasing their wandering livestock in various directions, and I felt the warm air rising from the scorched, barren earth. The dreary, moody cumulonimbus, king of the clouds, billowed high from the horizon like a giant, dark mushroom. Without much warning, the azure savannah sky filled, replete with heavy rain, dazzling lightning, and ferocious thunder.

Lancelot and I quickly rounded up our cows into the kraal and ducked for cover inside our mud-brick hut. We always had one troublesome cow that sneaked out of the herd, or worse, broke through the kraal's wooden barriers during the night. Our bad boy was Bantam, a stocky young bull. My father always called any calf with black-and-white dotted hide Bantam, but he doesn't remember why.

I relished Bantam's willingness for bullfights. He started most of these brawls of his own volition, kicking dust into the air and bellowing with fury if another bull encroached into his territory. I felt like Bantam's victories were my own — they filled me with a deep sense of pride. It was a consolation of sorts: if I couldn't beat Nduna, at least Bantam could trounce one of their bulls.

But he could be a nasty piece of work. His excessive libido created a litany of problems. He roamed around the savannah, sniffing cows in search of one on heat, hardly grazed. Or he used brute force to break into neighbours' kraals and cornfields.

Lancelot and I had a way to harness this playboy. Before shutting the kraal, we squeezed through the standing herd, got hold of Bantam's curly horn, and tied him to a giant corner pole using a strong rope made of cowhide. There he would stay, subdued all night, simmering with desire. Whenever anyone refers to their philandering partner as 'an animal', they take me back to the Bantam era.

That evening, however, overwhelmed by the heavy rain, we dashed into our hut without securing Bantam to his pole. We forgot to tell Baba of this blunder. The bad boy lived up to his reputation. Bantam forced his way through the old barricades, creating free passage for the entire herd to walk out and destroy a large portion of our ripe maize crop.

This pushed Baba too far; finally, he had had enough of Bantam. Early the next day, as the sky transformed into radiant gold, Baba summoned Lancelot and me to the kraal. He threw a leather rope around Bantam's neck and dragged him out of the kraal through the sticky knee-deep dung. He tied the bad boy to a giant gum tree and secured his legs with leather rope.

Bantam couldn't move. Baba and Lancelot vigorously pulled on their two ropes in perfect accord, sending the unsuspecting bull tumbling. *Mooooo!* the young troublemaker roared as his fat tummy banged on the dusty ground. The cows stuck close to each other in apprehension. Starving calves cried for milk from their enclosures, oblivious of their father's misery.

The worst was yet to come for Bantam. Baba looked completely unconcerned. He quickly pulled a set of green and silver pliers out of the pocket of his oversized grey overalls and snipped Bantam's balls. The bull mooed in agony, sending chills down my spine. It was game over for Bantam, the end of his dynasty.

Bantam was just reacting to forces of nature but nonetheless, that got him into trouble. His predicament reminded me of the words of Mr Mamvura, my grade three teacher. He constantly warned us, *Do not trouble until trouble troubles you!* Bantam became docile and lost his will to fight. We eventually released him from captivity since he had utterly lost his desire to mate.

CHAPTER 1

Village Life

I was born in May 1980, a month after the Union Jack was lowered for the last time and the five-coloured Zimbabwean flag raised, symbolising the end of almost a century of white minority rule. That makes me one of the 'born frees'.

I am the sixth of nine children and the youngest of three boys. My parents, Philip Zongo, born 1942, and Helena Mugavazi, born 1952, were traditionally married in 1967. My siblings are Osward Boza, born 1967; Viola Shonhiwa, born 1970; Cecilia Shonhiwa, born 1972; Maidei Zongo, born 1974; Lancelot Zongo, born 1976; Rosemary

Zongo, born 1978; Letwina Zongo, born 1983; and Salome Zongo, born 1985. Another baby girl, unfortunately, died soon after birth, in 1973. My parents named their next child Maidei, which means 'what did you want?' They strongly believed witches had a hand in their loss.

My mother had another son, Martin Mugavazi, born 1964, before she was married to my father. She was barely thirteen years old at the time of his birth. Big brother Martin, as we called him, stayed with my maternal grandmother, about twelve kilometres north of our homestead, and visited us on occasional weekends.

I grew up in Gonzo village in Mhondoro under the Rwizi chieftainship. Gonzo means 'rat', while Rwizi means 'river'. These communal, subsistence lands are tucked approximately 150 kilometres southwest of Harare, the Zimbabwean capital.

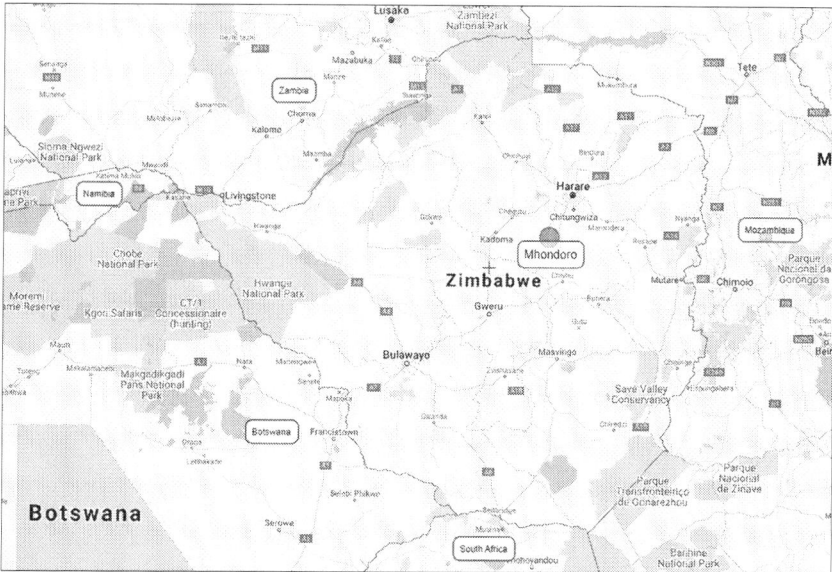

My paternal grandfather's name was Shonhiwa. White farmers named him Boza, which means 'constant wanderer'. He drifted from farm to farm as a labourer and the nickname stuck. Shonhiwa's father was Zongo, the son of Rugowo. The nine of us children ended up using three different surnames, due to unexplained administrative mix-ups at the birth registry office, but we are of the same blood.

We lived in clusters comprising several mud-brick houses. The majority of these houses typically had mud-plastered floors and grass-thatched roofs. Well-off families had houses with asbestos or zinc roofs and cement floors. Our homestead was set up just a kilometre from my school, Gavaza Primary School, and concealed within dense mususu, silver terminalia trees. It consisted of three round huts made of orange fire-roasted mud-bricks, all thatched with light-brown savannah grass. Each hut was a single room with tiny airings the size of a small brick. We called these windows. We stuffed old clothes into these ventilations before retiring to bed, fearing an owl would creep in at night and scare the hell out of us. The huts had uneven mud floors, plastered with hardened clay. During summer, my mother or one of my sisters crushed pee leaves and painted the floors green.

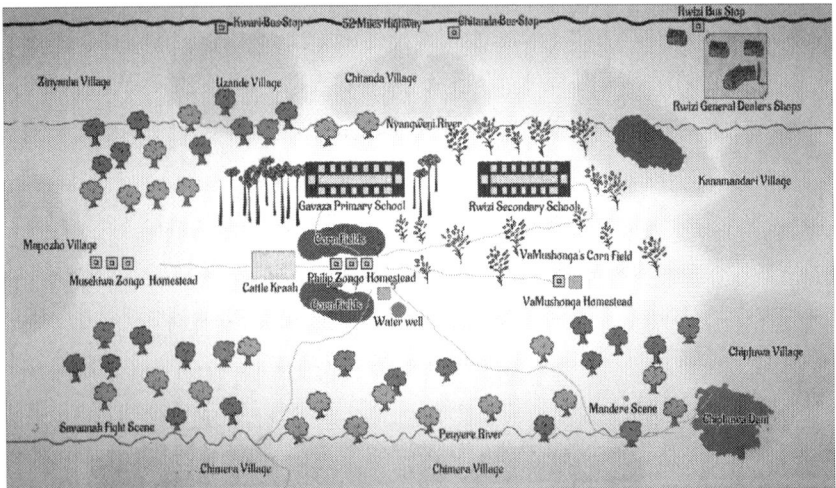

Our huts were arranged in a line and named after their purpose or location. They faced west to shield us from the frequent dust storms in spring, which almost always blew from the east. The main hut was the kitchen with a central hollow that acted as the fireplace. It also served as my sisters' bedroom and for any female guests. My mother or one of my sisters cooked on the stove, a rack of metal bars suspended over the cavernous fireplace. The clay shelves on the kitchen walls were always nicely decorated with brightly coloured metal plates, cups and pots. A mud bench, about fifty centimetres high, ran around one side of the kitchen. Men sat on the bench, while women sat on mats made of dried reeds or goat hides placed on the floor. Each hut had a make-shift wooden door, secured to the wall with rusty wire.

Next was my parents' bedroom, *imba yepakati*, or simply 'middle hut'. Then the end hut, *imba yekunze*. It served as a bedroom for boys and male visitors. Our *hozi*, or granary, was next to it, an elevated wooden cabin compartmentalised to store dried corn, shelled ground-nuts, sorghum, and millet. My father also kept in there his *pfumo* (a long, sharp spear), his *gano* (a battleaxe) and other items used during traditional rituals. The granary had no ventilation; its dark-ness and secrecy terrified me but there was no way around it. My older brother Lancelot shoved me into the pitch-black cubicles to collect the residual produce — I was the only boy small enough to fit through the tiny entrances.

Prolific mango trees grew in front of our huts. In the summer, their branches would sway with giant mangoes, which we sold to the local school teachers and other villagers. We had several fields surround-ing our homestead, approximately one acre each, where we grew the maize, groundnuts, sorghum and millet. Using a giant tin tied to a rope, we drew water to cook, drink or wash clothes from a twenty-metre deep open well, situated about two hundred metres away. The well was a sanctuary for huge bullfrogs, which we trapped with the tin and set free. Random villagers walking long distances stopped by our well to quench their thirst.

The kraal was about three hundred metres north of the huts, a rectangular enclosure of wooden protective barriers that housed our herd overnight and during storms. VaMushonga, my paternal grandmother, lived close by. Her name means 'medicine'. She lived a simple life, owning a granary and one hut that served as a kitchen, bedroom and guesthouse.

*   *   *

My mother, Helena Mugavazi, is a kind and strong woman. She was born into the tightly bonded and polygamous family of the Nhari Nyandoro totem, the majestic elephant. Biri and Ganyire were the original Nyandoros, brother and sister respectively, and renowned spirit mediums. They came to prominence when they descended on the mighty Zambezi Valley of Nyatsimba Mutota (Mwenemutapa) dynasty from the famed Great Zimbabwe. Nyandoros acted as respected advisors to Mutapa kings in the ancient city.[1]

Nyandoro people lived in Dande, along the Zambezi Valley, Northern Zimbabwe, from the tenth to the eleventh century. In their ancient poem of praise, the Nyandoros are referred to as 'the kings of kings', 'the thicket of thorns', those that crossed the raging Zambezi River in broad daylight, among other rich lyrical venerations. The Zambezi Valley was then the epicentre of Arab and Portuguese trade, which resulted in interracial marriages. Thus the Nyandoros are also referred to as 'vazungu vedande' in praise poems, the light-skinned people of Dande.

Over time, my mother's ancestors voyaged across Zimbabwe and eventually settled in Mhondoro, under Mashayamombe chieftainship.

The Mashayamombes are of the Impala totem and referred to as Mbuya Chikonamombe in their praise poem. They still control large swathes of land in Mhondoro.

My maternal grandfather, Mugavazi, was a wealthy man by rural standards. He was one of the first black school teachers during the colonial era. Mugavazi owned a large herd of fattened cows. He married his first wife in the early twentieth century and they had seven children. This wife's younger sister, Rebecca, routinely visited her. She was a tall, slender, and curvaceous African goddess. Mugavazi couldn't resist Rebecca's charm. The two fell in love and within a short time, Mugavazi sent a delegation, with a herd of cows, to Rebecca's family, locking her in as his second wife. Polygamy was deeply embedded in Shona culture but marrying two sisters was still an extraordinary act. My grandfather's younger wife gave birth to nine more children, including my mother, bringing his tally to sixteen in total.

I was perplexed that my two grandmas, one of whom had stolen the other's husband, had maintained such a loving and unbreakable relationship for decades. Their lives resembled the opposite of traditional polygamy, which was often punctuated with hate, love portions, gossip, and even physical tussles. My grandmas sat next to each other on traditional mats of interwoven dried reed, cracking nuts, peeling maize corn, or just talking for hours. Young grandma read an old Shona Bible as old grandma listened carefully and intently. If one of them slaughtered a chicken, a rare savannah treat, she cut off half and hobbled with it to her sister's homestead. They travelled together by donkey cart when they visited us.

We referred to them as 'young grandma' and 'old grandma'. Without context, this naming convention confused me because, by my early teens, young grandma was already in her eighties. Even when her older sister eventually passed on, we kept referring to Rebecca as young grandma. How my grandfather managed to enchant two sisters, and keep them so tight for more than five decades, remains a mystery.

*   *   *

My mother was an indomitable woman. Her life was defined by a fierce commitment to feed her children and give us access to education — toiling day in and day out in other people's fields, often with a baby tied on her back. No matter how uncertain our food supplies, my mother always went out of her way to share the little we had with visitors and fellow villagers. She joined several old maize sacks together to craft makeshift blankets, so we didn't have to sleep directly on the dusty floors. She improvised raincoats for me using empty fertilizer bags. I hated smelling like urea but this was quickly washed away when driving cattle in the rain. We had no money to buy tea so my mother burnt sugar on a metal plate instead. When the sugar turned black, she mixed it with water, giving it the appearance of black tea. We squeezed oil out of peanut butter to moisturize our faces.

During summer, my mother boiled heaps of pea and pumpkin leaves before drying them slowly under the scorching savannah sun. Once the leaves dried, she packed them into *mufushwa*, long-life dried vegetables, and stored them in the granary. My mother was a woman of foresight. She did her best to insulate us from rainy days. If my brother and I returned from a hunting or fishing trip empty-handed, my brother would shove me into the granary to retrieve a pack of *mufushwa*. It was bitter and always our last resort. And despite how much my mother prepared, the *mufushwa* eventually ran out.

Then she turned to plan C. She would fill a metal bowl with cold water, throw in a few pieces of rock salt, and stir it vigorously with her middle finger, occasionally testing to check if it had become 'salty enough'. That salt and water solution is called *nhanhamuto*, which means 'baby soup'. If a respected villager showed up unexpectedly, we'd push the *nhanhamuto* aside and pretend we had finished eating. Despite my strong aversion to baby soup, I had to stomach it because often that's all we could afford. Sometimes, when we had no matches to light a fire, my mother would send me to a nearby homestead to fetch burning coals on a sheet of metal. I ran as fast as I could back to the kitchen before the metal sheet heated to an intolerable temperature. If it did, I just dropped it and repeated the routine.

*   *   *

In the evenings, once we secured the kraal, Lancelot and I would dash into the kitchen. We'd sit around the fire, whose orange and blue glow illuminated the hut. My mother or one of my older sisters prepared sadza, a filling meal and staple diet across several African countries. Sadza is straightforward to make: all you need is boiling water, mealie meal or maize flour, and strong arms to stir the boiling porridge until it thickens to taste. Generally, Zimbabwean women prefer softer sadza, and rural men like it very solid, called *chidhinha*, which means 'hard as a brick'. The majority of rural Zimbabweans eat nothing else besides sadza — for breakfast, lunch, and dinner, all year round.

Snobs prefer to eat sadza using a knife and fork but that's less than half the experience. Sadza is best eaten using bare hands. Shovel as much as you think you can swallow in one go. Mould the soft lump into an egg shape, dig a hole using your thumb, then scoop in whatever accompanying dish. Sadza is an acquired taste, not good by itself, so you always combine it with another delicacy, such as fried vegetables, fermented milk, or beef curry. *If you eat well-simmered sadza, with dried golden mice roasted in paprika sauce, you will forget your mother-in-law's name,* my cousin Shonhiwa, better known as Shons, proclaimed.

My brother Lancelot is left-handed but my parents forced the habit of eating sadza with his right hand from a young age. *If you eat with your left hand, you will insult the ancestors that bless the harvest, and invoke terrible misfortune upon the entire family,* my mother screamed at him, until eating with his right hand was deeply wired in his subconscious. Lancelot wrote superbly and could accurately throw down a dove with his left hand. But he always ate with his right hand.

A giant black pot of thick sadza porridge was cooking, steaming the kitchen, and the smell of boiled pumpkin leaves with peanut butter hung in the air. My father, Baba, was a masterful storyteller gifted with a wicked sense of humour. He treated us to fascinating tales of our family, the history of the Shona people, and numerous hunting escapades. I forgot my grumbling stomach, momentarily carried into a magical realm.

Baba sat on an aged wobbly stool as we gathered attentively around him on the floor. My mother was busy with the pots. She pushed a giant metal dish of dried groundnuts to us so we could crack them as Baba narrated. Baba inhaled two heavy doses of *bute* (snuff), two per nostril, the dark brown powder made from pulverised tobacco leaves. The swift hit of nicotine led to big sneezes and tears down his cheeks. I was soon fascinated by Baba's personal journey, which he narrated with extraordinary passion.

During the mid-1960s, I left Harare for Wenera to look for a job in the South African gold mines. Wenera was the Shona version of the acronym WNLA, which stands for the Witwatersrand Native Labour Association — the recruiting body of the South African Chamber of Mines during the apartheid era. Over time, Zimbabweans started referring to South Africa simply as Wenera.

I stopped over at Sandawana, an emerald mine in Matabeleland South, to look for a temporary job as a labourer. The Second Chimurenga, the liberation struggle that eventually broke the century-old British subjugation of our people, was already in full steam. My rugged appearance aroused the white man's suspicion.

As Baba's narrative approached its climax, my mother screamed to one of my sisters.

'Maidei, the sadza has been boiling forever. Do you think we will have that same repetitive story for dinner?'

My mother had heard this one dozens of times but Baba was impassive to her diss. Maidei swiftly wrapped a traditional multicoloured apron, called a *zambia*, around her waist and started pounding the sadza into a creamy paste using a *mugoti*, a wooden cooking stick. My father paused to snort more *bute*. Sensing this, I whispered to Lancelot, 'May you please escort me outside for a pee?' My brother obliged and tiptoed with me into the pitch-dark adjacent field. I relieved myself and we ducked back to the kitchen.

Once Maidei handed the steaming sadza to my mother to dish out, Baba asked, 'Where was I with the story?' 'Somabhula!' I shouted back with excitement.

'Ah, okay!' Baba continued.

After detailed inspection by Sandawana's security guards, the white man summoned me to his office. 'Can you tell me, one by one, which towns lie between Sandawana and Salisbury [now Harare]?' he quizzed, with a concentrated gaze.

'Umm, Belingwe, Chegato, Shabani, Gwelo, Kwekwe, Gatoma, Hartley, Sinoia and Norton,' I thoughtfully responded.

'So, how the heck did you fail to find a job in all those towns and end up here, in Sandawana? You are a mujibha *[an informant] sent by Mashona fighters from Salisbury to infiltrate my mine!' Before I could even respond,*

he escorted me to the kitchen, and instructed his African cooks to 'feed this Trojan and usher it out of my premises.'

That's when I decided to risk it all and proceed to Wenera. I crossed the Mwenezi River and hitchhiked to Beitbridge. I saw successive large road signs inscribed 'Transvaal/Johannesburg'. But the night before I crossed the mighty Limpopo River, Mukwewo, my late grandmother, cautioned me in a dream to ditch the treacherous mission. I took heed, aborted my Wenera dream, and returned to Harare.

'If it wasn't for your caring and omnipresent ancestors, none of you would have been born,' Baba concluded with unwavering conviction.

He inhaled another good portion of *bute* and sneezed heavily. We all washed hands before indulging in our sadza. Baba started to sing his favourite chorus.

Oh, my darling, oh my darling. Oh, my darling, Clementine,
You were lost and gone forever, dreadful sorrow, Clementine.
In a cavern, in a canyon, excavating for a mine.
Lived a miner, forty-niner, and his daughter Clementine.

I was astonished that Baba, a barely educated communal farmer, perfectly recalled lyrics of this classic word for word.

'This old man is always reminiscing about some ex-girlfriend whom no one knows about,' my older brother Osward said, laughing this mystery away.

*   *   *

Our family history was passed on to Baba, through oral tradition, from previous generations.

We are descendants of the Mutasa dynasty, a powerful chieftainship located in Manicaland, a province of jagged mountains, deep valleys, and breathtaking streams bordering Zimbabwe and Mozambique.

Our forefathers left Mutasa two centuries ago on a hunting escapade and settled in Marondera, seventy-two kilometres east of Harare.

They then migrated to Dungwiza, which means 'the territory of long grass', present-day Chitungwiza, a city thirty kilometres south of Harare. There they lived in harmony with the Rwizi family. Our maternal grandfather, Dumba, was one of the most respected *mbira* maestros of that time. The mesmerizing thumb piano, *mbira*, is an integral part of Shona musical tradition, believed to connect our ancestors and the living. Dumba's younger brother, Zhanje, was so good he was chosen as one of the players for Pasipamire Chaminuka.

Pasipamire was the revered spirit medium of Chaminuka, the ancestor of the Shona people. A proficient military strategist, Chaminuka is best remembered for predicting the arrival of men without knees, referring to the European colonisation of Zimbabwe towards the end of the nineteenth century. He was the son of Rwizi II, Watambwanaye, chief of Chitungwiza. The Rwizis preside over our chieftainship in Mhondoro and are of the eland (Shava Mazarura) totem.[2]

Pasipamire Chaminuka was so powerful that Frederick Courteney Selous, the famous British hunter, featured him in his book *A Hunter's Wanderings in Africa*, referring to him as an *umlimo*, or a god. European hunters sought Chaminuka's permission to kill elephants in his territory, while chiefs from faraway lands paid tribute to Chaminuka through cattle, ivory and other treasures.

Chaminuka's leadership became paramount during conflicts with Lobengula, the king of the Ndebele people, when Europeans were invading southern Africa from Natal, forcing Africans to migrate northward and engage in conflict among each other. Chaminuka sent repeated messages to Lobengula advocating for peace but his words fell on deaf ears. Initially, Lobengula was respectful of Chaminuka — sending him gifts and sparing Chitungwiza from conflicts — in return for promises of rainfall. But Lobengula eventually grew uneasy as Chaminuka's influence expanded.

He invited Chaminuka to Bulawayo under the guise of a conciliatory meeting. Chaminuka was accompanied by his wife, Bavheya, their sons, Bute and Kwari, and a few warriors. Chaminuka's entourage included Zhanje, the mbira maestro.[3]

When Chaminuka and his procession reached the Shangani River, approximately two hundred kilometres from Bulawayo, they were ambushed by Lobengula's fighters. Bavheya begged Chaminuka to flee, but he remained, unflinching, in the face of death. The Ndebele warriors massacred several of Chaminuka's fighters, including my great grandfather Zhanje.

So our family has been deeply related to the Rwizi tribe for centuries. My great grandfather perished with the prophet at the Shangani River. When the white people drove the Rwizi from Chitungwiza, our ancestors moved with them and settled in Maunze, near the Skyline turn-off on the Harare-Masvingo Road. The British later annexed the fertile red Marirangwe land and drove us further south onto poor, dusty, grey soil. Chief Mashayamombe welcomed the Rwizi into his territory and gave them a piece of land. We have now been here for almost a hundred years.

Baba concluded his chronicle with an ancient song.

Chaminuka ndimambo; haye ndimambo — shumba inogara yega musango.

Which means, Chaminuka is the king, the solitary lion that roams around the forest.

*   *   *

In our society, a headman oversees homesteads based on patrilineages. The role is hereditary and the homesteads can be several and scattered. The headman presides as a judge over rudimentary disputes, such as land ownership or family squabbles. On top of several headmen sits the chief, a traditional leader entrusted to safeguard Shona traditions and rule over a clearly marked jurisdiction. Chiefs arbitrate more pressing matters, such as territorial disputes between headmen and other issues where either the plaintiff or the defendant is beyond a single headman's jurisdiction. They officiate sacrifices to ancestral spirits, host rainmaking ceremonies, and jealously guard the Shona cultural norms and values.

Each chieftainship designates one day of the week as 'Chisi', a holy day in which no one can work in the fields. In Rwizi, Friday is our holy day. Chisi honours Mwari (God) and the ancestors who provided rain and good fortune. It's also a smart way to force workaholics to rest, thus promoting social interaction and good health.

Mwari, also known as Musikavanhu (the creator), is the supreme deity for the Shona people. The Shona consider themselves unworthy of interacting directly with Mwari. All petitions are relayed via the ancestors, who intercede on behalf of the Shona people. Ancestors make their wishes known through the mediums they possess and often cause their descendants to suffer mild but persistent illness.

The Shona people are divided into clans, each identified through animal totems. People of the same totem share the same ancestor. We hold totems in a near-mystical reverence passed on from one generation to the next through oral tradition. There are at least twenty-five distinct totems in contemporary Shona culture. Totems are usually animals, such as the monkey, elephant, eland, and lion. In some instances they are body parts, such as the leg, heart, and lung. Totems provide an enduring form of social identity for each clan and have bonded people of the same lineage for centuries. These relationships run deep in our veins. Totems were introduced centuries ago to prevent inadvertent incest, preserve the environment, and reinforce good deeds through praise.

One cannot hunt or eat one's own totem no matter how enticing the dish might look. Doing so would be akin to eating your own flesh. If someone belonging to the Moyo Chirandu totem (the heart) visited, and my mother slaughtered a chicken, she would carefully cut out the chicken heart and throw it to my dog, Bhoki. Eating your own totem is a taboo believed to invoke misfortune. Didymus, my cousin and best savannah mate, is a Dziva Shayamombe, the river totem. He would donate all his fish to me whenever we went fishing as his family is not supposed to eat any creature that lives in water. I never competed with Didymus, knowing all the fish were mine at the end of the day.

Similarly, two people from the same totem cannot get married. When a Shona girl introduces her fiancé, her auntie quickly quizzes him, *What is your totem, sir?* If the fiancé shares the same totem, the auntie persuades the two to break off their engagement. Marriage would be unthinkable for those who firmly hold Shona beliefs — regarded in a similar vein to incest.

Dissuading two young adults from romantic union is easier said than done, however. In many cases, the two can insist that their chemistry has gone too wild to be broken by this ancient belief. The fiancé must then supply a spotless white cow to be slaughtered during a special ceremony to break the families' relationship. Once the union has been blessed by the elders, the two can proceed to start a new family, as they are no longer considered related. The difficulty of finding such a cow, almost never seen across the savannah, is meant to discourage the fiancé from pursuing this morally incongruous union.

Our totem is Samaita-Mbizi-Mutasa — the toned, swift, and harmonious zebra. The original Mutasa totem is a hybrid of the lion and the zebra (*shumba/mbizi*). The lion represents courage, fearlessness, and power; the zebra signifies beauty, harmony, and sophistication. Our ancestor created an enduring emblem by the amalgamation of these two remarkable animals. Consequently, Chief Mutasa was better known as the well-adorned one.[4]

Before any of our family members travelled, Baba squatted inside the hut and petitioned his ancestors to protect them.

We advise you, Grandpa Shonhiwa, of [so and so] who is travelling tomorrow. I pray that you guide them and protect them from the chariots of fire (road accidents). *May you kindly pass this message to your father, Zongo, and ask him to relay that message to his father, Rugowo.*

He then mentioned two or three other ancestors to whom the petition had to be passed before it eventually got to Mwari. Boy, there was an endless procession between the living and Mwari.

Every time a new teacher joined our village school, my parents, well regarded in our community, quickly enquired into their totem. If the new teacher was Samaita (a man) or Madhuve (a lady), my parents slaughtered a rooster and hosted a welcome dinner at our homestead. For the duration of their stay at Gavaza, they treated Samaita teachers as their own, gifting them savannah delicacies such as fresh maize cobs, ripened giant mangoes, sugar cane, and fermented milk.

Whenever I topped my class, or we performed our chores with distinction, mother ululated and praised me, using rich Samaita totem lyrics. 'Good job, Samaita.' 'Well done, Mutasa.' 'The majestic zebra, my beloved Tembo.' 'Howdy, the royal southern ground hornbill.' 'The hornless bull, mighty desert muley.' 'Well done, the one adorned with the white emblem of royalty.' 'The spiritually enlightened.' 'Beautiful and smooth like a young girl's skin.'

My parents rarely had treats to reward our efforts, but those beautiful verses had a more enduring and sweeter impact on me than any lolly from the Rwizi store. The charming totemic lyrics gave me a deep sense of pride and identity — I would never trade them for anything. They inspired me to do my best, push beyond my limits, and keep going even when the odds were stacked against me. If we were caught in a bad act, our parents used our real names when reprimanding us, never wanting to associate our enduring symbol with shameful behaviour.

By the time I was in primary school, my paternal grandmother, VaMushonga, was at the tail end of her life. Her birth was never formally registered but her firstborn son, Musekiwa, which means 'the one laughed at', was said to have been born in 1918. Assuming VaMushonga had Musekiwa in her early twenties, she would have been born in the 1890s, when Cecil Rhodes and his British South African Company arrived to colonise Zimbabwe. So, by the early 1990s, VaMushonga was already in her nineties. Her posture reflected her old age and lifelong toil. She walked with a stick, her back bent over at almost ninety degrees. Despite the physical handicap, VaMushonga was incredibly sharp: she remembered the names of the dozens of her grandkids.

The love between my grandmother and me was deeper than the ocean. She treated me as her son and there was a reason for that. Her second son, Phillimon, a gifted academic and proficient soccer player, had died in his late teens. She talked of him with the fondest of memory and kindest of words. Baba named me after his older brother to honour his memory and perpetuate his name, following Shona customs.

VaMushonga had a heart of gold. Whenever my father screamed at my mother, VaMushonga reprimanded him sharply, calling him by his first name, Phillip. I frequented the savannah with a sharp axe and cut large msasa trees, piling the wood outside my grandmother's hut to dry so she could light a fire. My grandmother reciprocated generously, giving me large chunks of cold sadza smeared with peanut butter. I gorged these delicacies inside her hut, fearing I would bump into one of my cousins. Sometimes she handed me two handfuls of dried groundnuts, which I quickly hid in my pockets.

One evening, my parents were invited to attend a Bira ceremony at Chikasa, a village of distant cousins situated about six kilometres south of our homestead. Bira is an all-night ceremony in which Shona people sing, drink, dance, and conduct rituals to appease ancestral spirits. Scared of the dark, we implored grandmother to come and sleep beside us in our large mud-brick kitchen. She wobbled to our homestead at around 7 p.m. After dinner, we blew out the fire and went to sleep on the floor. Grandma provided us psychological safety.

We rose before dawn to milk the cows before releasing them into the open, dry spring fields. An hour later, Grandma was still sleeping. My sister Maidei became worried. She knelt next to Grandma and shook her slightly. Grandma didn't respond. *'Grandma, Grandma!'* Maidei shouted. Grandma remained motionless, like a dried savannah log. We took turns to shake her but nothing changed. No movement, no word, not a blink.

'Run to Chikasa and tell Mother and Father that Grandma is not waking up,' Maidei instructed me in sheer panic.

I took off and ran the entire six kilometres non-stop.

'Grandma is not waking up, and she is not talking to us!' I shouted to Baba the moment I spotted him.

Later that morning, my grandmother was pronounced dead and was buried on a small anthill near her homestead. She left behind an enduring legacy of selflessness, kindness and deep devotion to Shona customs. She remains one of the kindest people I have ever known.

*　　*　　*

When someone dies, Shona people believe that their spirit goes wandering around in the wild. The next August, a year after VaMushonga passed on, the family gathered to organize a ceremony called *kurova guva*. This ritual was meant to welcome my grandmother's wandering spirit back into the homestead, bringing her eternal rest. Her *varoora*, or daughters-in-law, descended on VaMushonga's hut and started preparing a potent millet or sorghum brew called 'seven days'. (It takes seven days of detailed procedures to make.)

When the agreed Friday arrived, VaMushonga's extended family, relatives, community elders, and several spirit mediums packed her hut. *Mbira* players, called gwenyambiras, sat in an arc at the hut's top section, with several calabashes of fully fermented seven days.

Women, wearing zambias that fully covered their legs, played *hosho* all night, a percussion instrument made of gourds filled with dried seeds. Revellers showcased traditional dances — like Muchongoyo, Jerusarema, and Mbakumba — turning the clay floor into dust.

Gwenyambiras displayed their amazing abilities, playing rhythms until their long fingernails were reduced to the quick. They played songs like 'Nhemamusasa', a hunting song, which translates to 'temporary shelter', built by Shona hunters from fresh msasa branches. In its essence, 'Nhemamusasa' is meant to encourage temporary relief from life challenges. I was impressed by gwenyambiras' stamina and ingenious improvisations. These *mbira* virtuosos played non-stop, all night, only taking occasional breaks to pee in the nearby bushes.

Mhondoro is renowned for several *mbira* maestros, most notably Mhuri yekwaRwizi, which means 'Family from Chief Rwizi', an internationally acclaimed group led by Hakurotwi Mude and Luke Kwari Pasipamire. It has been playing *mbira* at the highest level since the 1960s.

The music played deep into the night. Different spirit mediums manifested, predicting future events or airing grievances, each competing for attention with intoxicated and drowsy revellers.

Before sunrise, a handpicked group of relatives, including the older grandchildren and her *sahwira* (best friend), made a procession to VaMushonga's grave to intercede with the ancestors and conduct various other rituals. Her grave was smeared with *masese*, a by-product of the seven day brew, and the insides of a slaughtered male goat. The *varoora* distributed the calabashes to elders and the seven days was passed around. They then swept around the grave using long dry grass before Baba led the singing-and-dancing procession back to VaMushonga's homestead. Women ululated and all clapped hands, celebrating her return, to be among her people forever.

As the *kurova guva* ceremony winds up, the *nhaka* ceremony kicks in. During this phase, the elders distribute the deceased's estate and designate one of the surviving brothers as official guardian to her children.[5]

The deceased's spirit becomes embittered if the family neglects this important ceremony, unleashing bad luck on the next of kin. When someone fails to secure a job, or succumbs to an inexplicable ailment, the family visits a *n'anga*, a witch doctor, to determine why. The *n'anga* often advises the bad luck will vanish once the spirit has been welcomed back into the homestead and appeased.

A family can host the *kurova guva* ceremony any time of the year except November, the goat month. November marks the beginning of the rain season in Zimbabwe when the savannah regains its vitality and creates new life. November is regarded as the month of fertility. Shona elders outlaw ceremonies during the month to avoid villagers inadvertently killing pregnant goats.

*   *   *

Our society is bonded by the spirit of Ubuntu, a Zulu word that means 'I am because you are'. *My humanity is tied to yours.* The Shona version of Ubuntu is Umunhu. Ubuntu speaks of our interconnectedness, selflessness and respect. We share the little we have and carry each other's burdens. What's good for the community is certainly good for the individual. Ubuntu is a deeply rooted belief that as individuals, our accomplishments are inconsequential, but as a village, we can rise past several seemingly insurmountable obstacles and solve big problems. As the African proverb goes, *Sticks in a bundle are unbreakable.*

Ubuntu is not just an idea — it is our way of life deeply engrained in our bloodstream. Nothing signifies our sense of community more than nhimbe, an ancient tradition that pools resources between the poor and well-to-do families. Nhimbe can rapidly smash tasks that seem impossible when viewed in isolation.

I vividly remember the last nhimbe hosted by my grandmother. She owned no cows, just a couple of goats that I looked after as she was too old to run around. VaMushonga was also short of excess grain and money to hire labourers. Nhimbe came to her rescue. When the word spread that she would be hosting a nhimbe, several community ladies joined forces to prepare large quantities of *chihwani* beer and *mahewu,* the fermented alternative for teetotallers.

Village men arrived way before sunrise and immediately got down to work. It looked like chaos from a distance as quad sets of oxen-pulled ploughshares ripped into the ground. Barefoot men whistled discordantly, wielding long *sjamboks* in the air. Two sets of plough-shares came close and a boy in the team behind got inadvertently smashed by a *sjambok* across the cheek. His father was unsympathetic, and told him to wake up. Women in an assortment of multicoloured zambias jumped in and methodically dropped maize seedlings. Everything worked to perfection, even without a team leader.

Once VaMushonga's fields were fully tilled, the oxen were disassembled and released into the savannah. It was now payback time. Everyone assembled under a giant mango tree. Adult men sat on makeshift stools while boys with shorts that severely exposed their buttocks sat on the dust. A handful of women served sadza to the starving men. After lunch, *chihwani* started coming out in traditional clay pots, called *chirongo*. Each man took heavy sips before the beer was passed to the next. Their dripping wet grey goatees and moustaches might put off a snob but the savannah men were having a great time.

CHAPTER 2

Gavaza Primary School

One thing was clear as I grew up. Education was the only way to eventually escape a hopeless life, to unshackle the chains of poverty that had gripped my family for generations. I have no recollection of anyone in our community who extricated themselves except through education. There was no plan B. I yearned for the day we could afford to buy school shoes and white socks. You screw up and you would be screwed your entire life.

Baba, barely educated but deeply wise, constantly reinforced that message. *Take your education seriously so one day we can also be regarded as human beings.* Baba's enduring words would anchor my resolve for decades. The absence of a plan B was not necessarily a bad thing: it forced me to focus intensely on school and chase my dream daily. My adversities entrenched an insatiable passion for self-improvement and obsessiveness with my goals. I know poverty because I lived through it for decades. Almost all homesteads in my village were poor but poverty is always relative.

There were families I regarded as rich back then because my perception was very limited. Some had relatives who occasionally visited them from the city and gifted them with used clothes and shoes. Others had cement-plastered houses with asbestos or corrugated iron roofs. But they too relieved themselves in pit latrines, or the bush, and drank water from open wells. We were just very poor — besides our cows, a handful of goats and a few hectares of infertile land, we had nothing else.

It was impossible to see through the many obstacles back then, to see the brighter side, which was still decades away. But I always believed a better life was eventually achievable.

I enrolled in grade one at Gavaza Primary School in the summer of 1987. I was seven years old. My first teacher was Mr Felix Naka. He was tall, bald, and a devout Catholic, the only founding teacher still at Gavaza. Despite being approximately fifty years younger, Mr Naka referred to me as Sekuru, Uncle, because his mother was of the Samaita totem.

The school, located about a kilometre east of our homestead, had been built some decades ago by the colonial regime to provide elementary education to 'natives'. The school comprised five asbestos or corrugated iron blocks, each subdivided into three or four classrooms.

The teachers shared three-room houses and pit latrines, known as Blair toilets. Apart from four locals — Mr Naka, Mr Thelingwani, Mr Marowa and Mr Garikai — all the teachers came from faraway places. The headmaster, Mr Dzoro, lived in a large pink and white house; it was isolated from the rest, in recognition of the headmaster's seniority. A crumbling barbed-wire fence demarcated the school from the surrounding villages. Cows, donkeys and goats often strayed across the school grounds. At recess time, teachers' wives, schoolchildren and villagers all lined up behind a blue metal push pump. They took turns to vigorously pump the lever and water gushed into their buckets.

We took over the playgrounds as soon as the recess or lunch bell rang. We played *chikweshe*, barefoot, with improvised plastic mini-balls. Some preferred *hwishu*, a made-up footy-cricket game, or *nhodo*, a pebble-throwing contest.

I had a love-hate relationship with the game *fongo* (derived from the Shona verb *fongora*, or 'bending with bum up'). It was not a game for the faint-hearted and I never saw girls play. We entered into *fongo* pacts by locking pinkie fingers in the presence of a witness. If your opponent caught you bending down unawares, they smashed your backside with impunity. If you snoozed, you got badly whacked.

Fongo threatened long-standing friendships: the target cannot retaliate if executed under the *fongo* code. I would wisely select *fongo* opponents who were slightly smaller than me. I caught a few unsuspecting opponents clean but also got my little bum cracked.

Some boys always tried to game the system. After kicking an opponent, they quickly sought to opt out of the arrangement, igniting occasional scuffles. I never saw anyone seriously injured by *fongo* because older boys rarely engaged in this game. At its core, *fongo* was devised to foster street smarts and constant vigilance, self-protection that would help boys cope with the twists and turns of life.

At 7:30 a.m., we assembled in front of the main school block. Each class arranged itself into a straight line, one behind the other. The headmaster officiated the assembly from an elevated square platform in front of the students. As the head boy slowly raised the Zimbabwean flag, the entire school hummed, 'Ishe komborera Africa. Ngaisimudzirwe zita rayo ...' — the national anthem at that time — whose lyrics translate to, 'God bless Africa. May her name be exalted ...'

The dreaded inspection came next. Each teacher slowly strolled down their respective straight line, scrutinising the class for hygiene. We extended our little arms, palms facing downwards, to show our fingernails. The teacher would smack you on your freezing fingers, with their wooden blackboard duster, if they found a student with long nails or unkempt hair. I would hastily bite off any dirty nails as the teacher approached, but without an afro-comb in my pocket, my kinky hair often landed me in trouble. I avoided standing at the start of the line to buy some reaction time. Some students simply hid, squatting behind bushes, before blending back into the crowd as the headmaster dismissed the assembly.

Around the age of nine, midway through primary school, I suddenly started stuttering. The impediment stuck with me for a few years. I fought to utter words, forcefully stomping the ground, rapidly blinking my eyes, and clenching my fists until I broke loose from my nasty speech block. The constant chuckles from other students who equated my struggles with intellectual impairment had a corrosive effect on my confidence. Cecilia, my older sister, had also battled heavy stuttering for years. Without any medical diagnosis or speech therapy, I feared my stuttering was chronic.

Luckily, by the time I reached grade seven, my speech impediment had miraculously vanished. My confidence was restored. Textbooks were scarce at Gavaza Primary School. We had no library. Often, a teacher had one textbook he read for the entire class and kept to himself. Sometimes that sole textbook had several pages missing. Mr Thelingwani was my grade seven teacher; he was chubby, tan-skinned and wore thick glasses. He had a way around this book shortage. He liked my English skills so often asked me to stand in front of the class and read entire chapters loudly. My classmates folded their hands on wobbly wooden desks and listened with careful intensity.

But the process was a painfully slow routine. If I read a section Mr Thelingwani thought was essential, he abruptly paused me and asked the entire class to repeat that segment after me. He rose from his chair and screamed, *Boys alooooooooone!* The boys yelled the sentence after me in near-perfect unison. Then he turned to the girls' section (boys and girls sat separately) and screamed, *Girls alooooooooone!* The girls also obliged, repeating after me in high-pitched voices. Mr Thelingwani then moved to the centre, spread his arms wide like an evangelical preacher and, with a voice like a foghorn, bellowed, *Everyoooone tooooogether!* I joined the boys as they yelled, shut my mouth during the girls' turn, then screamed again with everyone. The teacher then gestured to me to read on, before abruptly stopping me again. If the sentence was too long, some kids only remembered the first three words and mumbled along the rest. The process was so intense I can still recall perfectly my favourite definition twenty-seven years later, *Soil erosion is the removal of topsoil by the action of surface flow, moving ice and wind.*

Mr Thelingwani was dedicated to education in the extreme. No teacher at Gavaza could ever match him. He expected us to arrive around sunrise, two hours before school officially started, and to be the last to leave at the end of the school day. He dished out endless homework, sometimes questions in batches of fifty. Sunday, when everyone else from grade one to form four was relaxing at home, herding cattle or at the house of worship, we were stuck with Mr Thelingwani's unorthodox and arduous study learning routines. His wife was my mother's best friend, which helped solidify our student-teacher relationship.

The shortage of books instilled in me a disciplined devotion to reading whatever material I came across to improve myself. Thank goodness for my cousin Shons, the only son of Musekiwa, my father's oldest brother. We grew very close. Shons, fifteen years older than I, was employed as a guard at Gavaza. He roamed around the school during the night with a giant knobkerrie to fend off thieves.

Shons collected old newspapers from the teachers' houses, not to read, but to stuff tobacco and coil giant cigars. But he was very considerate: he let me read a portion first and then twisted his long cigars. Shons taught me to share; ours was a classic win-win situation. I voraciously read the old newspapers multiple times. I craved for the stories as a thirsty gazelle longs for water.

One late afternoon, I walked towards the teachers' Blair toilets to pinch old newspapers stashed on the floor inside to wipe bums. I snuck into the latrine labelled '*Varume*', Shona for 'Men's'. Unbeknown to me, a male teacher was busy relieving himself. As I extended my little arm to grab a chunk of the pink *Financial Gazette* in the semi-darkness, the teacher screamed 'Hey!' from his squatted position, *Iwe!* I quickly dropped the newspaper and sprinted away, vanishing into the eucalyptus woods.

*   *   *

For years my father had relied on subsistence farming to feed his nine children and keep us in school. In a stroke of fortune, around 1991, the Zimbabwean government offered to traditional chiefs two aides each to assist with rudimentary tasks such as: issuing summons to petty criminals, rallying headmen and their subjects to attend important ceremonies, or simply sitting stone-faced behind the chief to give him an aura of invincibility. After detailed consultations, my father, and Robert Bute, a direct decedent of Chaminuka, were chosen to become the first-ever aides to Chief Andrew Rwizi.

They were both paid approximately seventy Zimbabwean dollars for their work. That side gig allowed my father to gradually buy each of us shoes, thus giving us dignity in school. I was twelve years old, and doing grade six at Gavaza, when Baba bought me my first-ever pair of shoes from Chegutu, a district town he travelled to collect his meagre wage. I still did not have a school uniform but that pair of shoes brought immense joy to my life. But the thrill was not without a challenge. My shoes felt weird — adjusting my step was a delicate act that took months to master. My classmates lurked at any opportunity for me to leave my desk so they could laugh at my unusual gait. I further complicated things by attempting to walk with a swagger, as befitted the proud owner of a new pair of shoes. I ended up completely messed up, wobbling awkwardly like a baby buffalo.

Dakarai Choto, a nasty little pesterer from Maodza, an adjacent village to the east, took this further. He exploited every opportunity to bully me because he loathed me severely for my academic excellence. As soon as the teacher ducked out, he cynically reproduced my wacky step — the entire class cracked up. My first pair of shoes were the classic ankle-high Tenderfoot. They were made of hard black denim material with a matching rubber sole. That name was quite ironic because my feet were anything but: they were crackered and as rough as rhino skin.

*   *   *

We were born and raised in the Catholic Church. My mother rarely missed a Sunday service, as well as the Thursday afternoon gatherings of women, called *China*, Shona for Thursday. Baba was also a baptised Catholic but his commitment was marginal. He always referenced his favourite scripture, *Though shall drink, but not get too drunk!*, on departing for beer escapades on Sunday mornings. I never spotted that in the Bible.

The church was an imposing red and white structure with thick and towering walls, located a couple of hundred metres from the teachers' houses, deep in thickets of large msasa and eucalypts. The immaculate house of worship was a stark contradiction to the crumbling primary school buildings. We sneaked inside to look at the magnificent cream-coloured sculptures of Christ, the Holy Mother, the twelve disciples and other New Testament heavyweights, on the high walls and around the alter.

I liked church because it gave me a rare reprieve from the herd and the cornfields but found the services painstakingly long. Father David Gibbs, a tall and bearded white man who had devoted his life to the poorest and most marginalised people of Mhondoro, officiated the Mass. Father Gibbs was the only white man in our area and for a long time was the only white person I had ever seen. His life of stripped-down simplicity, profound humility, and extraordinary compassion had endeared him to everyone in the community, Catholic or otherwise. I was puzzled by Father Gibb's contrasted life. He was a white man but always wore flimsy sandals that exposed his crackered feet, usually the mark of rural native folks.

Father Gibbs read the Bible and preached in fluent Shona. Over time, many local preachers started mimicking Father Gibb's painfully slow and tedious musical tone, confusing his accent to piety.

CHAPTER 3

Savannah Adventures

The savannah was majestic and beguiling. Masses of birds — grey Chirinda apalis, little green-and-yellow bee-eaters, and heavily streaked cardinal woodpeckers — foraged for insects in the dense woodlands. Stunning, amber and red wine canopies of msasa trees sheltered large flocks of grey doves, black and yellow orioles, and lemon-breasted canaries. Pristine white egrets scavenged for cattle ticks before gliding over the valley back to their enclaves.

Captivating fauna: venomous *mhungus*, black mamba snakes, territorial duikers, and solitary steenbok antelopes coexisted within the lush, tall green grass that transformed into various shades of straw during dry spells. This was my savannah.

I often merged my cows with fellow herders from Chimera, a mud-hut cluttered village across the river. I developed deep bonds with these boys. We moulded makeshift bulls from the dark clay, as our cows grazed on the lush riverbanks. We left the clay bulls to dry in the sun, then pitted them one against the other in fiery imaginary fights. Now and then, our fingers got smashed by the clay horns but collateral damage was part of the game. Our bulls crumbled rapidly under pressure and we rebuilt them. The mud stuck inside our long fingernails, turning them dirty grey. It stayed there for days until we eventually bit the nails off.

The savannah grasslands were rich in natural fruits, such as *nhengeni* (sour plums), *nhunguru* (governor's plums), *hacha* (mobola plums), *matohwe* (snot apples), *matamba* (monkey oranges), *tsambatsi* (wild grapes), *hute* (water berries), and *maroro* (wild custard apple). We gobbled these treats until our bloated little bellies bulged over our skinny legs.

We dug deep holes and buried *matamba* to fast-track its ripening. After a couple of weeks, we retrieved the *matamba* and sat in the dust to suck the juicy and sour seeds. *Nhunguru* was my other favourite but they painted my lips, tongue and teeth maroon and made me look funny.

As the *hute* season rounded up, *matohwe* kicked in, hanging invitingly off giant trees. When *matohwe* ripened, the fruit split apart, unleashing thick lubricious natural sugars. It seemed *matohwe* sugars would gush out forever.

We ate stuff that most people would consider weird, food that my snobbish friends screamed *yaaaaark!* just at the sound of. Dried mopane worms (*madora*), withered crickets (*makurwe*), dried mice roasted in the paprika source (*mbeva*), flying termites (*ishwa*) that oozed from anthills after the rain, and many other savannah delights. Screaming *yark!* suggests one has better options.

My favourite was *mandere* (chaffer beetles), which I hunted adeptly. One super-hot summer afternoon, I was lying on my back, shirtless, under the cool shade of a giant msasa tree. We were on school holidays. My brother Lancelot had disappeared and I had no means to track him down. I was bored and whistling gently as my cows grazed on. I decided to take happiness into my own hands. I drove the cattle into a nearby forest on a *mandere* hunting escapade. I moved from one msasa tree to the next, shaking them violently until the very last *mandere* lost its tight grip and tumbled to the ground. I amassed my booty into a little sack. The hunt looked promising and I was pumped.

I moved on to the next tree and shook it viciously, exerting maximum force from my skinny arms. Suddenly all hell broke loose. About a dozen giant black wasps shifted into a defensive frenzy, shaken from their habitat. I was stung twice as I rushed to grab my sack, right on the scalp, penetrating my budding little afro. I had taken many stings before but I felt like these were of a more intense venom. Adrenaline coursed through my veins as I took off.

The devil entered my soul when I sat down to itch my head. I devised a plan to entrap my cousin Didymus in this menace. Didymus was more than a cousin to me — he was my best friend in the savannah. We often merged our herds before driving them deep into the grasslands and relied on each other to defend against young tyrants. It felt unfair that only I should endure such pain.

'Mate, I discovered a marvel of a tree, a holy grail of *mandere*. Only two shakes and you will have enough to feed your family for the entire month', I fabricated. 'But being the fair guy that I am, I want to give you a go. Whoever gets to the tree first can shake it hard and claim all of the *mandere.*'

'I am up for this, Sekuru (Uncle),' Didymus concurred, his competitive spirit aroused.

Once we arrived at the designated start spot, I shouted, 'Three, two, one, go!' Didymus took off at a menacing pace. I was normally slightly faster than him but he was fixated on the prize and didn't notice. I dragged it out, pretending to have pulled my hamstring. Didymus never looked back. He got to the tree and shook it with all his might. The script unfolded exactly according to my malevolent plan: the incensed swarm descended upon Didymus like rockets.

He took one on his upper lip, which hung floppily for several days. I cracked up from a safe distance as Didymus took off in the other direction shouting, *Maihweee, Maihweee!*, which means Mamma, Mamma! This vice troubled me for some time but I felt better when Didymus got over it. *I will catch you, Sekuru*, he threatened, laughing it off. Didymus never harboured bad feelings; he understood that these seemingly savage games were what made the savannah tick.

Unlike me, Didymus had a strong aversion to education. He vanished into people's fields and stayed incognito on some school days, stealing watermelons, groundnuts, sweet sorghum and whatever he could lay his hands on.

*   *   *

My brother Lancelot and I foraged for beehives in the bushes during winter, when our cattle roamed freely across open fields. If we spotted one, we bounced back in the early evening to extract the liquid gold. These missions were precarious, but we kept at it because our love for the liquid gold was much more intense than our fear of the angry bees.

Lancelot had the bravery of a lion and the pain tolerance of a mole rat. Sometimes I thought he bordered on recklessness. He got stung everywhere but nothing dissuaded him from his mission. He kept kneeling with one knee, extending his left arm deep into a hole dark as pit, to pinch the honeycombs. We preferred underground beehives as they were easier than the ones that hung on trees.

The furious bees defended with their lives. I lit up long dried grass in rapid succession and held this with one hand, using the other to fend off bees. If I got stung in my face, I dropped the blazing grass, but quickly regrouped.

Once Lancelot had drained the hive, we sat down on the dried lemon-yellow savannah grass and split the honey into two empty green Olivine cooking oil tins. We took one tin home to share with everyone else and buried the other deep in the thickets. When the honey at home was finished, we secretly went back into the woods to find our treasure. One day I mistakenly chewed a dead bee and the venomous stinger pierced my tongue. It swelled severely and looked like a small pink banana. It was karma of sorts.

*   *   *

Lancelot and I also went fishing now and then. We improvised fishing rods using old twine and sharp silver pins, which we plucked out of old books. We sat beneath the edge of Chipfuwa Dam, a communal dam, about two kilometres south-west of our homestead. We caught bream and flathead on a good day.

Fishing had its own risks. The mighty river Penyere was adjoined to Chipfuwa Dam. According to tradition, a prominent spirit resided in Penyere so public fishing was precluded. Violating this sacred place could invoke misfortune, it was said, even empty the dam abruptly.

The river was the deepest and richest part of the dam system for fish. It never made sense to me that the territorial ancestors, the custodians of Penyere, would relegate us to other parts that were overrun with reeds and fish-starved. *Us, the living, need protein, not the dead ancestors.* I always questioned the sacredness of Penyere.

Aggressors from Chipfuwa, who claimed jurisdiction of the dam because it was built by the government within their village, enforced this rule with partiality. They sneaked onto Penyere and caught large flathead while keeping everyone else at bay.

Fishing trips were risk and reward escapades. On a good day, we caught so much fresh fish that my mother had to dry some after feeding the whole family. We arrived early at our designated fishing spots and used large portions of *masese* as bait. (The fish were attracted to the home-brew by-product.)

There was a tyrant called Nehemiah Manomano, a brutal savannah hunter who carried half a dozen fishing rods, with about as many hungry and vicious dogs behind him. Nehemiah falsely claimed that he had cleared up several large parts of the dam several years ago — this was before we were even born — and he would never tolerate youngsters fishing at one of these spots.

'If I ever find you squatting on my fishing spots, even if you have sprayed a bucket full of *masese,* may the gods be with you', Nehemiah cautioned, and he meant every bit of his threat.

We all knew that Nehemiah was plain hell. If we spotted him from a distance, we abandoned any spot he claimed as his own. One day, however, Wellie, an introverted boy with a giant belly button, foolishly sat on Nehemiah's spot. 'Wellie is either the bravest or the dumbest boy in the savannah,' I whispered to Didymus. Nehemiah appeared from behind the dam wall, not his usual track that day, as fate would have it. Wellie was having a great time, filling his empty gallon with baby bream, oblivious to the imminent threat. When he turned around and noticed Nehemiah, it was way too late.

We were shocked Nehemiah did not beat up Wellie there and then but he had a more insidious scheme. He handed Wellie a giant hoe and commanded him to climb to the other side of the dam wall and dig a cricket. 'Don't kill the cricket; bring it live and healthy,' Nehemiah ordered Wellie, visibly shaken.

'If Nehemiah was really craving crickets, he would have instructed Wellie to dig at least twenty of them. What the heck is going on here?' I murmured to Didymus.

Wellie returned with a live cricket a few minutes later. Nehemiah ordered him to drop his pants and get the stridulating cricket to bite his private parts. As if that was not enough torture, Nehemiah commanded Wellie to make weird sounds, as if he were making love with a woman. This was the meanest act I ever witnessed Nehemiah commit — his tyranny was engraved in every savannah boy's mind.

*   *   *

Baba was a man of average build but had a short fuse. He reserved disdain for anyone who disrespected him because of his poverty. One autumn afternoon, Lancelot, my cousins and I went to play around the primary school. We entered a dilapidated workshop building, found broken pieces of chalk and started sketching pictures on the boards. We had no idea that Mr Dzoro, the headmaster, was lurking. He was fuming about our perceived 'mischief'. We panicked in all directions when we saw him, jumped over the school fence and most of us vanished into the woods. But Lancelot was not as lucky. The barbed-wire fence trapped his shirt and Dzoro pulled him back. He beat him with a dried log until his brown skin turned red.

Baba exploded when he learned of Dzoro's brutality. He had taken a few cups of *chihwani*, a potent and illegal alcoholic drink made of fermented sorghum. Fuming with rage, he jumped into the granary, retrieved his long spear, and took off towards Dzoro's house. Dzoro, anticipating trouble, barricaded himself in the pink and white headmaster's house.

'If you ever come out, I will rip through your belly, you bastard!' Baba cursed at Dzoro's door and waited for him to emerge.

Baba eventually retreated to our homestead after a couple of hours, shouting, *Brat shit!*, a misunderstood curse that mimicked white farmers swearing 'Bloody shit!' to their servants.

*   *   *

As December approached, I looked forward to Christmas, the most celebrated holiday across the savannah. Christmas is a time for Zimbabweans from all walks of life to loosen their belts, reunite with extended families, or simply wind down after a year of sweat. Christmas Day is venerated in the savannah. Everything shuts down, except shops and pubs. Harare people flock to Mbare, a bustling terminus on the outskirts, and catch buses to some of the remotest parts of the country to celebrate Christmas with their wider clan.

Every villager prayed one of their relatives from Harare would show up unannounced with bags loaded with gifts. On the 24th of December, we dressed up and waited at Rwizi bus station all day, hoping any one of our distant relatives would emerge, even those who had not shown up for years. The green-and-yellow Nyamweda bus, inscribed 'The Headmaster', would be jam-packed.

We often waited until dark, until the last bus arrived, the famed dark-green and gold 'Suffer Continue'. Most buses — like the Mhuriro,

Vazungu, Chivero and Nyamweda — were named after their owners. But Suffer Continue was clearly not named after anyone. It never made sense to me that someone could afford to own a bus and give it such a gloomy name. I just looked on, green with envy, when my neighbours rushed to embrace their elegantly dressed relatives disembarking the bus's steep stairs. 'Suffer' as we called it was always the last bus — and as the driver pulled away, back onto the gravel road — our hopes faded away and we dashed back to the village.

On Christmas Day morning, Baba opened the kraal and drove the cows into the savannah so we could enjoy the festivities. We would see him later. I dressed up in my oversized light-blue T-shirt, which dangled around the shoulders, and navy blue velvety trousers. Those pants, super tight around the thighs and baggy around the ankles, were called 'Revo', short for revolution.

Our *ruseros* (baskets) were already overflowing by 7 a.m. with slices of bread smeared with Sun Jam and Buttercup margarine. Large maroon teapots were simmering with 'heavy tea', thickened with sterilised milk. My favourite was the 'fat cooks', the round, soft and golden-brown buns made by deep-frying flour dough. If you squeezed a fat cook, it dripped with fat, hence the name. My mother prepared them best. Her fat cooks were juicy and succulent, but never greasy — they were just right.

After breakfast, we formed a procession across the lush maize corn-fields to the local shops. I was barefoot but feeling good. Sungura songs by Kiama Boys, Four Brothers, Leonard 'Musorowenyoka' Dembo, System Tazvida, Simon Chimbetu and others played full blast at the shops. Some villagers brought their own battery-powered cassette players. Multiple tunes played at the same time.

Kids whose relatives came from Kuwadzana, Highfields, Chitungwiza or other places we considered well-to-do indulged themselves with lemon creams, loose biscuits and multiple bottles of lukewarm Fanta, Cream Soda or Cherry Plum. None of our relatives showed up and that Christmas I could not afford any of those frivolities. But that was not a problem.

Baba had gifted me some coins and I could afford several hard, round and sticky candies, called 'niggerballs'. I was too young to understand the racist connotations of this derogatory term, coined in South Africa in the 1970s. Niggers came primarily in five distinct shades: red, black, yellow, green, and white. They presented the best value for money — they were sweet, long-lasting and incredibly cheap. When it was hot, the lollies stuck together inside their plastic jar. I walked up to the counter and screamed my order at the shopkeeper, *'Five white niggers and five black ones, please.'* I prayed and drooled as the shopkeeper struggled to break up a tightly glued bunch. *'Take them all, but I am not giving you any change!'* He vented his frustration and handed me the entire bunch of bonded niggers. The assortment gave an illusion of choice but this was just a facade. They all tasted the same beneath the coloured surface.

We indulged ourselves with large portions of rice and chicken stew before running deep into the savannah to find Baba and take over the cows. It was now his time to join the other men at the Rwizi Beer Hall.

CHAPTER 4

Mashayamombe

attained the highest marks in grade seven at my village school in 1993. This despite having been ejected from school innumerable days over perpetual school fee arrears. My parents applied for a form one place for me at Rio Tinto Mhondoro High School in an act of sheer faith. Built by the Rio Tinto Foundation in 1982, Rio was an exceptional school compared to its rural peers. It boasted stellar academic records and was an athletic powerhouse.

The headmaster accepted my application instantly. I had never been to Rio but I had heard lots of admirable things about the school.

For most kids in our village, their happiest memories were when they travelled to Rio to participate in zonal sports competitions. The news put me on cloud nine. My cows hardly had time to graze as I impatiently drove them across the savannah, telling any herder I came across about my imminent adventure.

I was ecstatic but a significant obstacle lay in the way. Rio was twenty-three kilometres from Rwizi, our nearest bus stop. Compounding matters, we could not afford the daily bus fare, which was fifty cents each way. Baba was a peasant farmer. He doubled up as Chief Rwizi's aide but was only paid seventy Zimbabwean dollars per month for executing the chief's errands.

My mother petitioned her younger sister who lived in her home village, Chihoro, about seven kilometres from Rio. Would she bring me under her custody? My auntie said yes. In the summer of 1994, I packed my few belongings and departed for Chihoro in pursuit of a four-year mission: to pass my O-level exams at the first attempt before departing for the city to look for a job.

The savannah was still reeling from the forbidding Southern African drought of 1992, considered the worst in living memory. Central and Eastern Tropical Pacific Ocean surface temperatures had risen substantially above average and created a phenomenon called El Niño. The drought reduced more than a million cows to carcasses, a third of the Zimbabwean herd. Light-brown cornstalks lay wilted on roasted earth. Thirsty villagers, cows, donkeys and goats lined up behind sporadic and failing boreholes as once perennial rivers, swamps and dams depleted.

My mother accompanied me to my aunt's. She walked at a fast pace and I had to occasionally jog to keep up. I was radiating with hope and anticipation. At the same time, I was deeply uneasy about being uprooted from my familiar savannah routines. I was fourteen years old and this was my first time living away from home. I would severely miss Didymus, my notorious cousin with whom I had an unbreakable bond. I also feared boys in Chihoro would test my prowess through arranged bouts. We arrived in Chihoro late in the afternoon, a densely clustered homestead of round thatched mud-brick huts. The homestead was located on the southern fringes of Mashayamombe territory, approximately ten kilometres north of our village.

*   *   *

Chief Chinengundu Mashayamombe was the architect of the First Chimurenga in Mashonaland, the first liberation struggle. (His first name means 'one with long unkempt hair' and he sported lengthy dreadlocks.) Leveraging his exceptional leadership skills, Chinengundu rallied several other Shona chiefs to join the resistance. His army won many strategic battles until they were blasted by dynamite in the Njatara caves, where Mashayamombe's men had retreated for cover. He was decapitated when the settlers finally got hold of him, the enemy believing that his dreadlocks were the source of his powers, like the biblical Samson. Sadly, Chief Chinengundu's skull, together with those of other illustrious First Chimurenga heroes such as Chief Chingaira Makoni of Rusape, are still held in Natural History Museum in London as war trophies.

Looking back, I am perplexed that such rich history, our own history, was barely mentioned in school. Chief Mashayamombe was the architect of the first Mashonaland Revolution, which inspired the Second Chimurenga (1966–1979). I sat next to Chinengundu's offspring in class. My history teacher, Miss Mashayamombe, was a direct descendant of the Mashayamombe dynasty. Similarly, my Shona teacher was a descendant of Chifamba, Chinengundu's pre-eminent military commander during the First Chimurenga.

We were taught everything about Cecil Rhodes and his friend Leander Starr Jameson, the Sarajevo incident and how it catalysed the First World War, the Bolsheviks and the Russian Revolution, Mao Zedong and the Chinese Communist Uprising, among endless foreign narratives. Oddly, very little was mentioned about Chief Chinengundu Mashayamombe, Chief Chingaira Makoni, Mbuya Nehanda Nyakasikana, Sekuru Gumboreshumba Kaguvi, and our many other gallant sons and daughters of the soil.

*   *   *

My mother returned to our village the next day, leaving me under the custody of my auntie. My auntie owned three round grass-thatched mud-brick huts, located near half a dozen cattle kraals on the western fringe of my grandfather's homestead. My auntie was a brave woman. Born around 1954, she became a mother in her mid-teens and raised six kids as a single mum. By the time I landed in Chihoro, two of my auntie's oldest children had already moved out to look for jobs in the city. She lived with her other four: Ruth, a girl two years older than me; Tsuro, a boy one year my junior; Sarudzai, a girl several years younger; and Clive, a toddler boy. My auntie was industrious — she worked very hard to provide food for her kids and pay their school fees.

After school, my auntie poured buckets of dried groundnuts onto a large silver metal dish and we took turns stomping them with our bare crackered feet until every nut was shelled. My auntie then roasted the peanuts in a giant metal pan before pouring them into a *duri*, a giant hollow wooden grain stomper. Next, we crushed the roasted nuts using a special wooden pole with rounded edges called a *mutswi*.

Once the peanuts turned into a crunchy paste, my auntie shoved the residue onto a *guyo*, a giant smooth rock, and pounded it further using a *huyo*, a smaller piece of flat stone, until it was semi-watery. She knelt there for hours, moving her arms back and forth in quick motion. She packaged the peanut butter into giant containers and caught a bus to sell it to her loyal customers in the Harare ghettos. She used the proceeds of the hustle to buy second-hand clothes at Mupedzanhamo market, an enormous Harare bazaar whose name means 'poverty crusher'. Once back in the village, she exchanged the clothes for buckets of groundnuts and started the cycle again. From this enterprise, my auntie provided for her kids and kept them in school. I am sure, however, if her clients knew that we pounded the raw peanuts using our bare feet, they might have thought twice before parting with their cash.

During school days, Ruth and I woke up way before daybreak and jogged to Nyangweni River, less than a kilometre east of the village, where my auntie owned a large vegetable garden. We knelt over the hanging granite rocks, drew water from the river using large tin buckets, and watered dozens of vegetable beds. Once we had completed this exacting task, we washed our faces, arms and legs in the same river, then sprinted back home to change, before running to Rio.

Rio was more than three times bigger than my village school. The school was comprised of several long cream-coloured blocks, a large staff room where teachers planned their work in between lessons, and two giant dining rooms. Unlike other rural schools, Rio provided its students with lunch meals. Lunch was always sadza with alternating dishes: luscious beef stew, nourishing beans or the thick, creamy and delicious 'Dairibord Lacto' (cultured milk). The teachers' lavish houses were located within the Rio estate, surrounded by a towering perimeter fence.

Rio was immaculate; you would hardly ever find litter on the ground. There were several running water taps installed across the school, which were powered by a giant electric borehole. Deep green bougainvillea plants were constantly in pink bloom. In spring, the jacarandas that lined the school's red sandy streets exploded in gorgeous violet-purple flowers.

Tsuro, my auntie's son, was thirteen. Old enough to be responsible for the cows, exempting me from this monotonous chore. I watered the garden, crushed the peanuts, tilled the fields, and performed several other domestic tasks. Unlike my mum, my auntie did not differentiate much between boys and girls. She expected me to wash dishes and cook, just as my older cousin Ruth did. After a few weeks, I was already proficient at cooking sadza and vegetables. I also occasionally relieved Tsuro with the herd when he was sick or during lunch breaks.

I was fond of my auntie and respected her just like my mother. I was polite and never complained about anything; I executed my chores conscientiously. My auntie returned the favour, constantly reinforcing my manners through praise. But my stay in Chihoro quickly became problematic. As soon as I arrived at my auntie's place, Tsuro resented my intrusion into his territory. Everyone around the extended homestead spoke highly of my smarts.

'This boy is a genius, he topped his entire class at Gavaza, he will go a long way.' My Uncle Simbisai spoke with boundless pride.

Tsuro on the other hand, like my cousin Didymus, had a strong aversion to school. He faked sickness and bunked off school at will, preferring to roam around the savannah than attend to his education. Tsuro got green with envy whenever someone praised my smarts. My auntie tried to neuter this simmering tension by loudly admiring Tsuro's looks. Despite being a spoiled little brat, this praise had merit: Tsuro was a light-skinned, striking-looking teenager. The century-old repressive colonial system ingrained a widespread belief that 'lighter was prettier' so Tsuro's melanin shortage earned him constant compliments.

The general admiration for my academic talents got under Tsuro's skin. He became bitterly aware of his intellectual inadequacy.

He engaged me in a few seemingly 'friendly scuffles' to test the waters but I always trounced him. Besides being a year older, my numerous savannah bouts had hardened my resolve. I was determined to never let him intimidate me. I leveraged both age and experience to fend off his amateurish challenges. But his nastiness hinted darkly at a graver trouble to follow. He resorted to a more insidious ploy when it became clear that I would badly smash his backside if ever our tussles escalated into a serious fight.

In the villages, boys ate together from the same plate, while girls ate from a separate plate. It did not matter if there were two, three or four of you; you received a plateful of sadza and another of an accompanying dish, usually vegetables. Way before the concluding 'amen' of the grace, we pounced on the sadza. It was survival of the fittest. We were the only two boys in my auntie's household so the boys' plate was for Tsuro and me. As everyone else began their meal, Tsuro simply said, 'I am not hungry yet,' and looked sideways. So, weirdly, I always started eating on my own. Even if we had not eaten anything all day, Tsuro still stuck to his strategy.

My auntie stared and cautioned, 'Please don't forget to leave food for your young brother.' I promptly complied with the implicit message and washed my hands as Tsuro looked on. A few minutes later, Tsuro, starving, demolished the rest of the sadza. His little tummy bulged.

The worst was when my auntie slaughtered a fat roadrunner chicken, the most prized of village delicacies. She dished out four pieces: the chicken head, the neck and two feet drowned in a bowl of glittering, mouth-watering soup. I knew Tsuro would undoubtedly play his dirty little game so I went straight for the head, leaving him to unhurriedly feast on three pieces.

The whole saga deeply confused me. I was surprised my auntie not only tolerated Tsuro's blatant abuse but encouraged it. This mum-son complicity went on for several weeks. Ruth detested Tsuro's hideous tactics. She seethed whenever he refused to wash his hands as the metal dish with cold water was passed around. She looked up to her mum to intervene but my auntie kept quiet. It never crossed my mind that auntie might hate me because I was an obedient kid, and now a key part of her peanut-butter hustle. Also, besides enabling Tsuro's abuse, my auntie never abused me. *She is able but unwilling to protect me from Tsuro's mistreatment*, I pondered at bedtime. My feelings boiled over with frustration and rejection. During the wintry savannah nights, my stomach grumbled with hunger but I kept my suffering bottled up.

I did my best to mask my anguish. I knew for certain that if I told my parents, they would instantly transfer me back to our village secondary school, Rwizi. But I badly wanted to stay — Rio was where my hope was anchored. I had survived savannah bullies but being mistreated by my auntie and cousin posed a graver challenge. It was a war I could not win. I had done everything possible to be loved, scrubbing the dishes with sand when we had no soap, watering dozens of vegetable beds, stomping dry groundnuts for hours, and never exacting revenge on Tsuro. But nothing helped. I even built a brick and mud bench in my auntie's kitchen, using some early skills I had mastered from building classes at Rio, yet the chorus played on.

I was willing to go as far as possible without throwing in the towel but Tsuro's bully tactics exerted an untenable physical and mental toll. I finally cracked and told my parents. Excited by the new opportunity at Rio, I had assumed everything would unfold smoothly. Now I had to deal with an unanticipated setback. The feeling of rejection and being treated differently by my new family was devastating. *What will I do if I have to move away from my auntie's place?* I pondered.

My mother suggested that I stay with 'young grandma', her mum, who lived two hundred metres away from my auntie's place. Young grandma was a compassionate woman but she was already in her eighties, too old to look after me really. She had raised several of my cousins, including my half-brother Martin, so politely pushed back, citing old age and failing stamina.

That left me with two options. I could stick it out at my auntie's place or quit Rio and go back to my village school. Renting in the township like other kids from faraway places, so-called 'bush boarders', was implausible as my parents had no idea how they would raise even next term's school fees.

Fortunately, destiny beckoned. I was selected as one of the Kristin Diehl scholarship recipients at the beginning of the second term of 1994. Kristin is a benevolent German citizen who worked tirelessly for decades to rally well-wishers in her home country and raise fees for disadvantaged but bright kids from Rio. She paired me with Marion Bertram, a benefactor from Hanover, Germany.

Marion's sponsorship radically changed my life. She opened a window of opportunity that was on the verge of closing forever. *Why would his benevolent stranger — twelve thousand kilometres away –take such a huge gamble on me, when my own family had slammed the door of opportunity right in my face?* I contemplated. Marion gave me a renewed chance, paying all my fees. This left me only having to hustle for food, clothing and accommodation. The combination of Kristin and Marion embodied the spirit of Ubuntu — I am because of them.

Without their kindness, no amount of heroism could have materially altered my circumstances. My life would look starkly different today were it not for Marion and Kristin's support. They rescued me and gave me one of life's greatest gifts — a chance to discover my boundless potential and shape my destiny. Hope anchored me as I walked through the dusty township streets, ran through storms or scavenged backyards for empty Coca-Cola bottles for their deposit refunds so I could buy food. There was no margin for error with this opportunity of a lifetime. I had to work hard in honour of Kristin and Marion's generosity and faith in my potential. There was one thing I knew with certainty: I would never let down my parents, or Kristin and Marion.

*   *   *

My Chihoro experiences had left me lonely, depressed and miserable. The scholarship removed those feelings and helped me move on with my young life. The school caretakers who hounded kids with fees arrears never bothered me again. I just shouted '*Bursary!*' as I walked past the checkpoint, holding my head high — the scholarship was highly regarded as a mark of academic excellence across the school. Some boys even claimed *Bursary rinonyengesa!*, meaning 'you could easily land a beautiful young girl because of a German bursary!'

The scholarship came with a condition — I had to stay in the top ten of my class. If I slipped, I could lose the bursary. That threat unleashed a new wave of determination — it concentrated my mind intensely on my academics. I was determined to outwork everyone. I was awake to the fragility of my four-year mission and shook off complacency. With only a small misstep, I could find myself back at the village school, my dream dead — something I could not countenance.

The concentrated focus on my academics helped me to detach from the past and cleanse my young soul. Nurturing bitterness would only compound things. It would be impossible for me to overcome the many obstacles I faced in the township while burdening myself with corrosive resentment.

Everyone at home was ecstatic when I received the bursary. My hope of staying at Rio was alive again. My parents decided to secure a rented room for me in the township. My sister Maidei donated a one-plate paraffin stove. She was a temporary teacher at Nyatsanga Primary School during this time.

My parents made this crucial decision during the school holiday. I packed my few belongings and moved in. Everything about that tiny and dingy room spoke of troubled conditions. My room was part of a dilapidated three-roomed 'boysky', a standalone flat-roofed cottage. In neighbouring South Africa, *khaya* means house or home. Boys at homesteads there usually stayed in isolated rooms. Zimbabweans corrupted the phrase 'boys khaya' to boysky in reference to any cottage.[6]

Lizzy and Masibanda occupied the other two rooms. They were arguably the township's most prominent prostitutes. The cement floors were littered with dust-filled potholes; rotting trusses supported asbestos roofs that dangled precariously. The ceiling was smoke-stained as the previous occupant occasionally burnt a fire inside. Myriad bugs hid behind the crumbling cement walls and crept out after dark.

The boysky had no running water. I filled my bucket from a tap that protruded outside from the landlord's house, an old three-bedroom house about forty metres away. There was no electricity so I jogged to nearby bushes to gather firewood to heat the room and prepare food. Fortunately, I had learnt to cook basic meals during the three and half months I stayed at my auntie's place. I lit a fire within the small verandah shared with the two prostitutes and used a paraffin-powered lamp for light. Whenever it rained, I lit the fire inside the room as the verandah had no roof. Once I finished cooking, I sat down inside the gloomy room to eat alone, my thoughts racing wildly.

The place was almost uninhabitable but all Baba could afford. Despite his meagre income, he consistently paid my forty-dollar rent and gave me about five dollars for food every month. That was a massive bet on my success — everyone back in the village had to make do with the remainder. Baba always regretted putting me in that place. No parent would ever want to expose his or her child to such conditions. But, given the limited choices, this was my only hope for a brighter future. I was and am grateful for my parents' sacrifices.

The shameful place smelt like mouldy socks and had no internal bathrooms or toilets. There was a small 'vent', roughly the size of one brick, about two metres high on the left wall, which was 'designed' to circulate the air in my room.

There was a little blue toilet between the boysky and the landlord's house. But because this toilet stood on open ground, vagrants had reduced it to a deplorable state. I ran to the beer hall to relieve myself and peed under the giant mango tree that stood between our boysky and the landlord's house. (I had no consideration for people who picked the ripened mangoes that fell onto this soiled ground.) Lizzy and Masibanda peed in a bucket and decanted the waste into the blue toilet from a distance, their faces frowning from the heavy stench. Some nights, I filled a bucket with cold water and took a quick bath under the same giant mango tree.

One chilly evening after school, I slowly opened my makeshift door, careful not to break it. I could not believe my eyes! There was a short, skinny boy with a disproportionately huge head and large piercing eyes sitting on the rutted floor. He was faintly aloof. Compounding my shock, the teenager was wearing a Rio uniform. *What the heck is this boy doing in my room?*, my mind raced wildly. He was Mudiwa. His mum had come from Kadhani, forty kilometres south of the township, to secure rented accommodation for him — the same as Baba had done for me. The 'landlord' was actually a police officer who rented the main house and claimed jurisdiction over our run-down structure. He instructed Mudiwa to co-share my room and told him to also pay forty dollars per month, thus doubling his gain.

I was upset the landlord had imposed a roommate on me without Baba's knowledge and opened my room without my consent. But my anger was short-lived. Mudiwa's presence was one of the best things that happened to me in the township; it was an act of God's grace. Mudiwa and I developed a bond, and although never as strong as the bond I had with Tindo (my childhood friend from Gavaza who also enrolled in the same class at Rio), having him under the same roof relieved me from my daily anxiety.

Most nights, we cooked sadza with cabbage or *mufushwa*. I hated *mufushwa* because it took forever to boil, wasting our firewood and time; it was bitter and we always seemed to have vast supplies of it. We burnt dried cow dung as mosquito repellent because we could not afford coils. The dung smoke made me cough but this was more tolerable than the torture of the mosquitoes that beset the boysky. The smoke put them off but only temporarily; as the night progressed and the smoke faded, dozens of hungry parasites descended upon us for their bloody meals. After a bite, we smacked angrily, but we only hurt ourselves. The old saying, *If you think you are too small to make a difference then you have never spent the night with a mosquito*, rang true.

My experience fostered resilience and focus. And it was not unique to me. I shared this hellish journey with so many never-say-die kids, some of whom went on to achieve great success. They did so by refusing to lament their lack of resources, defying negative stigmas associated with rural folks — and more importantly, by resolutely setting their minds on long-term goals.

Jim Watkins, the American businessman, rightfully observed, 'A river cuts through a rock, not because of its power, but because of its persistence.'

We did not take any shortcuts because we could not; that option was never there. We remained decisive and unyielding in the face of difficulty, knowing nothing meaningful ever comes easy.

*   *   *

Lizzy and Masibanda were both big and tall. Masibanda was alluring, voluptuous and tan-skinned, what this generation of Zimbabweans now call 'a yellow bone'. That made her more attractive to men, but Lizzy was the boss. Lizzy owned a salon and they both worked there as hairdressers during the day before turning to their main hustle at night.

Around sunset, in worn high heels, their large lips made up red, miniskirts almost bursting from their supersized hips, they walked down to Gaza, a notorious pub tucked on the edge of the township. There, all congregated: bus drivers en route to remote destinations, off-duty teachers, police officers, hookers of both sexes, boozers, and noblemen out for a good time. Penniless, barefoot cattle herders from surrounding villages showcased astounding footwork and body movements, doing a dance called 'Borrowdale' for its resemblance to racing horses, as *Sungura* songs played at full blast.

Lizzy and Masibanda closed many deals on a single night. They pushed back on unprotected sex, often lighting candles to verify that the client was wearing a condom before an encounter. I was perplexed by the number of men that insisted on unprotected sex. The HIV/AIDS pandemic wreaked havoc, annihilating otherwise healthy men and women. The risk rang clear as a bell: AIDS killed.

There were no anti-retroviral drugs in Mubayira at that time. When HIV penetrated someone's defences, it wrecked them with chronic pneumonia and other opportunistic virulent infections. AIDS patients' lips dripped with blood; their bodies turned skeletal. Some almost coughed their lungs out. Once kinky and curly hair turned straight and shiny. Others endured severe and unrelenting diarrhoea; their bodies weakened, making it impossible to walk unassisted. Awareness campaigns sprouted, warning people of this raging menace. But to these men, those words of caution seemed unimportant and were quickly disregarded.

The painful death of its primary victims was worst but the scourge had other outcomes. The innocent and sick spouses left behind: orphans left in the hands of elderly grandparents, teenagers left to look after their siblings, students left teacherless, and horrific recollections forever engraved in memory. For relatives, it was like a horror film in slow motion, watching their loved ones hopelessly deteriorate to their graves.

Unprotected sex commanded a much higher charge, dubbed 'the danger fee'. It was a premium to compensate the prostitutes if they contracted sexually transmitted diseases. I was shocked by the extraordinary levels of risk these men, including teachers, police officers or even healthcare workers, were prepared to take.

As the epidemic raged, fear spread like a fever, unleashing a kind of mass paranoia and ugly stigma. People burned their plates while some shunned latrines used by AIDS patients, fearing they would catch the contagion. Others wilfully fabricated, claiming their relatives had died from tuberculosis, natural causes, or, nonsensically, sudden death.

Admitting AIDS as the cause of death was taboo. It shamed the dead and their families. The dishonour kept people from getting tested. Some demanded their deteriorating relatives be discharged from hospitals to have 'demonic spirits' exorcised by *n'angas* or self-styled prophets. Those moves only hastened their demise.

I dreaded a scenario in which a mosquito would bite me after sucking blood from any of the philandering men who showed up daily at the boysky. Mrs Marowa, our counselling teacher, eventually rescued me from my anxieties — she explained that since HIV could not infect mosquitoes, the parasites could not transmit the deadly virus.

Lizzy and Masibanda each turned up at the boysky with two or three men every night for a predetermined stint, then walked back to the pub for another client. These short episodes often ended up in violent scuffles, especially when clients went beyond their time and failed to settle the unexpectedly higher bill.

'I gave you two rounds, but you want to pay for one, you bastard,' Lizzy yelled in the middle of the night.

Those brawls scared Mudiwa and me to the very core.

'I am not that weak man you beat up at Gaza, Lizzy. I will beat the crap out of you, you worthless piece of sh!t' a client threatened, smashing the door behind him and vanishing into the dark. The debt was instantly written off. They had no recourse as prostitution was illegal.

Lizzy and Masibanda lived on the edge. They threatened to beat up defaulting clients, only to be kicked in the gut, have their braided hair pulled or shoved to the floor by violent drunks. My neighbours had clearly lost sense of their own worth and lived in jeopardy. As one of them screamed in agony, I broke into tears. There were countless gloomy moments and those were among my darkest. I found myself submerged in an environment of constant violence. Fear became my world. During those difficult years, I learned more about the abuse of women, anger and pain than I had imagined possible. I felt like the angel of death was continually lurking around our ramshackle abode and always imagined one of them would be beaten to death.

The ladies lived wretched lives, in what the psalmist called 'the valley of the shadow of death', what the poet William Henley referred to as 'a place of wrath and tears', and what Zimbabweans called 'the departure lounge'. I never saw love.

None of these men showed up with flowers, bread or even a soft drink. They came for sex and always wanted to pay less than what was agreed. They treated Lizzy and Masibanda as cigarette stubs — trashed by the smoker once he has sucked out the nicotine. Clients arrived and departed incognito; no man wanted the world to discover their terrible dark secret.

With my fear came the need to worship — it reinforced my faith in God. I prayed for my safety and my academics. I prayed for my roommate, Mudiwa, who was struggling in school and continuously bullied by the landlord's oldest son. I interceded for Lizzy and Masibanda. I petitioned God to help my struggling parents back in the village. I prayed for Marion to live a long life, knowing that my hope relied on her. Living in this place of despair made me realise my life was not in my own hands — things could go awry anytime. It taught me to fight through the darkest moments and emerge on the other side. As Saint Paul wrote, *God's strength was made perfect in my weaknesses.* My faith bolstered my hope, which always hung by a thread.

When in our room, there was no way for us to insulate ourselves from the horrific abuse these ladies endured. Termites had ruined the frame of our small wooden door; it could no longer be hinged so we used makeshift wire to hold the door in position. The endless fights and noise messed up our sleeping patterns.

Lizzy had a permanent boyfriend in what Westerners call an open relationship. If he found Lizzy with a client, he simply walked away and came back later. This man also lived a terrible, miserable life.

The ladies had another side to them that was so wonderful. They habitually sent us to buy Everest cigarettes and 'scuds', millet beer sold in brown containers that resembled scud missiles. The name 'Everest' felt incongruous. In return, we were allowed to keep the change, which we desperately needed to buy vegetables or a packet of *madora*.

I deliberately hid my residence from my schoolmates for as long as I could. I walked my friends to their homes before sneaking into our shabby structure. This was a wise move. If mischievous friends — like Edmore Chasi, a cheeky, fit, light-skinned classmate from Mubayira village — discovered my place, they would bully me. My academics would suffer. Even the handful of friends who knew where I lived — Tindo, Ngoni and Danai — never entered my room. We always hung out on the small verandah before walking back to their dwellings.

Somehow all these difficulties did not faze me — I never made excuses or felt sorry for myself. I made do with what was available. I did this in honour of my benefactors, Kristin and Marion, and my parents, all of whom made unthinkable sacrifices for me. I refused to sit back and wait for circumstances to change or allow my situation to hold me down. I strived to do my best daily, anchored by the strong hope that if I persisted, my distant dreams would come to fruition.

*   *   *

Like everyone, Baba certainly had imperfections but he had a profound influence on my life. He demonstrated a foresight that was rare among his rural peers. For decades, my parents lived beyond the edge, making several sacrifices to afford each of their nine children the opportunity of education. Their meagre resources did not impede them but only sharpened their resolve.

Baba had a brown-and-black spotted dog called Juri. Baba claimed to have dedicated Juri to the ancestors when he was a puppy and that move paid off. Juri was the ultimate pet; his loyalty to Baba was unquestionable. More so, Juri was a skilful hunter: he picked up his prey's scent from a distance, swooping their safe hiding places. Baba reminisced with nostalgia.

One day, during a savannah hunting adventure, Juri, because of his velocity, failed to apply the brakes and sprinted past a rabbit, before somersaulting, turning and taking the bunny head-on. Every villager and their dog begged to hunt alongside me, knowing the presence of Juri assured them a fruitful trip,

But Baba's herd had severely depleted. Several of his rural peers made 'justifiable' excuses and dropped their kids out of school. In an act that epitomised his sacrifices, Baba exchanged Juri for a goat called Makaita, which means 'You did well'. He sold the goat to pay school fees for my oldest brother. Several years later, he bought a puppy with the same brown and black spots and also named him Juri — but he was only a shadow of the original.

Baba's resolve was an enduring lesson to me about the quick fix, the importance of playing the long game, and why we should remain resolute in the face of adversity. I also learnt that long-term success is not merely about hard work, but the sacrifices one is willing to make along the way.

He understood the significance of education, often reminding us it was the only path to eventually escape from poverty, something inflicted on our family for years. Living today in this age of instant gratification, it is easy to forget that lasting change results from consistently taking those mundane little steps. Take a miracle pill and grow a six-pack within a few weeks. Invest in a new cryptocurrency and pocket millions after a few months. The Internet is replete with such astonishing promises. People expect business-class travel to resort destinations to drink margaritas on white sandy beaches, but loathe the hard grind demanded by long-lasting success.

Baba's resolve taught me the opposite — the tenets of diligence, patience and firmness of purpose. None of these virtues can be side-stepped to success. Great and sustained change is never instantaneous.

At the end of each month, Baba passed through the township on his way from Chegutu, the district town where he went to collect his chief's aide's wages. None of us had phones so I had no idea which day he would pass by. The green-and-gold Nyamweda bus he took arrived around 1 p.m. Still, he always waited until I finished school at 4 p.m., drinking Shake-Shake, the famous sorghum, maize and millet beer: so called because to get the best out of it, you needed to shake it thoroughly.

I roamed around a few of his favourite bottle stores until I spotted Baba. We sat down and talked for hours as I slowly devoured the half bread he bought for me. I inquired about my mother and my siblings, about Bhoki, my faithful dog. I took large sips of Coca-Cola, which sometimes gushed through my nose, forcing me to slow down. He let me know he had paid my rent and the landlord's wife had passed on positive feedback about my behaviour. As the dark settled in, I walked him to the bus terminus, where he boarded a Vazungu or Mhuriro bus to Rwizi. We replayed that same routine for four years.

CHAPTER 5

The Attitude of Gratitude

'Gratitude is not only the greatest of virtues, but the parent of all.' —
Marcus Tullius Cicero

Some Tuesday nights, the landlord granted Mudiwa and me thirty
minutes access to his house to watch the wrestling on his tiny
black-and-white television set. There were two rules. First, we could
not look at his daughters. Second, we had to sit on the cement floor

while the landlord's family sat on couches. There was always space on the couch but this discrimination was symbolic of their self-perceived upper class.

The first rule, not to lust after his daughters, was easy to comply with as there were far better-looking girls at Rio. The landlord's younger daughter stole glances at us but we kept our inquisitive eyes on the little black-and-white screen, foolishly believing the wrestling was real.

The landlord and his wife had a 'foster' child called Simbarashe, whom I grew very fond of. Simbarashe, born in 1979, was a year older than me. His mum, a prostitute who rented from the landlord years back, dumped Simbarashe as a toddler and simply vanished. The landlord repetitively told this story. Simbarashe had no recollections of his mother or any family. The landlord claimed to have rescued Simbarashe out of compassion but that was a naked lie.

It was impossible to witness the life Simbarashe was forced to live without disgust and rage. The landlord and his wife groomed him for scandalous exploitation — his life was nothing short of modern slavery. He was fifteen and had never been to school. Simbarashe couldn't read or write. He hustled for them all day, squeezing through crowded buses to sell freezits or penny coolers to sweaty passengers, frozen syrupy drinks packaged in fifty-millilitre plastic cylinders. As soon as the driver revved the engine, Simbarashe jumped off and ducked back to resume manning the landlord's flea market stand. He toiled barefoot, wearing his trademark too-small grey shorts and a black, oversized T-shirt torn around the shoulders. He was not paid a cent for his never-ending toil.

Despite these depravations, Simbarashe was a strong, energetic and respectful kid who doubtlessly would have thrived under the right conditions. He cleaned the landlord's house and the toilets. He washed piles of clothes, including the landlord's wife's undergarments as she sat on the balcony drinking alcohol, on a small stool that splayed her large buttocks. Simbarashe took on the dirtiest and most menial work you could ever imagine. He was not allowed in the kitchen because of his filth.

They claimed to have 'adopted' him but deliberately failed to acknowledge him. He had no formal birth registration papers and they refused to call him by their totem. He was just Simbarashe, a boy with no familial or traditional identity.

The landlord's oldest son whacked Simbarashe for the smallest infraction. The landlord and his wife set such bad examples they turned their youngest daughter into a vitriolic little tormentor. Their dark, round-faced, spoiled little brat commanded Simbarashe to fetch water and clean up after her mess. It set my teeth on edge whenever she shouted, *Simbarashe, may I have some cold water, please!* I felt like unleashing a thunderous clap across her chubby face. But I was powerless. The landlord exerted enormous power over all our lives in the township.

Simbarashe was also banned from sitting on the couches; on very rare occasions he joined us, on the cement floor, to watch the wrestling. He dozed through it, utterly drained by his daily hustles. There seemed to be no way whatsoever to rescue Simbarashe from his predicament. The landlord was a senior police officer, leaving him with nowhere to turn for justice. Almost everyone I knew witnessed his abuse, yet no one stood up for him. I was too young and powerless to do anything, despite my boundless love for Simbarashe.

Occasionally, Simbarashe sneaked into our little verandah to play draughts with us. But as soon as one of his many masters spotted him sitting down, they scolded him for being 'a lazy glutton'. He was quickly assigned another task. Simbarashe was a gifted and obedient kid turned into a slave by those who claimed to have saved his life. My daily struggles over essentials dwarfed in comparison to his constant anguish.

Sometimes I couldn't prepare dinner as the firewood was drenched with rain or my alternate one-plate stove had run dry of paraffin. Still, I was way better off. I had access to quality education and I was already eight school years ahead of Simbarashe. Through his tribulations, I appreciated the freedom I had, the hope I hung on to, through education, and the fraternal bonds that were so dear to me.

My parents were poor but they were always there. Simbarashe never experienced that kind of love; to him my life was to die for, the life I deeply hated. We rarely had food but we had the freedom to grind out and define our future. As long as we stayed focused on our education, there was a huge possibility that our lives would eventually improve.

By the time I met Simbarashe, his relationship with his keepers was irretrievably broken. His fellow hawkers also tried to play a part, constantly urging him to do something about his situation. Eventually, Simbarashe disappeared. He just picked up a few of his belongings, not stealing anything from the landlord. He didn't say goodbye to anyone and I never saw him again.

A year later, I heard that Simbarashe had escaped deep into the savannah and took up a job as a cattle herder. He would be paid a pittance but the news greatly relieved me. *At least he will get paid for his labour. More so, it's unlikely that Simbarashe will experience the frequent beatings he got from the landlord's oldest son,* I thought to myself after hearing the news of his independence. Paradoxically, he had found refuge in the same place I was running away from, a place most of us considered a graveyard of buried hopes. Simbarashe had been dealt the worst possible hand for the first sixteen years of his life. I missed Simbarashe dearly, especially on the weekends Mudiwa was away, visiting his village.

*   *   *

After watching the wrestling, Mudiwa would give me a nasty tackle claiming to be the 'real Yokozuna'. He was slightly bigger than me. It was easy to perceive the landlord's act of relegating us to the cold cement floor as unjust but that never bothered us.

Life is about perception. 'We can complain because rose bushes have thorns or rejoice because thorns have roses', the French critic, Jean-Baptiste Alphonse Karr observed.

We were grateful to the landlord for giving us a glimpse of the TV entertainment many kids in the township never got. We lived simple lives, didn't expect much, and that made us incredibly grateful. Most people would never bother about two scruffy rural boys so this gesture was a bonus for Mudiwa and me. We clapped our hands and shouted '*Maita basa, Mhamha!*' to the landlord's wife, which means 'Thank you, Mum!', as we vacated the premises.

I was thankful for the chance of a good education. At least I had a chance, in time, to alter my situation. Many people weren't as lucky. I was thankful for the people who actually cared about me, such as my brother Lancelot who ran miles alongside me some Monday mornings to shield me from my fears, before boomeranging to the village. I was thankful for all my siblings — none of them ever complained about me going to Rio when they went to the village school. Everyone back home had faith in me and that sustained me during stressful moments.

I was grateful for the many friends I met at Rio and in the township who gave me unconditional love. The first was Edmore Bonda, a short, gap-toothed boy of the *Dziva*, river totem, who also came from Rwizi. Gifted with furious intelligence and near-flawless manners, Bonda, as we called him, was every teachers' dream student. He was one year my junior at Rio. I sometimes caught the same bus as him, when I had the fare, and we talked about our aspirations. Bonda's sheer academic dominance and strong disinclination to mischief in class greatly inspired me. He possessed a fantastic attitude, applied himself daily and refused to give up. He always handled adversity with courage and grace.

Felix Chinodyamari was another. He was widely known as Mutumba, which means Giant, because by the age of fifteen, he was already taller than a gum tree. Mutumba was Bonda's equivalent in my class — he defined standards for academic excellence and challenged himself to do the best job he could. In a class of stars, Mutumba was the brightest of us all. For four years, Mutumba consistently set a high standard that inspired me to work to the full extent of my capabilities.

Mvuto was an ironsmith from Churu village. He rented a dilapidated building next door. His moniker translates to 'furnace', for his ability to turn scrap metal into scotch carts, ploughshares, hoes, anything of value. I never got to know his real name. Whenever I stayed in the township on weekends, Mvuto requested I prepare very hard sadza for him and his cohort. These gormandisers took off their shirts and demolished large portions, long sweaty hairs protruding from their armpits. I collected the leftovers as a reward for my labour, which I then shared with Mudiwa. Most of the ironsmiths had permanent mistresses in the township. These underhand relationships were kept secret from their formal wives who lived in the villages and rarely visited.

Tindo, my best friend from Gavaza, joined me at Rio, together with his older brother Prosper. Tindo and Prosper rented a room from Chimupombi, a brutish old man whose real name I never got to know. Chimupombi means short pipe. He owned a couple of grinding mills and multiple clean boyskys on the outskirts. Tindo and Prosper were much better off than Mudiwa and me as their father had a job in

Harare. Despite this slight difference in relative economic terms, the bond I shared with Tindo was closer than most.

Our bond was reinforced by adversity. We teamed up to fend off bullies like Givemore, an older aggressor from Muponda village, who always threatened to bash us after school hours for no apparent reason. Both Tindo and I relied on each other for defence. We formed a pact that I named 'The Rindikiting Club', derived from the Shona word *kurindikita*, which means heavy bashing. This was all talk, however; we were both too skinny and small-boned to take on the bigger bullies.

Our allegiance to each other was unbreakable — I always covered Tindo's back. One Friday afternoon at school, during a practical building session, Tindo inadvertently broke his trowel. He rushed back to the storeroom in a panic and stuffed the broken trowel onto a shelf, smearing everything around it with red mud. He picked a clean trowel, dashed outside and continued with his prac, pretending nothing had happened. Tindo's spot was next to mine so I witnessed his transgression. No one else saw. Mr Mashakada, our building teacher, fumed when he walked into the storeroom and observed the mess. He rounded up everyone and demanded that someone name the culprit, but no one came forward.

I looked at Tindo and he looked downwards. I hoped he would confess his sins to save our innocent classmates but it was already too late. Mr Mashakada took no prisoners. Nevertheless, I kept my silence. Mr Mashakada quickly followed through with his threat, whipping our backsides until the bougainvillea stick frayed. I later reprimanded him for his selfish act but until now have never disclosed this to anyone. Tindo, and many other of my friends, were willing to help me in exceptionally compassionate ways even when they themselves were going through desperate situations.

I was grateful for Danai, a fine specimen of a young man and another classmate. He was the son of a police officer. My love for Danai was unquestionable but occasionally I got envious when I heard girls whisper of his handsomeness. Danai would throw himself under the bus for me. Sometimes, when he came to play, he smuggled fresh pieces of bread from his mother's kitchen for me.

Some weekends, Danai stole his father's work bicycle so he could teach me how to ride on the dusty roads on the peripheries of the township. It took a while for me to find my balance and cycle independently but Danai stuck with me.

Danai's friendship sheltered me from my loneliness. For four years, he never left my corner. The pain I felt later, when I learnt he had been fatally hit by a car was beyond words. The tragedy happened at Morris Depot, Harare, where he was training to become a police officer like his father. I will remember him forever with deep affection and gratitude.

The last but by no means the least was Ruth Munemo, one of the brightest and cheekiest girls in my class. She was raised by her ageing grandmother in the village. She kept going even when the opportunity looked lost and poverty proved almost inescapable. Like many other brave girls, Ruth demonstrated character when others around them felt the game of life was unfair and cruel. Ruth eventually rose to become a top corporate lawyer in South Africa. I admired girls like her who set their own terms and remained optimistic. Such girls were determined never to allow their selfhood to be weakened by difficult circumstances or to be seduced by manipulative older men. Ruth never lost the urge to fight through dire situations, to grow in pursuit of her dreams like a seed planted deep in the dirt.

We took the time to pause and relish the little joys we had. Choosing to appreciate life's simple pleasures and graces, rather than resent what we couldn't afford, significantly uplifted our spirits. Gratitude lightened our hearts and had a profoundly positive impact.

'Whether your cup is half-full or half-empty, remind yourself there are others without one,' the author Matshona Dhliwayo admonished.

I saw my world as half-full. I had daily struggles, but if I stayed in the top ten of my class, my fees were assured. I was surrounded by amazing friends and was a favourite of several teachers. I constantly dreamt of possibilities but gratitude liberated me from needless anxieties. I thanked God for my blessings as well as my challenges. My life in the township was tough but I would die to remain there.

* * *

And life in the township was not all gloomy. On some weekends, I joined up with other township boys to play with improvised plastic balls on the streets. These games always gave us something to look forward to and cheer about, temporarily distracting us from our challenges. I learnt that I was responsible for my own happiness. If there were not enough players to make up two five-a-side teams, we hung around shops patiently waiting for someone who had a twenty-cent coin to play foosball, a table soccer game also known as slug. But this pastime once got us into trouble. The slugs had a loophole we loved to exploit. When you inserted a twenty-cent coin and pressed the metal lever, ten balls, equivalent to one game, gushed out. You needed another twenty-cent coin to unlock a new game. But if the lever remained pressed, the balls just kept rolling back forever.

Danai and I talked each other into this mischief one day. We paid for one game and chocked the lever using a stone. We played the longest foosball game ever until we could no longer keep score. It was too good to last. Zvichanaka, the stout shop owner whose eyes had turned red from smoking tobacco, couldn't believe such scruffy boys could afford so many games. He was suspicious but too old and heavy to catch any of us. We laughed about our near miss the next day at school.

CHAPTER 6

The Blessing Of Hardship

'Someone I loved once gave me a box full of darkness. It took me years to understand that this too, was a gift.' — Mary Oliver

passed by my auntie's place to check on her family whenever I visited my grandmother. I didn't harbour any grudges. My scholarship, my chance of a lifetime, instilled an ironclad focus on my studies. Besides, my life in the township was already difficult. Bottling resentment would pile on additional baggage and only weigh heavily on my mind, and ultimately my academics. It was important to embrace the future and stop looking backwards.

In the words of T. D. Jakes, the American bishop and author, 'This was a time for me to step out of my history to step into my destiny.' Resentment towards my auntie was not going to benefit me. A lot of people allow bitterness to take deep root and control over their lives — I wasn't one of them.

I had done my best to please my auntie. I was a decent kid and rarely engaged in mischief. My cousin Ruth and I jogged home as soon as we finished school for the day. We arrived before sunset and executed our chores conscientiously. We never loitered aimlessly in the township like other ill-disciplined kids. Yet, that didn't help my situation.

No one wants to run into unnecessary life hurdles. I am not here to romanticise suffering as a necessary means to success. But my rejection at a tender age revealed something to me: obstacles are a fact of life — it is how you respond that matters. This helped me cope with later pressures in positive and adaptive ways, rather than easily capitulate like makeshift savannah clay bulls. I had no way of telling what the future held, the opportunities and challenges. It was only when I looked back and joined the proverbial dots that I realised this situation was a disguised blessing. It hardened me and helped me fight through difficult moments instead of succumbing easily to defeat.

*   *   *

Mudiwa and I never hounded people for money. We toiled for food and made do with what we had. We maximised tiny opportunities. We learnt to be self-reliant, scavenging backyards looking for empty bottles to exchange for deposits so we could buy food. Our struggles forced us to improvise.

I saved the proceeds from my Coca-Cola bottle hustle, and the change I got from doing errands for Lizzy and Masibanda, and bought a large packet of toffee sweets from Metro Peach, a large wholesaler on the fringes of the township. I put the packet between my feet during lessons so they couldn't be pilfered. Between lessons, random classmates walked over to my desk and bought one or two sweets. I craved the mouth-watering deep-brown toffees but resisted, knowing this was business.

Some girls knew how to manipulate my boyhood feelings. They walked over my desk, tilted their heads to one side as their pretty little faces slowly lit up, whispering in gentle voices, 'Phidza, may I please borrow three toffees? I will pay you Monday morning.' I capitulated, gradually bankrupting my venture. If a boy tried on a similar request, I stared at him expressionlessly, telling him to go back to his desk and learn to live within his means.

In 1996, aged sixteen, I combined with some other insatiable youngsters and founded the 'gyming club', a group that wandered around the dining area after lunch and volunteered to clean up heavy-duty pots and plates and sometimes the floor. The head cook paid us in kind with leftovers, which we ate until our tummies bulged like balloons. Other kids formed their own groups creating fierce competition.

One day the head cook picked a different mob and after several minutes of loitering, we gave up. My cheeky classmate, Edmore Chasi, learnt of our predicament. He ran to the class and inscribed large text on the board, *The gyming club bites the dust!* Everyone cracked up at the joke when we walked in, defeated.

My circumstances also forced me to make responsible choices. I stayed away from alcohol, tobacco and teenage relationships, knowing that any simple mistake would take me back to the village school. Such an outcome was unthinkable for me.

Was the solitude that came from living by myself when Lizzy and Masibanda entertained their clients from pubs, a bad thing? Maybe not. I hated being in that wretched place: there was no electricity and my lamp rarely had paraffin. But I responded by multiplying my effort.

When other kids were plugged into the TV — watching *Mvenge-Mvenge* or *Ezomgido*, a popular music video show; *Mukadota*, a comical show featuring the brilliant Safirio Madzikatire; or English Premier League games — I packed my textbooks and ran back to Rio to study at night. This routine helped turn my proverbial lemons into lemonade. It was serendipitous and created long-term advantage: unearthing competencies I never knew I possessed and transforming me into one of the academic stars. The school was vacated so I could focus on my studies without distraction for hours. Over time, a few friends joined me creating a small army of bookworms.

The mindset of grit I developed turned out to be much more important than the preceding hardships. My experiences were lessons in grace, patience and empathy from a school of suffering, not motivational videos. My determination was born out of daily struggle, like a tree fighting through thickets to compete for the sun.

I detested the thought of going back to my village the same as I was when I first went to the township. I was obsessed with improving my circumstances through education. I turned my disadvantage into a powerful tool. My hate for our ramshackle home energised my love for books. School was an escape from my reality. There was no one to cry to so I reacted by throwing myself deeply into my studies. Meanwhile, Mudiwa, who was a grade ahead of me, was struggling badly. Lizzy and Masibanda, when they were around, appeared sombre and withdrawn.

All this pressure at 'home' encouraged me to perform and helped me maintain my scholarship. I learnt to push myself because no one else was going to do it for me. I certainly wanted it enough.

*   *   *

I trusted that if I kept on keeping on, I would eventually live in better conditions like some of my classmates. I was consumed by zeal and became an avid reader. When Lizzy and Masibanda were at their hair salon, I sat on our shared little verandah and binged on Nigerian Pacesetters borrowed from the school library. Pacesetters are a collection of more than a hundred works of fiction by notable African authors published by Macmillan from 1977.

Pacesetters provided a lens through which the citizens of newly independent African states could express their aspirations, as well as examine the joys and contradictions of post-colonial urban life.[7]

I read *Wages of Sin* by Ibe Oparandu, *Too Cold For Comfort* by J. Oguntoye, *Forever Yours* by Helen Ovbiagele, *Evbu My Love* by Helen Ovbiagele, *Naira Power* by Buchi Emecheta, *The Black Temple* by Mohmed Tukur Garba, *Crossfire* by Kalu Okpi, *Felicia* by Rosina Umelo, *Extortionist* by Chuma Nwokolo, *Mark of the Cobra* by Valentine Alily, *Things Fall Apart* by Chinua Achebe and countless more. For a while, I spent more time reading Pacesetters than doing anything else.

The Wages of Sin, a tragic love story between Ojiji, a philandering girl, and Obi, a man who loved her dearly but was repeatedly distraught because of her promiscuity, stuck with me as it resembled the life of Lizzy and her on-again-off-again boyfriend.

Some weekends, I couldn't find friends to hang out with and the solitude was almost unbearable. Pacesetters never let me down. They became my outlet and rescued me from a bleakness that threatened to engulf me. My love for storytelling was born as a result and a bridge to something else, unknown to me at that time. I might not have written this book without those experiences.

I also devoured Shona novels voraciously. I remember fondly the likes of *Kukurukura Hunge Wapotswa* by Edward W. Kaugare, *Garandichauya* by Patrick Chakaipa, *Pafunge* by T. K. Tsodzo, *Kutonhodzwa kwaChauruka* by David Chiguvare, *Jekanyika* by Francis Mugugu, *Kusasana Kunoparira* by Mordecai Hamutyinei, *Karikoga Gumi Remiseve* by Patrick Chakaipa, and *Zvaida Kushinga* by Charles S. Makari.

Muchadura by Father Emmanuel F. Ribeiro, a terrifying story of *ngozi*, a relentless vengeful spirit, gave me the chills at night when I was alone in the boysky.

The American writer Will Durant was right when he said, 'I think the ability of the average man could be doubled if it were demanded, if the situation demanded.'

I multiplied my efforts because I had no choice; my situation was untenable. My love for books intensified; the obsession became a refuge from solitude, a beautiful hiding place from the miseries. Books became a necessity for me — like food — and pushed my English skills to higher levels.

It was during these years I developed an affinity with narratives. I carried a Pacesetter to read whenever I travelled back to my village, whenever I took Baba's cattle deep into the savannah plains. I no longer felt too lonely when I couldn't find fellow herders to merge with. I would just lie in the cool shade under a giant msasa tree and devour my Pacesetter as my cows grazed nearby. Now and then, as the plot thickened, my cows strayed and mowed peoples' crops. Justice was swift and bitter.

As the old saying goes, *The wolf on top of the hill is not as hungry as wolves still climbing the hill.* I was that wolf at the bottom of the hill and there wasn't much there. I yearned to get to the top.

*   *   *

Today, I can help my family, underprivileged kids from my community and orphans because of the life I have lived. My lived experience has expanded my capacity for compassionate understanding. There were lessons I could only get from a place of pain. 'What is to give light must endure burning,' as Viktor Frankl put it.

I understand the plight of those at the bottom because I spent two and half decades there. I have seen, touched, and lived poverty. The stress that I went through stripped away the gloss at an early age, helping me discover the core of my existence. I was rejected by close relatives during my most vulnerable and neediest days, then accepted and believed in by assorted strangers.

Everyone judged Lizzy and Masibanda, as prostitutes who had succumbed to a deplorable morality. But I observed things from a closer distance. Lizzy and Masibanda also once had big dreams, like most village girls. The door of opportunity had been slammed in their faces through no fault of their own.

Lizzy never brought boyfriends home when her father visited from the village. She cleaned up the place, wore a long skirt, and prepared a decent meal for him. She politely asked Mudiwa and me to clear up the verandah for a few hours. It was heartbreaking to see daily struggles rob her of a decent life.

Through my trials, God gifted me with an opportunity to encourage others through lived struggles, not theories. I embrace everyone the same way, be they an executive vice president from Goldman Sachs or a shoe repairer in Mubayira township. We are connected by our common humanity, regardless of where we come from.

CHAPTER 7

Running Away From Problems

'The cowards never started, and the weak died along the way. That leaves us, ladies and gentlemen. Us.' — Phil Knight (founder of Nike)

Clarity of goals honed my focus and resolve to keep pushing in the absence of instant rewards. I knew that education was my only exit door. Not a day passed over the course of two and a half decades where I did not reflect on my ultimate goal. I yearned for the day I would leave my village for the city, become gainfully employed and afford my family a dignified life. The path was long, tedious and uncertain, but settling for shorter-term goals would have buried my potential. I wanted to succeed in my academics more than anything and was determined to do everything necessary to make my four-year mission at Rio a success.

Most Friday evenings, I ran back to my village. I never measured the distance but our nearest bus stop, Rwizi, was marked twenty-three kilometres from the township. I had an option to stay in the township, hang out with friends and study, but usually my food was running precariously low. Running back home guaranteed much better meals than I could prepare in my boysky. I was only fourteen years old — I badly missed my family and my dog, Bhoki.

As soon as the headmaster dismissed us, at 4 p.m., I grabbed a Pacesetter and took off. I held the Pacesetter in my left hand and my shoes in the other. I feared that if I left my shoes in the boysky, a vagrant would break in and steal them. The first few Fridays, I ran with my shoes on but I felt the extra weight impeded my high jogging tempo and needlessly burnt more calories. In bare feet, I maintained a light, efficient and fast stride. Besides, my feet were already harder than a rhino's skin, thanks to the perennially harsh savannah conditions.

Running with my shoes on would have quickly depreciated them. I determined it was much better to endure freezing winters, muddy summer tracks and occasional injuries than damage my shoes, as I had no way of replacing them. Unlike Gavaza Primary School, Rio did not allow bare feet, so it was a responsible choice.

I took off past the imposing Metro Peach Wholesale before disappearing into the msasa woods, right through Mubayira and Matemera villages, towards my roots, on familiar dusty and meandering tracks. I was almost always the first to leave because, as far as I know, I had the furthest to run of all Rio students in my direction. I never saw any kids in Rio uniforms once I had passed Goroni Primary School.

I refused to be drawn into any after-school chit-chat in the knowledge that, if it turned dark before I reached my village, I would be on my own. Fear of darkness terrorised me. There were countless (unproven) tales of ruffians, hired by local businessmen, who would waylay pedestrians, dismember private body parts and mix them with *muti*. The concoction was believed to attract new customers.

I jogged past sparsely populated hamlets, undernourished dogs barking at me from a distance. Sometimes there was hardly anyone in sight; sometimes I ran into *sjambok*-cracking herders rounding up their livestock. The melodious sound of *nyenze*, cicadas in the blooming savannah woodlands, distracted me from the agony of my legs. The shade of the lush msasa trees that lined the dusty tracks kept me cool.

When I was parched, I pleaded for water over degraded barbed-wire fences at random homesteads. Warm-hearted villagers always responded with extraordinary Ubuntu, rushing to the fence with a large brown *mukombe*, calabash, full of cold water. I gulped it down, conveyed my gratitude and ran on. I could hear the water sloshing in my little stomach as I jogged.

The first few runs were agonizing. My body was not conditioned to run half-marathons. I did not have any complex drinks, glucose supplements or anti-blister aids. The first miles were the hardest. I slowed down when I needed to but I never stopped. Sometimes thoughts of quitting engulfed my mind but my love for school was so intense it diverted me from the knife-like pain on freezing winter mornings. The thought that if I kept at it, I could eventually own one of those cars whose gas I smelt long after they had overtaken me, motivated me to run on. If I overcame my pain, eventually I would matter like those well-to-do city dwellers who visited the village during Christmas holidays. It was mind over matter: as long as my mind did not give up, my body complied, but when my mind doubted, my legs weakened.

My lungs screamed for oxygen and my body begged me to stop. My mind fought every urge to quit, powered by a deep conviction that if I kept chipping away, I would maintain my scholarship and be on a pathway to a better future. I discovered there was always more untapped potential, the harder I dug.

I have since responded to several bizarre questions from my Australian friends. A workmate once quizzed, 'Were you sponsored by Nike during those runs?' As if that was not even enough, the same colleague persisted, 'What were the readings from your Fitbit?' There were no Fitbits in even the US in the 1990s — the chances I would have owned one in the savannah are zero.

*   *   *

The hardest moments came when I ran through a storm or heavy showers. But I knew that Marion, Kristin and my parents deeply believed in me — that bolstered my perseverance. I had received an opportunity that my siblings and peers in the village could only dream of. Giving up would have been an unthinkable let-down. My parents would easily consent if instead I chose to transfer to the village school but they never pressured me into this. I had a responsibility to make the most of my chance and not squander it.

I ran back to school before sunrise. About halfway, I encountered teenagers jogging in the opposite direction, to my village school. Although Rio was a much better school and nearer their homesteads, their parents could only afford the same village school I was literally running away from. I looked at the world through the eyes of those kids running in the opposite direction. I reminded myself that, no matter how gruelling my runs, I was still in a much better situation.

On my way home one Friday, soon after passing Matemera village, an elderly gentleman overtook me in his scotch cart. He would have been in his sixties; his cart was of the donkey-drawn, two-wheeled, spring-less, wooden type. He was singing, 'Pamsoro, pakudenga pane vatsvene voga', an ancient hymn, which means 'Only the holy shall make it to heaven', with incredible passion. He whistled gently and his four dark-brown donkeys came to a halt. This stranger had a large, shiny, bald head, heavily contrasted by a long grey beard that extended to his pot belly. He was clad in pure white oversized garments and wore brown leather sandals. I could immediately tell he was a *Mupositori*, a sect that follows hard-line religious beliefs, although I was unsure which particular faction. His Old Testament appearance made him look like Elijah but his old donkeys and antiquated cart were no chariot of fire.

'Where are you going, young man?'

'Gonzo village, sir,' I responded enthusiastically.

'Okay, jump in, I am going to Rukuma, so I will drop you near your kraal.'

Rukuma was approximately ten kilometres further south of my homestead. I made myself comfortable on the cart. The Good Samaritan unleashed a thunderous *sjambok* on his donkeys and steered them back onto the dusty track.

The Good Samaritan fired the usual question at me, one that always blew my fuse.

'Youngster, why are you punishing yourself running to such a faraway school when Rwizi, Neuso, Rukuma, Ndori and other second-ary schools are way closer to your kraal?'

I felt people always questioned my determination with a conde-scending undertone. No one ever asked me why, with an open mind;

theirs was a rhetorical question to expose my 'remarkable foolishness', by older people who considered themselves wiser. But I didn't need their approval. No amount of negativity or sarcasm could ever cage my ambition.

I pondered for a few minutes before firing back.

'None of the secondary schools you have mentioned squares up to Rio, sir. My school boasts a stellar academic record. We even have about half a dozen expatriate teachers.'

'You are taught by white people?' the Good Samaritan's eyes widened with amazement.

'Yes, my biology teacher, Mr Schneider, is from Germany,' I politely responded.

The mention of the word *biology* seemed to disorient him. Maybe fearing this line of conversation would expose his illiteracy, the Good Samaritan quickly redirected the dialogue towards his comfort zone. He enquired instead about my totem.

'We are of the Tembo Samaita, but my mother hails from the Unendoro dynasty.'

'Are you serious?' he interjected, his wide grin exposing protruding yellow teeth. 'I am therefore your Sekuru, as I too am *Mhukahuru* (majestic elephant). I feel so good having given a lift to my Muzukuru.'

After we had established our distant familial bonds, the Good Samaritan turned to religion: coaxing me to dump my Catholic beliefs. He dismissed these as a Western faith system imposed by colonisers and zealously tried to persuade me to convert to his Johane Chishanu Masowe beliefs.

The founder of their sect, Sixpence Shonhiwa Masedza, was born in 1914 in Manicaland Province. He was believed to be the reincarnation of John the Baptist: Johane Masowe means 'John of the Wilderness'. He went on to detail how only Johane Chishanu Masowe believers were predestined to inherit the kingdom of heaven. Everyone else, including me, would burn eternally in hellfire. However, if I chose his proclaimed light over my darkness, he would steer his cart towards Nyangweni River and baptize me.

I gently shook my head, hiding my true disgust at his proselytising. His message got creepier when he dismissed the Bible as stale, arguing that the only redemptive truth was through special Johane Masowe Chishanu prophets. I appreciated his transport but not the preaching as he rambled on.

The Good Samaritan whistled gently and his donkeys obeyed, slowing down as we arrived at my kraal. I thanked him, grabbed my Pacesetter and shoes, and jumped down from the cart. Bhoki spotted me from a dim distance and sprinted, jumping onto my chest and almost tearing my school shirt. I never met that Good Samaritan again.

*　　*　　*

Baba woke up before sunrise and read the time using the position of Nyamatsatse, the bright morning star. Nyamatsatse was my family's trusted guide for decades as none of us owned a watch. I washed my face, legs and arms, with freezing water in a silver metal dish, then Lancelot and I took off through the savannah landscape.

Lancelot dictated the pace, running on his toes, twenty metres or so in front, holding the small sack of food my mother had packed for me. I did my best to keep up with him, stride for stride, but occasionally fell behind as my stamina waned. Lancelot was four years older so he was a much stronger and more experienced runner than me. Creatures leapt through the dry grass that towered beside the tracks — the resulting spikes of dopamine forced me to accelerate and keep up.

I was so scared of the darkness but Lancelot was always there for me. He was an unwavering comrade and for years my secret weapon. He stayed tight, never listened to his moods, ignored weather conditions and just ran on. Lancelot had no designated turning point: as long as it was dark, he kept running and only turned back after daybreak.

One Sunday night, Mother Nature unleashed a fearsome thunderstorm, an unrelenting downpour and gusty winds across the savannah. When we woke the next morning, the swamps were heavily flooded. Bullfrogs had been evicted from their habitats and there were dead crickets floating everywhere. Lancelot, sensing danger ahead, decided that it was better for us to use our alternate route — to run up east towards Kwari bus stop then jog along the highway to the township. That way, he could help me cross Nyangweni River on its upper and safer side. The Nyangweni runs into the Mupfure, a tributary of the Sanyati River, which in turn feeds into the mighty Zambezi. The longest east-flowing river in Africa, the Zambezi runs an astounding 2,700 kilometres across six African countries to the Indian Ocean.

We could hear the river from a distance; when closer, we could see the situation was grim. The swift flows had ravaged the riverbanks. This was the worst that I had ever seen it.

Lancelot usually had an unadulterated appetite for risk. He plundered beehives and trapped black mambas. That morning, however, he exuded a rare unwillingness. We stood there for several minutes until Lancelot eventually whispered:

'Give me your hand; we are going to cross together. Keep your feet as close as you can to the ground. If you lift them high, you will soon be history.'

I hesitantly extended my right hand to him. I lifted my left high to preserve my Pacesetter.

About one-third of the way across it felt doable. But without warning, a vicious undercurrent swept us and we struggled to maintain balance. Lancelot grabbed on to the reeds with one hand. I could feel his grip around my wrist tighten like a bobbejaan spanner. My survival instincts kicked in and I dropped my Pacesetter. I staggered but Lancelot kept tightening his hold. We made it to the other side but the powerful river had pushed us north. I felt closer to death during that escapade than any of my innumerable savannah trials. We recouped and kept running, the adrenaline pumping hard. Lancelot ran alongside me until the break of dawn, before boomeranging back to the village. He never complained or made any excuses.

*   *   *

The running bolstered me. If I had had it easy, I would have been like a half-baked mud brick that crumbles at the slightest exposure to rain.

The runs demonstrated the invincible tenacity of the human spirit and uncovered hidden capability. I became a long-distance runner at school, demolishing five-thousand-metre races with relative ease. When the teacher blew the start whistle, I closed my mouth, breathed in through my nose and just took off at high speed. Five kilometres felt like a walk in the park after my half-marathons runs to and from home. Without this involuntary training, I would not have had a credible chance in big races against kids who were actually two years older than me.

Let me explain why. Like most communal farmers, my parents did not consistently, formally register their children's births — they only did so out of necessity. When my sister Rosemary, two years older than me, needed to register for her grade-seven exams, my parents travelled to Chegutu to acquire birth certificates for both of us. But they messed up and registered us as twins, using Rosemary's date of birth. My birth certificate still reads 'Twin-2'. I became two years older than by my real date of birth. The error was never corrected and the school treated me in accordance with that mistake. I therefore competed against kids who were much bigger than me. And it was even harder when competing against kids from other secondary schools who showed up with their younger brothers' birth certificates. By form three, I was already running in the 'Open' age group.

Pushing through pain gave me strength to draw on whenever I felt doubtful, incapable or disinclined. Running taught me to be 'a closer', the important habit of finishing what I start. The physical exertion toughened my mindset. Others complained they had no bus fare and Rio was too far; I responded by running faster.

When I was alone and fearful, I avoided the bush tracks and ran along the tarred road. Cars, lorries and bicycles overtook me but I kept running until I got to the Kwari bus terminus then turned right, towards my kraal. Occasionally, a benevolent driver stopped just past me but I slowed down deliberately to indicate I wasn't taking up their generous offer of a lift. My mother had sternly warned me against hitchhiking with strangers. I only took up the offer if I spotted other Rio kids in the car.

Some village teachers told me that my long runs to and from the township would amount to nothing. Initially that agitated me but over time, I was unbothered by such negativity. It only fuelled my resolve to succeed. I ran faster — I was determined to prove them wrong.

My focus intensified on what mattered, de-emphasised what was non-essential. If I could maintain my running tempo through the first two villages, then I tapped into a new reservoir of energy. The pain became more tolerable, over time diminishing to trivial.

I kept running because education was at the centre of my ambition; nothing else mattered. In golf, there is the mulligan: a second chance to reload if the first shot is wasted. I had no mulligans. My determination came from the certainty that if I missed this one chance, my future would be unbearable.

Running became a powerful tool for introspection and self-discovery. It narrowed the gulf between my self-imposed mental limitations and what I could do. Running taught me that I wasn't born with grit: it is something I can muster and constantly nurture.

By the age of fourteen, I had grown sick of the monotony of village life in the savannah. Rio provided the most plausible opportunity to extricate myself from this life, characterised by toil, bottomless poverty, and hopelessness. It forced me to dig deeper until I excavated mental and physical abilities previously masked by a weak belief I had always previously obeyed. I had to run forward in the absence of alternatives.

Unfortunately, this was a tough reality for my siblings. They had to juggle demanding chores — cutting down trees for firewood, tilling other people's fields for a pittance, herding cattle — while doing their best at a village school starved of books and other essentials. They toiled daily with little reprieve. I had my own challenges but I would rather those than wander hopelessly around the savannah. It was my home but it was also devoid of hope; there was not much to look forward to there. Here and there, you heard of someone who eventually became a teacher after several attempts to attain O levels. That script did not inspire me; I wanted to walk a different path.

*   *   *

I defaulted to my old routines when back in the village during school holidays. I took over the herd from Lancelot and wandered across the savannah grasslands. At the age of sixteen, I was old enough not to be coerced into any bouts. I was admired for a higher quality of education that others had no hope of accessing. Most herders would not have seen a television, let alone know who Yokozuna was. I demon-strated double kicks, takedowns, and head-and-arm throws as they looked on with interest.

I used imagery to segment my half-marathon runs into smaller chunks. At first, I took off at unsustainable speeds and inevitably imploded after a few kilometres. Over time, I trained myself to just chip away the next mile, then focus on the next. I learnt to stay focused on the moment and resist the urge to waste precious energy thinking too far ahead. I fixated on one village at a time to avoid becoming overwhelmed by the enormity of the distance.

Besides my constant desire to excel at Rio, I was also motivated to run as fast as I could because our headmaster, Mr Hungwe, severely punished latecomers. Short and stout, Mr Hungwe had been at the helm of the school since its inception in 1982. He was a firm believer in the use of corporal punishment to weed out troublemakers and create a culture of sustained high performance. That doctrine worked to a great extent. Rio had impeccable academic and sporting records. For several consecutive years, Rio crushed surrounding schools in athletic competitions. When Mr Hungwe left the school, Rio quickly became a shadow of its former glory.

The headmaster treated us to a four-hour disco whenever Rio topped the zonal athletic competition. DJs travelled all the way from Harare to entertain us. This inspired teamwork, with the entire school screaming 'Disco, disco, disco!' as our athletes decimated competitors, especially in the short distance sprints and relay competitions.

But I hated this 'spare the rod and spoil the child' regime. Rio main-tained half a dozen 'groundsmen' whose main duties included main-taining the lush flower beds, picking up mail at the post office, and cooking lunch for the students. Simply put, groundsmen were school labourers. Mr Hungwe delegated sweeping powers to them and the prefects, who then abused this authority by booking students for the smallest misbehaviours. The groundsmen exploited the students, getting them to do some of the manual chores they had been hired to do. They were heavily conflicted by this self-fulfilling arrangement.

On Friday afternoons, the head boy read out the names of dozens of offenders who had to show up on Saturday to till the school fields, water the garden or wheelbarrow large rocks from the river. I was booked several times for being 'greedy at the dining', the most ambiguous and embarrassing of offences, despite my conscious efforts to avoid these excruciating punishments. Sadly, some prefects exacted vengeful measures on kids they disliked or those who outmanoeuvred them in romantic battles.

*   *   *

Rio had several teachers whom I greatly admired. Mr Takawira was my geography teacher. He was a towering giant and walked with a straight, confident posture. Mr Takawira believed in my academic potential and greatly trusted me. I sold his freezits during the break. In return, he gifted me one back, which I sucked during the dying minutes of the interval. When Mr Takawira travelled to Harare, where his family lived, he entrusted me to stay at his lavish house. He would remain a close friend for decades.

I also loved my biology teacher, Mr Schneider. He was a twenty-seven-year-old expatriate from Germany. He executed his duties with extreme professionalism. When the bell rang, Mr Schneider packed his books and left. Other teachers stayed longer than necessary, eating into our study or playtime, which I hated. The German expatriates endeared themselves to students because, despite their hard-to-understand accents, they never caned anyone. On the contrary, most local teachers flogged wrongdoers on the spot. (I was surprised that Mr Schneider, an extremely pale white man, born and raised in Europe, spoke in broken English. I naively assumed that every white man was fluent in English.) But Mr Schneider was not always smiling. He looked extremely distressed one Monday morning. Soon after walking in for our thirty-five-minute biology lesson, he lashed out:

'I stay in Germany for twenty-seven years, I never see a *tsotsi* [a mugger]! I come to Zimbabwe two months, I see a *tsotsi*.'

Word later spread across the school that Mr Schneider had been mugged in Harare and lost a few valuables. I had no idea why he was angry at us; we were not the *tsotsi*.

I loved being at school more than anywhere else and made great bonds with so many teachers. These include, in no particular order: Mr Berejena, who took over from Mr Hungwe as the headmaster, and briefly taught us geography (his name means 'the white hyena'); Mrs Marowa, our guidance and counselling teacher who sternly warned against the consequences of teenage pregnancy and STDs; Mrs Chinhoyi, a descendant of Chief Mashayamombe, who was my history teacher and public speaking mentor; Mr Marikisi, the gentle giant whose knowledge of chemistry was almost encyclopedic (who, also, had been through Fidel Castro's Zimbabwe-Cuban teacher training program); my building teachers, Mr Matekenya and Mr Goho; and Mrs Matekenya, a woman with an unerring eye for mathematical details who forced me out of my comfort zone.

*   *   *

On occasional Fridays, when I had fifty cents, I caught a bus with Bonda and a handful of other kids who commuted daily from the nearby villages. This was significantly less toll on my body but had its own challenges. There were three buses that left Mubayira for Rwizi every evening, although the time was never guaranteed: the light-and-dark green Vazungu (which weirdly translates to 'white people'), the yellow-and-dark-green Mhuriro, and the gold-and-green Suffer Continue. It would already be dark when the bus arrived at Rwizi. I was too terrified to run home alone, which was approximately five kilometres away.

There were always teachers from my village school drinking in the beer hall. I hung out with them until the pub closed and then we walked together through the cornfields and dusty tracks. But these teachers did not like that I chose Rio rather than my village school.

'Why are you subjecting yourself to so much torture, young man?' Mr Mabhiza always quizzed. (His surname translates to 'horses'.)

'Do you think teachers at Rio are any better than us? We trained at the same colleges. I even know some of them. I am not sure why you think we can't give you the same education here. Be careful, because there is a wide gap between what you fantasise and reality, youngster.'

Nothing the village schoolteachers said could alter my view — their negativity only fuelled my determination. I knew that one day, if I held on to my opportunity, I would prove them all wrong. I itched to rebuke them but restrained myself. If I were in their shoes, I would probably feel the same; they felt rejected by a teenager and that might hurt. They may have despised my 'uninformed fanaticism' but these were the teachers who taught my brothers and sisters. I simply had to suck it up — I needed their protection in the dark and sometimes rainy nights.

I performed poorly in maths during my first two and a half years at Rio, up until the age of sixteen. I excelled in other subjects but mathematics remained my soft underbelly. I barely made the 50 per cent mark in major exams.

But from year three, I realised maths would be central to my future ambitions. Except for a few occupations, like the police and army, most vocations had O-level maths as a prerequisite. I decided to take action during the winter of 1996, to throw off the mental and other limitations I had imposed on myself.

I stepped up my effort, solving complex equations and deconstructing formulae during my free time. I started paying attention during maths classes. My maths teacher, Mrs Matekenya, really liked me and was a big influence on me. I also frequently sold her freezits during breaks or inter-school sports competitions. Our close teacher-student relationship played a crucial role in boosting my confidence and passion for maths. I felt I had an obligation to live up to her expectations. When I dropped the residual freezits at her house, Mrs Matekenya gave me several past exam papers, and sometimes, her textbook. My weakness in maths morphed into a strength through a year of consistent practice and intense focus.

I persisted through setbacks, equated effort with a path to mastery, found lessons and inspiration in the success of others. When Mrs Matekenya announced the 1997 mid-year maths results, everyone was surprised — I had topped my class. I had made myself strong in what was my weakest spot. I had beaten my friend Mutumba for the first time in three and half years.

CHAPTER 8

Ran a Good Race

Chegutu Rural District Council moderately raised Baba's wage during the summer of 1997. That allowed him to do what he had always wanted: to rescue me from the boysky and the distressed conditions I had been living in for more than three years.

Baba secured a room for me at Samanyemba General Dealers, the small grocery store next door to Mhondoro Arms, the beer hall where we met on his monthly payday trips. The owner, Sekuru Samanyemba, allocated one of the three rooms in his main boysky to us. (Mudiwa moved with me.) Sekuru was a retired headmaster and strict disciplinarian, now in his mid-seventies. He was an imposing, flabby, wrinkly giant with large droopy lips, sagging jowls and teary eyes. He had never touched alcohol or tobacco all his life and always boasted about these achievements. My feelings towards him were complex. I feared him but also admired his work ethic and expectations of excellence.

His wife, Gogo Samanyemba, was starkly different to him. (She was his second wife; his first had passed on.) She was harmless and softer than wool. Gogo was twenty years younger than her husband and barely five foot tall. From a distance, one might think she was half-white because of her natural tan, but her kinky African hair indicated her Bantu heritage. She still, in her fifties, possessed features that suggested, during her prime, she was dangerously beautiful.

It seemed Sekuru had muted feelings. He was a man devoid of ordinary warmth. He rarely smiled at anyone, including customers. Sekuru was, to put it mildly, frightening. Gogo, on the other hand, was lively. She stood on an empty wooden soft-drink crate, with an African scarf elegantly tied around her head, and cheerfully greeted customers. It seemed to me that alcohol was her only vice, but she never drank in Sekuru's presence. Whenever he travelled to Harare for his frequent medical check-ups, she sent me to Zvichanaka Bottle Store to buy two or three scuds. She sipped the booze under the giant mango tree shade whose overhanging branches extended into Mhondoro Arms beer hall premises until she was pie-eyed. If Sekuru didn't disembark from his usual 5:30 p.m. bus, Gogo asked me to run to Zvichanaka again and buy a Castle Lager pint, to 'wash off' the *masese*.

I quickly developed a strong rapport with both Samanyembas. When Sekuru was away, Gogo occasionally asked me to relieve her with shopkeeping duties while she indulged in alcohol. The love she showed me constantly ignited loving memories of my grandmother, VaMushonga. Some Saturday mornings, the Samanyembas sent me on bicycle to deliver foodstuffs to workers at their rural homestead near Chinengundu Township. This was several kilometres away from the township. I rode the bicycle at terrific speeds, crossed the Nyangweni River and off into the rugged Mashayamombe terrain. But Mudiwa never developed the same level of trust. For some reason, Sekuru thought Mudiwa had potential for mischief. He never wanted to see him near the wooden shelves that were stacked with tempting delicacies.

One of my older cousins, Tarzan, visited us one Sunday afternoon. He lived near Goroni, a primary school situated about halfway between my village and the township. If notoriety were taekwondo, Tarzan would already have attained the ninth dan black belt, grand master status. Tarzan was a thief by his mid-teens, stealing chickens, goats, groundnuts, sugarcane, anything of any value. He snuck into the tall savannah grass just before dawn and took mice from their other people's traps. He leapt over the protective wooden barriers into kraals, strapped cows' legs and milked them straight into his wide-open mouth. Tarzan had predictably dropped out of primary school; he did not even make the seventh grade.

He frequented the township and loitered around, exploring targets to hit during the night. When Tarzan rocked up at Samanyemba's and saw me standing behind the shop counter with absolutely no supervision, Machiavellian plans besieged his mind. Later that night, he came over to our boysky for a 'sleepover'.

'Phidza, next time those oldies let you in behind that counter, let me know. I want you to grab the cash box, creep back to the boysky, and hand it over to me. I will give you a good portion of whatever amount we get.'

There was no way in a thousand years I could sacrifice everything I had endured for three years to participate in Tarzan's evil ploy. Besides, I could never steal even a lolly from Gogo Samanyemba. She treated me like her own grandson. For the three days, Tarzan roamed around our boysky. I kept a close eye on him. He eventually lashed out.

'People like you, Phidza, are good for nothing! Those muscles are just for eating sadza, nothing else worthwhile!'

This was a senseless dig. I was so skinny and barely had a fibre of muscle. Eventually he gave up and retreated to his village.

Unlike some wine, Tarzan never got better with age. He was later locked up in prison with hard labour for battering his aged father, who had chided him for stealing his grain.

*   *   *

Our new place was certainly better than the one before, the dilapidated and hazardous place we lived in alongside Lizzy and Masibanda, but it still had several shortcomings. There were potholes on the floor and we always had to lock up as it was located so close to the Mhondoro Arms beer hall. I was grateful for the 'upgrade' but Mudiwa was discontent. We were treated differently by the Samanyembas and this intensified Mudiwa's distaste for the new dwelling. He voiced his frustration.

'I want to look for a better place; I am sick and tired of these shabby boyskys!'

His intentions were clear. He would probably go mad if he stayed any longer at Samanyemba's. Mudiwa hurriedly secured another place at Nkomo, a homestead situated on the outskirts of the township, along the old Harare road. I agreed to go and view the room. The landlord, Gogo Nkomo, was a lovely woman who had let out to dozens of Rio kids over the years. The room was much cleaner and secure than ours, but the thatched huts, kraal and roaming chickens put me off. The village ambience reminded me of my own homestead. I also did not like the abruptness of Mudiwa's move. And it was impossible for me to move away from the Samanyembas without Baba's knowledge.

Mudiwa was obsessed, however, his frustration unrelenting. He confronted Sekuru and abruptly gave notice.

'Sir, Phillimon and I will be moving out to a cheaper place in three weeks.'

The little shop was instantly engulfed with tension as Sekuru stared down Mudiwa, his oversized lips trembling with rage.

'You found somewhere cheap! You pay heavily discounted rent here, because I was a teacher my entire life, and want the best out of you. So, how dare you want to stay for three more weeks here, you unappreciative and unruly boy?'

Mudiwa had come with the intention of dressing down Sekuru Samanyemba. Little did he know he was jumping into a boiling tub.

Gogo was paralysed by her husband's volcanic burst of rage and stood there, motionless, like a deer in the headlights. Sekuru forcefully pulled his drawer, grabbed a blue twenty-dollar note and a red ten-dollar one and threw them over the counter.

'Here is the portion of your rent; go spend it at the cheaper place. You have a head the size of Suffer Continue, but you are as thick as a plank. I want you out in two days!'

My mind raced at full throttle. Mudiwa, by invoking my name, had thrust me between a rock and a hard place. As I struggled to recover my position, Sekuru, madder than hell, turned to me. Holding another thirty dollars in his hand, he yelled:

'Are you leaving for the cheaper place too, Phillimon?'

'No, no, not me, Sekuru. Baba is unaware of this and I have no intention of leaving.'

Mudiwa stared at me with a wide-open mouth. He felt I had betrayed him but that was not the case. There was no way I would move away from the Samanyembas without Baba's knowledge. Mudiwa's moves were too hasty for my liking.

'Okay, you stay and pay me the same thirty dollars you have been paying, but I want this idiot out in two days!' he lashed, stashing the money back in his drawer.

Two days later, Mudiwa vacated. He commuted from his village, Kadhani, some forty kilometres from the township, until his lease at Nkomo kicked in. That episode marked the end of our close three-year association. I missed Mudiwa dearly.

*   *   *

Sometimes I walked to the shop next door and sat down with Sekuru Gava, another shop owner.

While his name means Jackal, Gava was one of the most thought-ful and caring people I ever met in the township. He was a small man but radiated authority. His passion and enthusiasm were infectious. I never heard Gava speak ill of anyone. I am not sure if he had a wife back in the village or not. Gava had a stamina that would be uncom-mon in people twenty years younger than him. I estimated him to be in his mid-seventies, about Sekuru Samanyemba's age, but he cycled several kilometres every day, to and from his village, navigating potholes and gradients on an old black bicycle that didn't have gears.

Gava's hollowed cheeks betrayed his old age. As Zimbabweans love to say, he had enjoyed too many Christmases. But I was impressed by his unconstrained drive. He arrived just after sunrise and left at sunset. Unlike Samanyemba's, Gava's shop was almost empty: a handful of packets of brown sugar, *kapenta* (dried baby fish), boxes of matches, jars of multicoloured niggerballs and one or two other groceries scattered on the shelves. Expiry dates had faded away; nonetheless, he sold to customers who cared more about prices. Most days, Gava sold not a single item but he remained cheerful and undeterred. He lived his frugal, modest lifestyle; the store was a pastime. He earned a living from his herd of cattle and subsistence farming back in his village.

Gava showed up daily wearing a khaki shirt, matching pants, and shoes. His shirt was always neatly tucked in, with a thick dark-brown belt tightened high up, on his belly button. I was more than sixty years Gava's junior but we quickly developed a strong bond. He acknowledged me from a distance, shouting, *Hama yemurume!*, which means 'beloved brother!' Sekuru Gava's salutation made me feel manly and important. We basked in the glorious savannah sun sitting on his wooden bench outside his tiny shop for hours, Gava oozing timeless wisdom. When I was at school, he would just sit alone on his bench, looking incredibly serene.

I had been at Samanyemba's about five months when my older sister Maidei married Stanley Chiweshe, a health officer at Mubayira General Hospital. He was a tall, skinny light-skinned and introverted man. Stanley was also a diehard English Premier League fan. He stayed up late into the night, until the final whistle, getting up and down to fetch bottles of Lion Lager.

Stanley was sympathetic to my lonely circumstances: he invited me to live with Maidei and him in their modest marital three-bedroom white-and-green painted house. It was close to school, located a few hundred metres from Rio. Stanley had an electric stove, maroon-fabric sofas, colour television, and a fridge. He even had a spare bed, which they generously donated to me. Their place reminded me of the teachers' houses that I frequented to sell freezits.

For about one and half terms, I stayed there mostly with Stanley and his mother, Gogo Chiweshe. She visited frequently from Hwedza, her communal lands, situated 130 kilometres south-east of Harare. Maidei, after graduating from the village school, was now employed as a temporary teacher at Nyatsanga Primary School, about twelve kilometres west of our village. She came back to the township on Friday nights and caught a bus back on Sunday afternoons. The timing of my move was opportune. After I had finished preparing dinner, I jumped over the fence and ran to Rio to study, now a stone's throw away. I sat for my last O-level exam in November 1997 then returned to my village to resume my savannah duties.

*   *   *

It was February 1998. Word spread that the eagerly anticipated O-level results were out. I was back in my village, rounding up my cows into the kraal, when I heard the news. I was overcome by a deep sense of anxiety and could hardly sleep that night. The next morning, I took off towards the township. I ran almost non-stop and arrived at Rio soon around 9 a.m.

'Zongooooooooooooooo!' an excited teacher shouted from the staff room. I kept my head down and proceeded to the headmaster's office in a state of unbearable anxiety. Mr Berejena quickly pulled my exam slip from the drawer. His face was translucent with joy; he handed me the slip and said, 'Congratulations, Zongo, I am very proud of you, man!'

As I looked at the slip, all the emotions I had constrained gushed out in full force, like ocean waves. I had just passed nine subjects, five of them with distinctions. I came out the best of all students who pursued the 'pure sciences' syllabus (maths, physics, chemistry and biology). I could not comprehend how I — a skinny boy who had experienced some of the deepest hardships — had topped my class. The magical moment catapulted my spirit to towering heights. This was the greatest triumph of my life, and to this day, remains one of my most unforgettable days. I quickly thought of Marion, Kristin and my parents, and was overcome with tears of gratitude.

I had reserved my best performance to last, waiting until the end to make my big move. A dream most considered near impossible had come true, an achievement that exceeded what everyone in my village thought possible. It was a moment I had been dreaming of for so many years. I could have stayed in that blissful moment forever.

I could now go on to do much more than I thought. Money aside, with those grades, I could be accepted for A levels by any high school in Zimbabwe. All the hard work, the half-marathons in bare feet, the endless hustle, the physical and emotional pain — it had finally synthesised into a victory that defied prediction and expectation.

It had appeared to be a long shot four years prior. I remembered the teachers at my village school who told me that my endless travail would amount to nothing, and simply smiled. My grades had shattered that narrative. I had proved the doubters wrong despite my deprivations. I had attacked my goals with the zest of youth, given every fibre of my being to this mission, utilised every tool in the box. I had excelled despite the odds.

I felt a surge of emotions. I vaulted into the staff room and hugged all the amazing teachers who had nurtured me. I screamed until my voice grew hoarse. A little voice whispered into my head, *Phidza, look at you, how far you have come.* Where I came from, people did not come this far. In my village, students averaged two to three sittings to attain a mere five O levels. That summer entrenched a lifelong lesson, one that would anchor my ambitions throughout my lifetime. I learned that I could do anything as long as I was willing to make significant personal sacrifices — to keep moving with dogged persistence even when I felt like my internal engine had lost its energy.

I had beat kids with superior academic skills. I had outperformed kids who had a comfortable existence: those who carried toast with butter to school; who lived in houses with electric stoves and heated geysers; who slept with mosquito nets over their beds; and those who attended prestigious private schools alongside rich white kids. Nothing was impossible if I wanted it badly enough.

My high distinction despite the odds was not because of my intelligence. It resulted from a convergence of three factors. First, Marion and Kristin's unconditional love for me. Second, my parents' foresight and sacrifices, as well as support from my siblings. Third, the many teachers who believed in me and mentored me. Equally important was my mindset: the refusal to acknowledge glass ceilings, the disinclination to make excuses, and the disposition to keep going when life constantly felt hard.

I ran around the school like a crazy boy, showing my slip to younger students, caretakers, cooks and anyone I came across. I lingered around for hours, celebrating with classmates who had also passed, while feeling bad for those with lowered heads, who had not.

*   *   *

I ran home like the legendary Pheidippides, the Greek messenger dispatched from the battlefield to Athens. After running about twenty-five miles to the Acropolis, Pheidippides burst into the chambers and gallantly hailed his countrymen with *Nike! Nike! Nenikekiam*, Victory! Victory! Rejoice, we conquer! Pheidippides collapsed from exhaustion soon after announcing the famed victory.

Everyone was in awe. My family believed I could achieve five O levels but passing nine subjects, five of them with straight As, was a first in the village. My mother ululated and danced in bare feet, sending grey dust up into the air. She slaughtered a ripe black rooster (which had miraculously survived the previous Christmas.) As darkness set in, Baba, incandescent with pride, crouched inside the kitchen and recited our zebra totem poem, in praise of our ancestors, who he believed had stealthily guided me through my mission. We bowed our heads in veneration and clapped our hands in unison.

Maita, Samaita / Maita, Mutasa / Maita, Mbizi / Maita, Tembo yangu yiyi / Hekani, Matendera.

Ngwere / Nzuma isina nyanga / Zvaitwa, Mbizi / Zvaitwa, Chivara / Nzuma yerenje / Hekani, Tembo; Mashongera; Manjenjenje; Ganda revasikana.

I found myself waking up every hour or so that night to make sure it was not all a dream. Early the next morning, I grabbed my exam slip and sprinted to the village secondary school. I wanted to share my heartfelt gratitude to the teachers who had walked with me through the dark from Rwizi bus stop to my village on those Friday nights. I also wanted to prove how wrong they had been for always telling me my uninformed zeal would amount to nothing. After I handed my slip to Mr Mabhiza, he shouted across the staffroom:

'Guys, our education system here at Rwizi is trash. Look what Rio has done to this boy!'

*   *   *

The headmaster handed us forms to apply for A-level places before we sat for our final O-level exams in 1997. After completing O levels in Zimbabwe, a small proportion of students progressed to forms five and six to tackle A levels. Rio did not have A levels at that time so we had to look elsewhere. Only a tiny proportion of students applied, however. The majority shied away because they believed they were not up to it intellectually.

Some just knew that their parents, already struggling to pay school fees at Rio, could never afford boarding schools. Some perceived secondary education as the ultimate achievement; they had cleared the normal benchmark widely accepted as 'success' in our communal lands.

Many boasted of having 'finished school' once they passed with five O-level subjects.

My academic performance had significantly improved by then. I was excited by, not afraid of, A-level studies. My economic situation, however, was worse than most: I relied on Marion's scholarship. My parents had depleted the entire herd to give each of their nine kids a chance at education. They were already struggling to send my two younger sisters to the local village school. It was unrealistic to expect them to send me to a boarding school.

In a sheer act of faith, I grabbed an application form and sat with my friend Mutumba to fill it in. My first choice was Goromonzi High School, established in 1946 as the first-ever black boarding school. The school boasted stellar academic records. A famous saying, *Why worry Goromonzi after form six*, insinuated you were set for life once you graduated from there with A levels. This claim had merit: Goromonzi had produced notable alumni, such as Dr Herbert Ushewokunze, Dr Herbert Murerwa, Dr David Karimanzira, all cabinet ministers.

A local girl, Mary Majoni, was already studying at Goromonzi. She lived nearby our run-down place. Mary had smarts, and was an exemplar, topping her class of 1996 at Rio. I admired Mary greatly and wanted to follow in her footsteps. Mutumba followed suit, listing Goromonzi as his first choice too.

My next choice was Kutama College, a reputable Jesuit institution located in Zvimba, rural lands situated 120 kilometres north-west of Harare. My appreciation for Kutama College was simple: Mugabe, who was still regarded as a great thinker and African statesman before his metamorphosis into a dictator, was a product of Kutama College. Like Goromonzi, Kutama had produced several notable scholars.

My third and last choice was Moleli, a high school near Chegutu, a farming town one hundred kilometres along the Harare-to-Bulawayo highway. We competed against Moleli in sports and I envied the elegance of its students. That said, Moleli did not have quite the same appeal as Goromonzi and Kutama.

Applying for a place when I had no clue where my fees would come from was a life-changing throw of the dice. It was easier to listen to my inner fears and stick to schools within my zone. That would guarantee a smoother transition but my growth would be capped prematurely. I would rather face indignity while growing than remain comfortable with my village routines.

Financially, I had nothing to lose (application was free of charge) so I just applied for the best possible schools without compromise. If I did not believe in myself, no one would. Academically, this was a gamble. I had never before scored five As, without which Goromonzi or Kutama would not admit me. Moleli had a lower bar but my heart was not there. That requirement forced me to rewrite my goals and I responded. I intensified my efforts over the ensuing six months to O-level exams, regularly returning after school to study and dissect past exam papers with a near-compulsive level of intent. Even if I failed to reach my ultimate goal, my grades would improve.

A few weeks after my O-level results, I received an acceptance letter from Goromonzi. I quickly borrowed some money from Mr Thelingwani, my grade seven teacher and great friend, and hitchhiked to Hurungwe, where my oldest brother Osward now worked as a primary school teacher.

Osward had eventually managed to pass six O levels after multiple sittings at our village secondary school (Rwizi). He worked several stints as a temporary teacher in various rural schools, then secured a traineeship at Nyadire Teachers College, located in Mutoko, 140 kilometres north-east of Harare. I petitioned Osward to pay my fees but he advised that, while he loved the idea, he had too much on his plate and could not afford to send me to Goromonzi.

'This, however, is not the end of the world, brother. I can hook you up with powerful people here in Hurungwe and within a few weeks, you will be a temporary teacher,' Osward reasoned.

His proposal made sense at face value. If I took up the offer, I could immediately buy myself some clothes and start helping my family, something I had long aspired to. But I knew that settling for this, albeit reasonable proposition, would be short-sighted. Turning down my brother's advice carried consequences; my stubbornness could be setting me up to fail. But I figured I had nothing to lose. If my plan flunked, I could always come back and beg for assistance into temporary teaching.

Hard-nosed, I jumped on a yellow Pioneer bus going back to my village. I stopped off at Mubayira township and used the small change I had left to buy an international stamp and an envelope from the post office. I sat down and wrote a long letter to Marion, advising her of my academic triumph, imploring her to extend her kind hand for two more years, and send me to Goromonzi. I felt terrible about appearing thankless to someone who had already transformed my life in the most unimaginable way, but eventually, I slowly licked the edges of the red, white and blue envelope. I closed and dropped it into the post office letterbox.

Even if Marion declined my request, she would remain in my heart to the grave. She had done for me what my government or my relatives could not do for me. There were no phones in my village so for several weeks I travelled back and forth to Rio. I foraged through piles of letters. A week went by, then another, with no word. I knew time was running out and I was filled with anxiety.

Eventually her letter arrived. Crazy with hope, I tore the exotic-looking envelope apart. I rushed through the first congratulatory paragraph. I hoped not to see the word 'sorry' — that would have shattered my heart into a thousand pieces. But Marion wasted no time. In her second paragraph, she informed me that she would be sending eight hundred Deutschmarks — enough to pay my fees for the whole year at Goromonzi, buy uniforms and pay for my transport. I felt so alive as a blast of adrenaline shot through me. This was unthinkable until now. Everything felt unreal.

*   *   *

I handed over Marion's letter to Mr Berejena, the Rio headmaster. He glanced over the good news, looked up to me, nodded his head a few times and gently smiled. Mr Berejena had been my geography teacher before taking over the reins from Mr Hungwe as headmaster. He had become a great mentor and friend and over my four-year stint at Rio.

It was a decisive moment, one that would forever alter my trajectory and thrust me into previously uncharted terrain. Nobody in my family had proceeded to A levels before. I felt incredibly blessed by the sense I was creating history and setting a new standard.

Poverty can confine us; it can force us to settle for much less than our God-given capabilities. Unchecked, poverty can cut deep into our souls and precipitate insidious self-hate; it can force us to throw away our individual identities and render us who we are not.

CHAPTER 9

Goromonzi

Towards the end of the summer of 1998, I left the village to pursue my A levels at Goromonzi. It was profoundly gratifying to be accepted by such a revered academic institution, one of Zimbabwe's best public schools. I had given my body and soul to attain excellent O-level grades despite my squalid living conditions, and my half-marathon runs to and from school. Now I was stepping into the unknown; I was about to do things I had never done before.

Baba accompanied me on my first journey there. I was apprehensive about my new challenge, but deep inside I was glowing with optimism. He stuffed the envelope containing the Deutschmarks Marion had sent into his side pocket, which he tied off tightly using an old shoelace. This was to deter pickpockets at Mbare Musika, a hectic bus station on the outskirts of Harare through which we passed. We alighted from Suffer Continue and strolled across to check in on my cousin Didymus's father. Sanyama, whose name means meat lover, had a small shoe repair business near Chitungwiza terminus at Mbare. From there we proceeded straight to Barclays Bank on First Street to convert the Deutschmarks to Zimbabwean dollars, as directed by Mr Berejena, the Rio headmaster.

We encountered our first obstacle in Barbours, a large and prestigious department store located at the corner of First Street and Jason Moyo Avenue. We had no clue regarding most of the stipulated items on the school's list. *What on earth were swimming trunks?* The word 'swimming' was a good hint, but 'trunk' confused the hell out of us. The only trunk I knew of was an elephant's. It also made little sense you needed to buy clothes to swim; in the savannah, we swam naked and doggy style — heads held out of the water.

After wasting a considerable amount of time, we swallowed our pride and a store assistant came to our rescue. *It's just underwear,* I whispered in disgust as the assistant pointed to a rack of tiny maroon swimming trunks. This phase was the beginning of a realisation that the world was much bigger and complex than my communal village or Mubayira township. The swimming trunks ended up being a complete waste of money anyway — my next swim was still fifteen years away.

Secondary school boys from form one to form four wore grey shorts and matching short-sleeved shirts, while the girls wore plain maroon skirts and short-sleeved white blouses. A-level boys (form five and form six) wore long grey pants and white shirts, while the girls wore pleated maroon shirts and white blouses. That demarcation was replicated in the dining hall; seniors ate in their own section.

Everything was different. Goromonzi introduced me to cornflakes, mashed potatoes, and other treats. We had breakfast twice. Around 7 a.m., we were served the cereal and jars of cold fresh milk, eggs, sausages, and several slices of Proton bread. Later, around 10 a.m., we had morning tea with large butter sandwiches. The lunches and dinners were abundant, delicious and varied. My favourite was the *dunha*, huge and crusty pieces of chicken, which oddly translates to just 'the dead'.

Thanks to my extroversion, I quickly developed strong bonds with a dozen or so boys. Most of these boys — the likes of Oscar Makausi, Isaac Kurasha, Mike Tafatawona — came from rural secondary schools like me, so naturally we were united by the same anxieties and hopes.

My days at Goromonzi were wonderful and unforgettable despite my initial struggle to adjust to the school's etiquette and the demanding A-level studies. At school, I never worried about my previous burdens. For those two years, I was never hungry. When I first arrived, I was short and bony, but the food had an extraordinary impact on my body. I shot up in height and gained mass. Whenever I returned to my village, everyone exclaimed, *Phidza was a dwarf all these years. He goes and attends boarding school for a year and grows faster than maize stalks.*

*   *   *

The intervening months were characterised by steep learning and adjustment. Silently I observed and imitated those kids who were more polished in handling issues, especially in the dining room. I embraced the fake-it-until-you-make-it mantra. I found it bizarre that Goromonzi kids ate rice with a fork, when it was clearly easier and faster to use a spoon, as I was accustomed to. Back in the village, we always ate with our right hand so as to appease the ancestors who blessed the harvest, so I found myself conflicted that I had to hold the fork in my left hand. Internally I questioned the logic behind many things, but I never let my bewilderment show, not wanting to stick out.

Everyone laughed at some villager who naively mixed up the order of things, drinking his tea with the cornflakes before eating his toast with the milk. I never wanted to end up like *that* boy. Over time, practices that previously felt weird and foreign to me became second nature. I started wielding a knife and fork with more ease and confidence, although never as perfectly as the kids from well-to-do families. My gluttonous tendencies had earned me a bad reputation at Rio; slowly they mellowed at Goromonzi. There was so much food; my survival instincts could relax.

You'll never walk alone, goes the famous song Liverpool Football Club fans love to sing. There was more than a dozen of us from so-called 'upper tops', a stereotypical term used to describe rural secondary schools. Those stigmas had a uniting effect on us; most of us guys attacked our academics with undivided attention and went on to achieve remarkable things.

My insular view of the world was about to change dramatically. Everything at Goromonzi was so starkly different. We listened to the Sungura genre of music back in Mubayira. Songs like 'Upenyu Mutoro', which questioned why the poor had to suffer in perpetuity; 'Samatenga', which ignited dark memories of death; and 'Jojo', which cautioned against the perils of political activism. These songs were rich with cultural meaning; they ran deep and were inextricably linked to our identity.

But several kids at Goromonzi shunned this traditional genre. They listened to artists I had never heard of, the likes of Snoop Dogg, Mary J. Blige, Busta Rhymes, Whitney Houston, Mariah Carey, Backstreet

Boys, Kirk Franklin, CeCe Winans, Boyz II Men, and Westlife. They took sides in the West-Coast-versus-East-Coast US hip-hop rivalry. They knew the exact dates and places where Tupac Shakur and the Notorious B.I.G. were slain. Even more bewilderingly, some seemed to know who had killed each of these hip-hop greats. In perfect unison they effortlessly sang along to 'Mo Money Mo Problems' by Biggie Smalls, 'Everything' by Mary J. Blige and 'California Love' by Tupac as the Saturday night disco exploded into life. The rhythms were too fast for me at first; I could hardly understand anything. But with the passage of time, I started to enjoy the ambience of those discos.

I was also astonished by the affluence exhibited by several kids. Some had multiple pairs of Jordans, Nikes and Filas. Basketball sessions served as showplaces of privilege. Even those who could hardly jump dressed up for basketball sessions to display their arsenal of expensive footwear. Most boys wore their unbuckled grey pants, called 'zeros', half dropped, exposing their upper buttocks. Weirdly, this was an emerging hip-hop trend, which supposedly girls liked. I never understood why intelligent girls were attracted to such idiocy.

Well-to-do kids referred to themselves as 'salads', a term that reflected their preference for Western food, entertainment and clothes. In turn, others referred to them as 'nose brigades', an older, prejudicial term used to describe black people who spoke through their nose, like white people. In the end, the nose brigades and the salads were the same people; they labelled most traditional stuff *chibharanzi*, which means primitive. Salads worshipped Valentine's Day: it was an opportunity to flex their financial muscle. Teenage boys bought lavish gifts like Christian Dior perfume and handed these to girlfriends during 'see me' time, a brief romantic window after school, around the telephone booth. Those without the same material privileges could only express their affection through quick hugs or rapid-fire kisses.

We bunked in open-plan hostels. Aft er study, we would pull togeth-er our silver-spring single beds and talk about all kinds of things before retiring. We confessed the girls we liked and rated each other on a 'sexy index' of one to ten. Most 'maseke', a made-up word for sexy boy, were salads. It was very rare for someone to be both a museke and an SRB (a rude acronym for 'strong rural background').

*   *   *

I enrolled in maths, biology and chemistry. My choice was purely driven by ego. At Rio, I was one of the few students who studied the so-called pure sciences — maths, chemistry, physics, and biology. We spurned physical science, a hybrid of these three subjects, thinking it diluted and weak. I quickly struggled to cope with the pressures of my chosen combination because my heart was never there.

On one occasion, during a biology experiment, I panicked and broke a glass measuring cylinder. Chemicals spilled everywhere and soiled Peter Tagwireyi's paperwork. Peter was racing against the clock, next to me; he was incensed but later accepted my apology. That episode marked a tipping point. I dropped biology and chemistry, picking up geography and economics instead. Being the first in my family to get to A levels was a considerable advantage in more than one way. I had the freedom to experiment with subject combinations without anyone imposing a course of study on me.

My struggles resurfaced during school holidays. I went back to my village while most of my classmates travelled back to their urban homes. I hopped off the bus at Mubayira before hitchhiking to Rwizi. I wore my maroon blazer, grey pants, and fl ashy Weinbrenner shoes. Everyone stared at me, in admiration and envy I thought. I was now 'educated' and smart-looking. Girls who had previously shunned me because of my deprivation now smiled and greeted me. I smiled back but pretended to be in a hurry and walked on — the table had been turned.

I lost momentum in my studies during these holidays because there was no electricity to study at night. Fortunately, my parents exempted me from working in the fields so I could maximise the daylight. But if it rained, I relieved my younger sister Salome with the herd and wandered across the savannah. The other boys were curious about my life at Goromonzi, the nuances of boarding, and what I hoped to do after form six.

*   *   *

Goromonzi girls represented nothing I had ever seen before. A girl called Tinevimbo quickly stole my heart. She was of medium height and two years my junior. Her flawless tan pigment, chiselled jawline, and effortless elegance sent shivers up my young spine. Tinevimbo was beyond perfection; nothing like her existed at Goromonzi, let alone Mubayira. Every time I made contact with her enchanting eyes as Mr Makainganwa fervently directed 'I dreamt I went to heaven', 'El-Shaddai', 'Nearer to thee', and other hymns, my heart melted. I could sense some magnetism. But every time I contemplated a move, negative thoughts prevented me. *What will you say if she asks where you're from, Phidza? Remember some of these girls don't even entertain boys from Chitungwiza, Mabvuku, Tafara, and similar Ghettos. How good are your odds, Mhondoro boy?*

As my confidence grew and emotions towards Tinevimbo intensified, I decided to surrender my life to Jesus Christ and join the Scripture Union (SU). My Christianity eventually diverted my attention from Tinevimbo; I never tested the waters.

Scripture Union kids met on Saturday nights in the chapel, para-doxically, located next door to the Beit Hall, which hosted the Saturday night discos.

The entertainment patron, Miss Murehwa, had a nasty repulsion towards the Scripture Union. She lobbied incessantly and convinced the headmaster to ban the Scripture Union, under the pretence of 'letting kids be kids'. The headmaster passed the appalling decree. Miss Murehwa pounced, shutting down the chapel and commanding everyone to attend the Saturday night gigs.

'If you want to read your Bibles, you can read them inside the dance,' she declared.

A small number stayed in their hostels in protest, but the major-ity, unsure of the consequences, conformed. Being forced to read our Bibles inside the Beit Hall, in dimmed light and with hip-hop music at full blast, intensified the feeling of gross injustice. I boiled with feel-ings of irritation: *Some of us are already eighteen; who the hell is she to impose her belief system upon us?*

I decided I was sick and tired of this inequity one Saturday night. I carried my Bible to the dance. I stayed patient — only two of my friends, Peter Pasi and Tinashe Badza, knew what I had planned. I also knew they had my back. When the disco reached peak hysteria, I vaulted onto the podium and implored Wallace, the DJ, to surrender the microphone, stop the music and switch on the lights.

'Just give me ten minutes, Wallace,' I pressed.

I was surprised he so quickly complied. The Scripture Union kids were stunned, the revellers were angry, but everyone stayed still and there was dead silence. Those who were touching and flirting disen-tangled. I read my Bible and preached about responsible choices. I kept my promise, under ten minutes. I handed back the microphone to Wallace. Everyone from the Scripture Union was fired up.

Word spread around that Zongo had stopped the gig and preached. Miss Murehwa summoned me and gave me a stern warning but that only deepened my zeal. Some form four boys were infuriated by my move and sought revenge. They graffitied 'Zongo Massive' in several places, threatened to beat me up, but never followed through with those threats. There were weeks of relentless protests until the headmaster gave in to our plight and lifted the decree. Feeling liberated, we returned to our place of worship.

CHAPTER 10

Midlands State University

I sat my last A-level exam in November 1999. I bid farewell to Goromonzi and hitchhiked to Magunje, a township thirty kilometres from Karoi, an agricultural town north of Harare, along the Chirundu Highway. My brother Osward lived there with his wife, Charity Moyo, and their two young girls, Mercy and Melissa. Osward was now teaching at Charles Clark, a local primary school. His wife taught at a village school several kilometres away and frequented Magunje on weekends.

In a stroke of luck, the Zimbabwean government had embarked on a mass recruitment campaign, hiring form-four graduates to register voters for the June 2000 general election. My application, and Ruth Moyo's, were soon accepted. Ruth was my brother's sister-in-law; she had also finished her A levels, hers at Chinhoyi High School. In January of that year, we got down to work. We travelled across rough terrain into the remotest parts of Hurungwe, registering villagers who had never voted before, and striking deceased voters from the electoral roll. The registration process was as good as we chose it to be. If we found a homestead unattended, because the villagers were tilling distant fields or had gone to fetch water, we just proceeded to the next. At the end of each week, we submitted all the voter registration forms to the Hurungwe District Council office, located at Magunje township, and travelled on to the next village.

I learnt in February that the A-level results were out. The next day, I was on the bus to Goromonzi. I was apprehensive all the way. On arrival, I proceeded straight to the headmaster's office. I flipped over the white slip and my chin dropped when I saw my results. I had scored eleven points: a 'B' (four points) in maths, a 'B' in geography (four points) and a 'C' in economics (three points). I had worked hard — awake during endless nights in the hostel at Goromonzi; holed up in my cousin Shon's poky room in Gavaza, which reeked of tobacco, for bottomless hours on weekends. For two years, I had dreamt daily of studying finance at university. I thought I had done everything I could to reach that goal but had fallen short of my target by two points.

Eleven points was commendable, all things considered. But at that time, Zimbabwe had only two government universities and there was intense competition from thousands of A-level graduates. Eleven points was mediocre in that context.

The University of Zimbabwe (UZ) was the country's oldest and largest university. UZ was established in 1952 as the University College of

Rhodesia and Nyasaland, then renamed after independence in 1980. Nyasaland is the colonial name for present-day Malawi. The National University of Science and Technology (NUST) was established in 1991 in Bulawayo, the country's second largest city. NUST swiftly asserted itself and was popular with many commerce and science aspirants.

I hung around Goromonzi for a while, humbly congratulating classmates who were running around in delight after scoring straight As. The world had suddenly become their oyster; the possibilities that lay ahead of them must have felt infinite. Those distinguished grades pretty much guaranteed them unhindered access into medicine, law, and business, at prestigious universities. Eventually, I dragged my feet back to the bus terminus and vanished.

*   *   *

I stayed in Chitungwiza with my sister Cecilia for a few weeks, carefully assessing my options. The money I had raised from my voter registration job proved handy. I commuted to the city several times alongside Tapiwa Mupereki, a kind-hearted Goromonzi classmate who lived at Makoni Police Station. Tapiwa worked as a temporary assistant at a medical centre at Chance, Epworth, just south of Harare. Over the next few weeks, I travelled to UZ and applied for a bachelor's degree in business studies (commonly referred to by the acronym BBS).

'You have zero chance of getting into BBS with eleven points, young man. You are just wasting your time and money', the middle-aged woman on the admissions' desk warned me.

I put economics as my second choice. I had slim chance of getting in and my heart wasn't there anyway. Everyone I knew who had studied economics ended up teaching the same subject at A level. Undeterred, or foolishly, I submitted my application and walked back along the jacaranda-lined Second Street to Harare CBD.

A few weeks later, I bumped into Paul Machipisa, a close friend at Goromonzi. He had smashed maths, physics and chemistry and was guaranteed to get into the UZ Medical School. Paul possessed the maturity of a forty-year-old.

'Zongo, I don't think you will be admitted into BBS. A new university has just opened in Gweru, called State University in the Midlands. It's offering a new degree called Bachelor of Information Systems. I am not really sure what it's all about, but I think it has something to do with cell phones. I suggest you check it out.'

He handed me a large advert he had cut out of *The Herald*.

I wasted no time. Within two days, I was on a bus to Gweru — Zimbabwe's fourth largest city, located in the Midlands Province, about 280 kilometres south of Harare — and had filled in the application forms. It was my first-ever trip along the Harare-Bulawayo Highway.

A few weeks later, a large envelope arrived at my sister's place. It was an offer to study information systems under the faculty of commerce. I was thrilled by the opportunity to advance to university. The villagers got right up me, insisting that my university story was a fib.

'Phidza is lying. There is no university in Gweru. He is going to attend Gweru Teachers' College,' many pushed back.

*   *   *

In March 2000, together with approximately four hundred pioneers, I arrived at State University in the Midlands, with an old blanket and a few clothing items, in pursuit of a new dream. As the regret letters from UZ were to prove, the opening of the new university represented a golden break. My brief voter registration job was also crucial: without it I would have never been able to travel to Gweru or raise the application fee.

Our university was soon renamed Midlands State University (MSU). Some stakeholders had argued that State University in the Midlands sounded like a sentence, not a name.

MSU wasn't built from scratch. The government established MSU through the State University in the Midlands Act of April 1999, by taking over the premises of Gweru Teachers' College (GTC). When MSU opened there were hundreds of ex-GTC students.

My Christian beliefs and banter endeared me to many people at MSU — I quickly developed strong ties. Ranganai Zvakafa was a short, fast-walking native of Zvimba (Mugabe's communal lands) with a witty sense of humour. He had joined GTC to study computer science one and a half years prior to my arrival. Varaidzo Mhembere, a wonderful friend and Goromonzi classmate, also enrolled in the computer science degree program. Our friendship would remain strong for years. I also developed a close bond with Nqobizita Siziba, a baby-faced Ndebele young man and biology student, whom I deputised for at the Christian Union.

Because we were the first stream, there was university accommodation for the majority of our intake. With the exception of a few Gweru natives, and some married couples, most of the March 2000 class stayed on campus. I was assigned a cubicle within a ground floor room in Uhuru Hostel (*uhuru* is Swahili for 'independence'). The hostels had double floors; I shared our main room with three other first-year students. Tragically for him, Tsungai, one of my roommates, was in the final stages of HIV/AIDS. He was about four years my senior and had worked as a teacher before re-enrolling to study African languages. I had witnessed the raging monster exterminate lives in Mubayira and

Magunje but living with a terminally ill AIDS patient was confronting. The virus had completely disabled his immune system. He coughed ceaselessly from his cubicle and the stubborn sores on his throat had become so painful they prevented him from eating.

I was amazed by Tsungai's determination to stay focused on his studies in the face of the inevitable. He got around campus slowly and attended as many lectures as he could. True to his name, Tsungai fought to the bitter end. Fortunately for him, he was still on the government's payroll as a qualified teacher and occasionally sent me to the tuckshop to buy milk and soft foods he could swallow. Inevitably, Tsungai's physique sharply deteriorated and he was then transported to his village in Masvingo. My heart sank when finally the news of his death reached campus.

*   *   *

Life at MSU was tough. The government paid us a meagre allowance every six months called the Vocational Training Loan (VTL). If you filled your forms incorrectly, the VTL could be delayed by several months. We endured crippling food shortages as the VTL was our mainstay and it quickly ran out. Student union leaders routinely called for organised protests but Mugabe's well-oiled police machine consistently quashed these. The university also responded with a heavy hand, permanently dismissing student leaders to send a message to the wider student body; alleged ringleaders were suspended for two years, if the university was lenient. This understandably scared off wannabe protestors, the majority of whom were the first from their families to attend university.

My best days at MSU were at the Christian Union. We sold packets of *maputi* (puffed corn) and raised money to travel to nearby schools, mines and villages to evangelise. I also became an active member of the Glad Tidings local church, led by Pastor Mugari and his wife, Sylvia. Both Mugaris had big hearts. Pastor Mugari ran a large and successful Dairibord franchise and sent his children to an exclusive private school. But despite their opulence, they treated us as equals. Most weekends, we frequented Pastor Mugari's posh homestead in the exclusive suburb of Ridgemont, in the north of Gweru. Sylvia Mugari treated us as if her own kids, preparing lavish meals with large portions of ice cream for dessert.

The Bachelor of Information Systems degree was a mix of business and computer science subjects. I enjoyed the computer science lectures but found the business and accounting sessions dry and mundane. I liked the fact that lectures were optional. I skipped several lectures, preferring to spend hours behind the Windows 98 Pentium 4 computers in the lab, fiddling with code. MSU had about two dozen computers when I joined. It was 'first come, first serve' as soon as the computer science lab opened. Occasionally I got sucked in — on Microsoft FrontPage, Macromedia Dreamweaver and Photoshop — from 6 p.m. until daylight the next day.

CHAPTER 11

Industrial Attachment

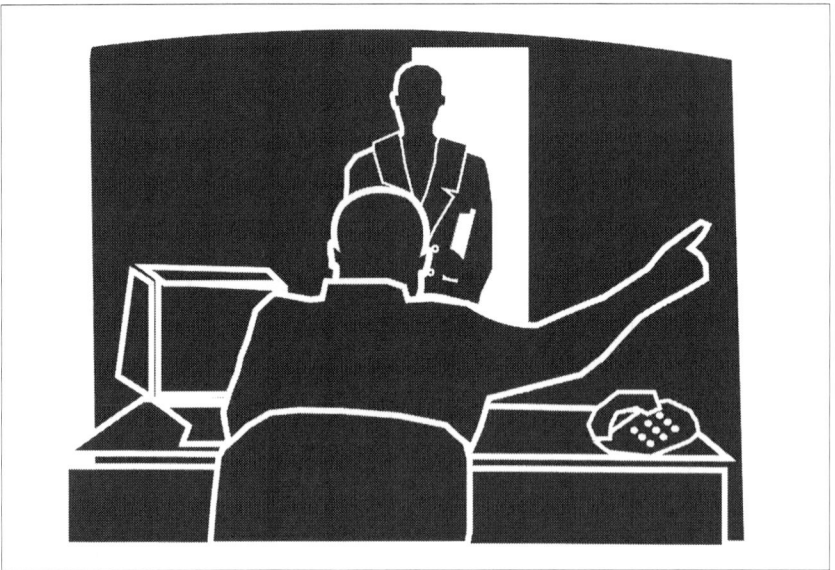

MSU required students to participate in an internship program, known as industrial attachment, during their third year. This was a critical phase in which students were exposed to the realities of the corporate world; students could put theory to practical use and discover potential career paths. The university secured a handful of attachment places but prioritised students with higher grades. I didn't make the top selection because up until then my grades were mediocre. I had developed a habit of skipping lectures, bored by academic theories, instead spending countless hours coding in the computer lab. So, I had to secure an industrial attachment place on my own.

Gweru was a relatively small town. Besides Zimglass Corporation and Bata Shoes Limited, there weren't many other opportunities for internship. I packed my belongings and jumped on a yellow Marcopolo bus, headed for Harare. I knew it would be a challenging mission. I had nowhere to stay in the capital and didn't know anyone in a senior position, anyone who could vouch for me. I would be starting from a blank canvas as I had done so many times before.

My brother Lancelot had moved to Harare two years before to look for a job. He had barely passed his O levels and his chances of gainful employment were slim. The Zimbabwean economy had by then reached breaking point and a state of advanced continuous decay — the wheels were falling off. However, he had recently married his savannah sweetheart, and as a man, he had to give it a go.

He stayed with our cousin Senzeni, a self-styled 'prophet' who lived in Dzivarasekwa (DZ), one of Harare's oldest ghettos, twelve kilometres south of the city. Senzeni was a respected force in the prophet industry. As the Zimbabwean economy collapsed, many flocked to these self-professed miracle makers to rescue them from hard times. They claimed to possess cures for HIV/AIDS, cancer, and other diseases. Senzeni made a lot of money exorcising goblins, known as *Tokoloshes*, and a host of misfortunes from cabinet ministers and prominent businessmen who visited her house in secret at night. She claimed to engage in an intense spiritual jiujitsu to vanquish these evils for her wealthy clients. None of them wanted the public to discover their superstitions.

Zimbabwean society is deeply superstitious, even among the educated and elites. In 2007, another self-styled spirit medium, Rotina Mavhunga, fooled several respected politicians into believing that refined diesel was oozing from a mountain rock near Chinhoyi, a provincial capital north of Harare. The prophetess claimed this miracle was a gift from national ancestors, one that would arrest Zimbabwe's economic troubles. It would turn the country into an oil-producing nation and clear the long, snaking queues at service stations.

She convinced the government to organize a Bira ceremony to thank the ancestral spirits for this gift. Soon after, the mountain was surrounded by people camped at the foot, including government officials, intent on seizing the 'duty-free' diesel to on sell. Some came from as far away as Chiredzi to witness the miracle, more than five hundred kilometres away.[8] Mavhunga instructed government ministers to take off their shoes when they arrived. Pictures of highly educated politicians sitting in the dust, barefoot, clapping their hands in reverence, went viral on social media — a stark and enduring symbol of the nation's endemic superstition.

Unbeknown, Mavhunga had arranged cleverly placed drums full of diesel on top of the mountain and connecting pipes that slowly delivered the black gold to the rock. The scam paid off initially: she received a large sum of money, a farm and a big house. The purported discovery was a smack in the face to George Bush and Tony Blair — the diesel would neuter the oil sanctions imposed on Zimbabwe. Mavhunga eventually ran into trouble, however, when tankers arrived to load the fuel.

*   *   *

Lancelot was hired as a digger by the Ministry of Housing several months after arriving in DZ. He woke up early and joined dozens of other labourers employed to dig trenches for sewerage and water lines in new urban developments. The government paid them a pittance but Lancelot was still grateful for this chance. He moved out of Senzeni's place and away from her bizarre rituals as soon as he was 'financially independent'.

He secured a single room in an old three-bedroom house in the heart of DZ 2. The house was owned by Bere, a native of Zvimba, a short, brutish man. (His name also translates to Hyena.) Bere had two wives: the younger one lived with him in DZ and the older old was the custodian of his rural homestead. This arrangement wasn't uncommon — a few men practised this form of polygamy, comprising the city wife and the rural wife.

Lancelot invited his wife to join him from Mhondoro and she happily obeyed. Then a friend tipped him to a budding, 'risk-free' business opportunity. For some reason, several white Zimbabweans had deserted numerous large building structures in nearby Mount Hampden (historically, the location initially chosen by the British for the capital of Southern Rhodesia). These buildings had become no man's property, creating a 'brick rush'. Unemployed men from DZ, Kuwadzana, Tynwald, and other low-income suburbs flocked to dismantle the buildings and salvage the high-quality red bricks for sale. Lancelot couldn't resist the allure of the brick hustle. He resigned from his excruciating government job, bought a few tools and went all in.

There was no shortage of buyers. Throughout the day, dozens of archaic AVM and DAF trucks rattled down the potholed roads into Mount Hampden, as hustlers flocked to buy cheap, durable bricks to on sell to Harare builders at exorbitant prices. Lancelot was working long and arduous hours but he felt fairly rewarded for his toil. He now earned more in a week than the Ministry had paid him for an entire month. Life couldn't be better!

Lancelot felt he alone couldn't profit from this glorious opportunity. He hitchhiked to Mhondoro one Saturday morning and convinced Tsuro to join him in DZ and make 'a lot of money from the brick business'. This was the same Tsuro, my auntie's son, whose bullying had forced me out of Chihoro a decade prior; he had always been a long-brewing problem. Predictably, Tsuro had failed his O levels and was now a Tsikamutanda, a rural version of the bone-throwing fake prophets, who roamed from village to village, claiming to be able to banish goblins in exchange for maize grain, groundnuts, chickens and sometimes, goats. But Tsuro was a lightweight fake prophet: he couldn't compete and earn a living in the overcrowded Tsikamutanda industry in Mhondoro.

Lancelot returned to Harare with Tsuro and they formed a pact. They hustled bricks together and shared the proceeds.

I rocked up in Harare during the summer of 2002 and went straight to stay with Lancelot, my sister-in-law and Tsuro. I was cool with Tsuro despite how he had mistreated me. I felt he was young and stupid; he deserved another chance to rebuild his life. Or maybe, as the proverb warns, I was just being naive and simply forgetting the pain because the scars had healed.

My brother rented a tiny room. We tied a perforated grey blanket between opposite walls at night to divide it into two sections. This was humiliating: I was a university student, a graduate from Goromonzi High School, but found myself sleeping in such shameful conditions. The previous years had insulated me somewhat from the realities of my situation. I had to get on with it, however, because my future demanded I do just that.

Tsuro and I retired on the floor on one side of the blanket barricade. My brother and his heavily pregnant wife remained on the other, pushing kitchenware aside to make more room. The toilet was located outside the main house. We tiptoed out to unlock the door so we wouldn't disturb Bere, snoring in the main bedroom.

*   *   *

My cousin Didymus, my savannah best friend, occasionally visited us in DZ. I was very excited to see him as it had been years. Didymus had never liked school, and bad choices were already catching up with him.

'Long time no see, Shayamombe!' I addressed him with his totem, which means the one who constantly loses his cows. 'What do you do for work now?' I quizzed, surprised he was dressed well, in new baggy light-blue jeans and a multicoloured viscose shirt.

He quickly laughed it away. 'We just touch this, then touch that, Samaita.'

Didymus, sadly, was either unwilling or unable to reform. He had long since morphed into one of the most notorious of Harare's thieves. He was part of a gang that raided homes in posh suburbs at night — like Westgate, Avondale, Bluff Hill, and Malbereign — retreating to DZ and blending back into ordinary life. They used whatever means necessary to plunder. Didymus ran a makeshift carpentry business outside their rented place in DZ 3 as a front for his criminal activities. One late evening, Didymus turned up at Bere's home with a khaki box containing a much sought-after Panasonic 3 CD player and an assortment of brand new CDs.

'May you keep these for me, Sekuru? I am off to the bombi-stombi [slang for pub],' he petitioned Lancelot, with no further explanation before vanishing into the night.

Lancelot took a walk to Didymus's place in DZ 3 the next day. As he drew close, he spotted heavy-handed police shoving Didymus into a four-wheel-drive Santana SUV. *Oh my God, that CD player is stolen!* Lancelot quickly joined the dots and was gripped with terror. He rushed back to his place and dumped the stolen loot.

Didymus only visited my brother to chill; he never robbed his own. He was part of a big boys' club: tough muggers who took enormous risks, like vandalising electricity transformers, stealing the oil to on sell on the black market. They targeted large colour television sets, expensive stereos, and other high-value consumer durables.

He always had cash and was willing to part with it. Whenever Didymus visited us, he brought a loaf of bread and soft drinks. We would sit on the cement floor and share the stuff, reminiscing over savannah memories.

'Sekuru, I will never forget the day you unleashed giant black wasps upon me!' Didymus reminded me of my old transgression, as he sipped the fizzy soda.

'LOL, I exploited your insatiable love for *mandere*, Shayamombe. Those were the days, mate.'

'Same thing, Sekuru,' he pushed back, before laughing it away, the same way he had done all those years ago.

He bid us farewell around 5 p.m. that day and disappeared into the dark. In the end, Didymus's inclination to dance with danger cost him dearly. He was gunned down by an AK-47 during a botched armed robbery and died instantly. His compatriot managed to escape but then kept the terrible, dark secret to himself for fear of being detained. Because Didymus didn't have any formal identification on him at the time of his death, the police couldn't contact his family. His body stayed unidentified at a government mortuary for four months. The compatriot eventually became too restless about it and opened up to Didymus's family. The prize my cousin paid for his bad choices was steep — he perished at a tender age.

* * *

DZ was my first experience with a full-on Zimbabwean ghetto. On Sundays, Tsuro and I cruised the DZ streets to kill time. A passer-by screamed one day, *Get off the way, you idiots! Who do you think you are? Can't you see the Nyau coming along?* I looked up the street in panic and ran into an alleyway to join other curious bystanders. This was my first encounter with the Nyau, a highly reclusive and secretive cult, known as Zvigure in Shona. *Nyau* means 'mask' in Chewa, the major local language in Malawi. The Nyau is a secret brotherhood of initiated men that exists predominantly in Mozambique, Malawi and Zambia.

The crowd's feelings towards the Nyau were mixed. Youngsters whistled and jumped in excitement, while some women gripped their kids tightly with apprehension. After a minute or so, the group of Nyau passed through. Their faces were covered with feathered and wooden masks that realistically resembled animals such as hyenas, baboons, lions and snakes, as well as mystical creatures. Some had towering horns affixed to their masks, magnifying their aura of wickedness. *This is the closest personification of the devil I have ever seen*, I thought nervously, passing judgement on the Nyau, with absolutely no context on the spectacle.

'As long as you don't encroach into their path, you will be fine, youngster,' someone next to me said in an attempt to calm me down. Almost everyone I knew in DZ was scared of the Nyau. They had a reputation for being sporadically aggressive.

Meanwhile, the Nyau drummers were in perfect accord and rhythmic dancers displayed extraordinary vitality. They kicked up dust with their bare feet and threw it into the air, apparently to further disguise their identity. Some acrobatically somersaulted into the air, drawing huge applause. Others abruptly stopped dancing and took off rapidly in different directions, deliberately intimidating petrified onlookers.

I was transported into a magical world by a combination of fear and captivation. I was scared of and excited by the Nyau at the same time. I saw two giant Nyaus walking slowly at the rear of the procession, each towering more than twelve feet high. They were walking on stilts, I realised, which gave them the illusion of being giant brutes. I was intrigued by such extraordinary balance. The Nyaus eventually passed, turned into another bumpy street, and kept moving.

What fascinated me the most was the secrecy that shrouded this ancient cult. In DZ, one's husband, sibling, landlord or tenant could be a Nyau, and no one might ever know. They guarded their secrecy as tightly as Coca-Cola preserved its formula.

The origins of this ancient tradition can be traced to the Chewa myth about creation. According to their beliefs, Chauta (God) descended to the earth with a man, a woman, and animals. They all lived in harmony until the man accidentally discovered fire by rubbing two sticks against each other. All the animals fled in dread and rage as the forest and the grasslands blazed in flames. Only three animals — the dog, the goat and the cow — chose to stick with their man. There has never been harmony in the world since that day. The Nyau dress up like beasts to personify their ancestors — ancestors who lived in harmony with God and the animals, until their descendants discovered fire and disturbed the natural order on earth.[9]

Very few people in DZ knew who was behind those masks. *I think so and so is a Nyau; please don't get messed up with him. He sometimes disappears inexplicably before resurfacing again*, people gossiped about neighbours.

*   *   *

On weekdays, I took a quick bath before jumping onto a Sagombeto bus to Copacabana, a bustling shopping district in central Harare. Barbers, many other vendors, and Nigerian shop owners plied their trades here. I walked from company to company, dropping my slim resume at reception and imploring staff to pass it on to HR or the IT manager. I naively believed the receptionists would do as I had asked. I walked out of the city along Chitungwiza Road, doing likewise at Telecel, the telecommunications firm; Art Corporation, the conglomerate; Coca-Cola; and many others.

Fawcett or Guard Alert security guards frequently prevented me from walking past the main entrance. *We are not hiring, young man!* These dismissals were humiliating and infuriating. But there was nothing I could do except move on to the next company. I had no mobile phone or Google Maps — I was guided by my intuition. If I felt the company could have an IT department, then I dropped off a copy of my resume.

I walked along the Samora Machel banking precinct, Sam Nujoma Avenue and First Street, where giant financial corporations were headquartered. I rode escalators and got off on random floors in skyscrapers like Karigamombe, First Mutual Life, and Livingstone House. I squeezed my sweaty self into lifts packed with serious-looking men in expensive dark suits, holding shiny briefcases, and wearing sunglasses. They had smooth and healthy brown skins, embodying their wellbeing.

I stood next to elegant ladies wearing various shades of foundation, which gave their skins a consistent, shine-free finish, heavily contrasted by their bold lipstick. They smelt like warm cinnamon, jasmine or grapefruit. Some sported racy miniskirts and sparkly high heels, their luxury car keys dangling on show; others brandished Nokias, holding their phones up high in search of the elusive cellular network. I could only wish to become one of these people in the future. I envied their class but detested the arrogance displayed by some, those who moved sideways in the lift to distance themselves from me in my oversized olive-green suit.

I walked to the light-industrial eastern district of Msasa, where the food giant Jaggers and the telecommunications giant Econet were headquartered. After an exhausting day, I walked back to the city and proceeded to a cheap Internet cafe around Copacabana to print more resumes and cover letters. I bought ten minutes and printed another batch. The dial-up modem was painfully slow but ten minutes was just enough to do what I needed to do.

I logged into my Yahoo email and scanned through unread messages hoping for an interview invitation. But all I found was an email from one of the widows of the late Nigerian dictator, Sani Abacha, petitioning me to help her recover thirty-five million US dollars, in return for a staggering 30 per cent payout for my services. The system abruptly kicked me out when my ten minutes ran out.

Next I headed towards Southerton, a massive industrial zone that boasted the likes of Unilever Company, PG Industries, and Olivine Corporation. I was hungry, fatigued and smelt like a locker room at the end of that day.

*   *   *

I had bumped into Cosmos in Harare. Cosmos was an economics graduate from MSU, now working for a micro-finance firm. He owned a Nokia 5110 phone and had given me permission to put his number as a contact on my resume. Periodically, I would line up at a silver pay-as-you-go telephone booth and call Cosmos to check if there had been any messages for me. I kept hoping for good news but Cosmos told me no potential employer had called him looking for me. I replayed this routine for weeks, insanely repeating the same thing over and over again, something that clearly wasn't working.

I frequently encountered classmates from MSU who had secured their attachment roles. Some were just lucky but some knew someone who knew someone. Others claimed to be 'database administrators' for large banks or boutique investment management firms, clearly exaggerating as no business would delegate such duties to students who could barely develop a Microsoft Access database. Nevertheless it all induced a sense of panic and made me feel left behind.

My friend Barnabas had a graduate trainee role at Mashonaland Life, one of Zimbabwe's largest insurance firms. Barnabas was at NUST and we had developed a strong bond on his frequent visits to MSU for Christian Union conferences. True to his charismatic nature and can-do attitude, Barnabas quickly moved to exercise his influence. He advised me to contact the Mashonaland Life Insurance HR manager, provided the manager's full name, and the address on Julius Nyerere Way. I was at Mashonaland Life reception at 10 a.m. the next day.

'I am here to see Mr [so-and-so], the human resources manager,' I said calmly and confidently.

The receptionist reciprocated my politeness, without questioning me. She dialled his extension and advised there was a Mr Zongo here to meet him. The HR manager confirmed, no doubt curious. I was escorted past a giant Mugabe portrait and into the manager's lavish office. Things were unfolding faster than I had anticipated. I felt upbeat — this could be it, the opportunity I had long been dreaming about. I walked in assertively, dressed as ever in my olive-green double-breasted suit. I held my resume and cover letter high, up to my chest. I had read somewhere that such a posture exuded confidence. *If the HR manager offers me coffee or tea, I will play safe and go for tea,* I mused.

He stared in disbelief and invited me to take a seat. The receptionist slammed the door behind her.

'Who the heck are you?' he questioned from his oversized, black leather chair.

He waited intently for my response, his colossal head hunched forwards, his palms intertwined, resting on the massive, shiny, dark-brown mahogany desk.

'My name is Phillimon Zongo, I am a third-year IT student at MSU, and I am looking for industrial attachment.'

His face contorted with disdain and rage, the HR manager swiftly cut me off. 'Young man, who brought you into my office? Who brought you into my office?'

I freaked out. My self-confidence was shot. I quivered like an impala sensing danger. The room was silent as the HR manager's demeanour hung in the air. I was numb with shock.

'My friend Barnabas advised me to approach you as ...'

'How dare you!' he screamed louder. He peered at me with blazing intensity. Every muscle in my body screamed at me to flee, but I remained still like a wooden pole. 'You don't just come into my office! Do you hear me?'

'I am sorry, sir. I didn't know who else to contact.'

'I forgive you, but tell your overzealous friend Barnabas to respect my office, and never do this again.' It felt like his rage had subsided and there was a slight chance to re-engage. But he yelled finally, 'Now, get out of my office!' and pointed to the door.

I slunk out, tail between my legs. I walked past the receptionist without saying a word, but enveloped by deep feelings of dread and humiliation. I had barely slept the previous night, excited by my first-ever 'interview'. I had shared the good news with Lancelot and sincerely hoped to walk out of that office with a job. Instead, all I got was quick-fire abuse from a chubby man who treated me like a bug and then 'forgave me'.

*   *   *

I had no idea that things were about to get even worse before they got any better.

Lancelot and Tsuro left DZ for Mount Hampden to dismantle as many bricks as they could. They threw their jackets onto the grass and got down to work. The future looked bright: there were still massive structures to demolish — this hustle would carry them for several months. But they were to learn there is no such thing as 'risk-free' enterprise. They were collared by plain-clothes police officers while waiting for their truckers to arrive to cash in. Some of the other brick hustlers escaped but Lancelot and Tsuro weren't so lucky. They were rounded up with dozens of other labourers and held up in a deserted office structure until around 5 p.m. They were sternly warned against engaging in 'criminal activity' and told never to show up in Mount Hampden again. That marked the end of their red-brick venture.

The little cash Lancelot had saved soon dwindled, making it extremely difficult for four adults with no income to survive. Baba came over to Harare one weekend and was shocked by the extraordinary struggle that we endured. He was sympathetic to my plight but lashed out at Lancelot and Tsuro.

'I wish you two bastards starve to death. Why the heck would you live like this, when we have plenty of food back in the village? What's so special about city life when you live like vagrants?'

He asked my sister-in-law, nine months pregnant, to pack her bags and travel with him back to the village. She gave birth to my niece Helena a couple of days later at the township hospital.

Our landlord, Bere, trusted Lancelot greatly. That trust was merited. Growing up, Lancelot was engaged in occasional mischief but he would rather starve than steal. When he started renting at Bere's place, he occupied a room in a boysky outside of the main house. Bere 'promoted' him after a couple of months to a larger room in the main house, entrusting Lancelot to look after the place when Bere travelled to the village. That arrangement was absurd because one of Bere's sons stayed in the boysky. Bere accused his son's wife of pilfering his groceries, so he decided to promote my brother to the main house instead of his own son.

Bere's unfounded distrust of his daughter-in-law was soon to work against him. Tsuro stayed in the ghetto when Lancelot and I left for the city to look for jobs. (Without O levels, Tsuro's chance of landing a job in the CBD was close to zero.) Leaving him alone in a room with no mealie meal, no cooking oil and no vegetables was a terrible blunder. As the Shona proverb goes, *A bird never changes its melody.* Tsuro's childhood proclivity for mischief had stuck with him. He was about to strike again.

Tsuro snuck into Bere's kitchen when everyone was out and helped himself to a plateful of mealie meal. He then pinched eggs from the ladies who ran the makeshift vegetable markets at Bere's house. He prepared his sadza and mashed boiled eggs. He always boiled rather than fried the eggs because he was scared the smell of fried eggs would tip off the hardworking ladies.

It took a while before Bere realised something was amiss because Tsuro took only one scoop at a time. He confronted us when he eventually worked out his mealie meal was running out faster than usual. Tsuro was wily; he didn't give Lancelot a chance to respond, telling Bere that he occasionally saw his daughter-in-law sneak into the house.

'I can't say for sure she is the one stealing your mealie meal. But what I can tell you with certainty is she inexplicably sneaks in and out of the main house during the day.' Tsuro exploited Bere's, unfair and deep-seated distrust of his daughter-in-law.

Bere lashed out at his son, accusing him of bringing a thief into his homestead. Tsuro's thievery was eventually exposed, however. He pinched Bere's mealie meal on a day the daughter-in-law had visited her family. When Bere realised Tsuro had tricked him, he told Lancelot that one of his relatives was coming from the village to take over our room: *Please make sure you vacate in two days.*

Luckily, we secured another room in the same neighbourhood. When my government grant ran out, Lancelot and I resorted to walking from DZ to the city, twelve kilometres one way. We parted ways in the city and agreed to meet underneath Karigamombe Tower, along Samora Machel Avenue, later in the afternoon.

*　　*　　*

After weeks of trying, Lancelot eventually got the attention of Elias Kamoto, an extravagantly rich uncle who ran several foreign exchange shops in Harare. He offered Lancelot a supervisory role at one of his farms near Chegutu. Lancelot packed his bags and left for the farm, leaving Tsuro and me in DZ2. Tsuro no longer had any business in the city — the brick hustle was history and he had no money to commute to the city to look for jobs. So, he just loitered in DZ and washed our plates. I could have sent him back to Mhondoro but my focus was on finding an internship, not sponsoring Tsuro's return to the village.

I ran into Kundai, a classmate who had been lucky to land an attachment soon after getting to Harare. Kundai was sympathetic to my predicament. He forwarded my resume to his boss, an entrepreneur who owned a thriving accounting software firm in Hillside, along the Airport Road, on Harare's fringes.

I was invited for an interview at ERP Systems and the MD hired me after just thirty minutes of conversation. Not only was I glad to land an attachment position after weeks of searching, but also ERP Systems paid a decent wage (compared to government institutions). And just in time. In fact I was running out of time — attachment was a year-long work-related learning and as a core part of the curriculum, it had a significant weighting on our final overall mark. Besides, by now I had exhausted my government grant and was cash-strapped.

At last! I would be able to pay my rent and buy food.

The first two weeks of my attachment unfolded predictably. I shadowed Kundai for this initial period. The driver dropped us at client sites to deploy new applications, or troubleshoot and fix software issues.

But the honeymoon didn't last. I was thrown into the deep end in my third week. I was assigned to a backlog of long-standing technical matters to resolve at client sites. The MD expected me to work as a level 2 support, a semi-autonomous role, fixing all trivial and moderate issues and escalating any complex issues to him, via a phone call.

My skills were weaker than Kundai's, who had studied accounting and dealt with the company's software for weeks. The MD held us to an equal standard but I really needed a bit more time to understand the accounting processes and the nuances of his bespoke application.

I ran into trouble just when I felt my life had found a nice groove. The MD summoned me to his office.

'Over the last two weeks, I gave you client-facing responsibilities, but you have failed.' Without allowing me to respond, he concluded the conversation.

'Failing in this department doesn't mean you are useless; it means you might be useful, but not in a client-facing role. I will reassign you to a different role and give you two weeks to redeem yourself. If you fail again, it doesn't mean you are useless; it means you might be useful somewhere else, but not in my company.'

I spent the next two weeks creating design documentation and operational manuals for clients. I faked confidence, but I was engulfed by fear and a deep sense of unease. The stakes were high. It had taken me three months to secure this role. I not only harboured ambitions to succeed, but do so well that ERP Systems would promptly hire me after graduation. My plans to buy my parents some clothes and school uniforms for my little sisters now felt improbable.

Those two weeks went fast. As expected, the MD called me to his office again. I felt like I was walking into a savannah storm. He quickly shut the door and asked me to take a seat. I tried to put on a poker face but I was quietly freaking out.

'I gave you two weeks to redeem yourself, but you squandered that opportunity. I don't like the quality of your documentation. But this doesn't mean you are worthless; it means you might be useful, but not in my company,' he underlined, reasserting his philosophy. He gave me an envelope with my wages and a final payslip before instructing me to vacate the premises.

I felt like a wounded buffalo deserted by its herd. I was certainly not new to adversity, but the MD's words felt like a dagger through my heart. His viewpoint, that I was useless within ERP Systems and somewhat useful somewhere else, rang hollow to me. I knew I had to move on but my feet were heavy. I had hoped for this to end much differently. I felt awful beyond words and plummeted into a state beyond despair. *I have got some difficult days ahead*, I thought.

The entire saga had been questionable. The likelihood that I could produce quality documentation for a system I barely understood had felt remote from the start. I dissolved into tears as I left the premises. I stuffed the cash envelope into a pocket inside my jacket, fearing pickpockets would pinch it at Fourth Street, pushing me deeper into the swamp. I needed every cent. I was disoriented and embarrassed. I felt like a failure, sinking in a quicksand of shame.

The thread of hope I had been holding on to the previous two weeks had finally been cut. The way ahead was uncertain, to put it mildly, and looked bleak. A dark cloud, like the savannah cumulonimbus, now hang on the horizon. My friend Kundai was at a client's site — none of us had cell phones and as a result, I couldn't say goodbye to him.

The startling rejection by my employer precipitated a cascade of self-doubt. I could not help feeling that I had failed my first test in the corporate world. I had hit another rock bottom and started questioning whether I would ever complete the mandatory industrial attachment.

∗   ∗   ∗

I felt terrible for letting Kundai down as he had vouched for me. It had taken three months to stumble my way into ERP Systems. I was aware that no matter how bad things had become, they were likely to get worse. My suffering was clearly far from over. I felt like I was climbing Mount Kilimanjaro with a heavy pack.

Sometimes failure is also redirection: it takes you to a different place. All this is difficult to fathom in the moment. Finding the right path in life involves missteps. I had to be decisive and make a move. I could try to learn from the experience, stay positive, and return to spraying my resume around until I secured another paying attachment role in Harare. Alternatively, I could catch a bus to Gweru and inform my lecturers of my predicament. I had informed the university of my gig at ERP Systems but my situation had now reverted to the same old, same old.

If I stayed and nothing materialised, I would certainly fall off the cliff. My last wage would soon deplete, leaving me in an untenable position. I had asked several people for help over the months leading up to my short stint at ERP Systems. Some had stopped picking up my calls even if I was just calling to check on them. I felt terrible doing it — I wasn't the young boy Marion and Kristin had helped before. I was twenty-two and not a child anymore. I hated being regarded as a sponge. I yearned to be independent but at the same time, I lacked the means.

Remaining in Harare and not securing an internship carried both financial and academic implications. I was running out of time in which to complete the minimum required duration of industrial attachment. Taking five years to complete my degree instead of the standard four years was unthinkable. But I had already delivered hundreds of resumes and it was hard to be optimistic. I felt like I was going backwards.

I was badly hurt but not crushed. The MD's criticism and my subsequent firing pained me but nothing compared to the distress life had inflicted during my secondary school years.

I decided to leave Harare and return back to Gweru the following week. I told Tsuro he was better off packing up too and catching a bus to Mhondoro. I gave him the bus fare and advised he had to leave in the next couple of days, about the same time I would travel to Gweru. I was fully aware of his thieving habit and so took precautions. I stuffed my money in a shorts pocket and wore trousers over this, even in bed. But he always found a way. One day before his departure date, I returned to our room and discovered he had gone. All my clothes, except what I was wearing, were also gone.

Infuriated, I decided to catch a bus and go after him in Mhondoro. But as the emotions subsided, I realised doing so would be unwise. There was no phone to call ahead and verify if Tsuro had indeed travelled to Mhondoro. Furthermore, it was likely that he had already sold the clothes in DZ. Tsuro had stolen my clothes but I still had my cash. I decided to write off my losses and stick to my Gweru mission. Tsuro had beaten me three times now. Attaining my degree was, however, far more critical than seeking revenge.

*   *   *

I bid farewell to the landlord and travelled back to Gweru. That was April 2002. I went straight to Mr Moyo's office, the chairperson in the Department of Computer Science at that time, to explain my dilemma.

'You have already lost a considerable amount of time. Your only option is to join Privilege Simango and work here in the computer science lab. You know you won't be paid, hey?'

I nodded and quickly got down to work. I taught Microsoft Office basics to first-year students. Privilege was a classmate in Information Systems, a tan-skinned, fine young man. He and I administered the lab and were responsible for rudimentary tasks such as joining computers to the network, replacing motherboards, formatting floppy disks, and slaving hard drives.

Mr Moyo trusted me. I kept the keys to the lab most of the time and took them with me overnight. He sent me down to the tuck-shop several times a day to buy the cigarettes he smoked in his office. Occasionally he shouted Nandos peri-peri chicken and chips for us as a token of his appreciation for our hard work.

He delegated sweeping powers to Privilege and me. The university didn't pay us a cent for our work; nevertheless, that aura of authority boosted our egos. We suspended anyone we caught streaming porno-graphic videos. The hardest part of our job was chucking out Internet addicts in order to shut the lab. By chance, we stumbled across a program called Remote Shut Down. Boy, I loved this tool. *Five minutes to go, ladies and gentlemen!* I shouted across the lab, giving everyone time to save their work before vacating. There were always one or two students who thought they were smarter than others or the girl who thought we would exempt her because she was pretty. Once the five minutes elapsed, I clicked the remote shutdown command, blackening every computer screen, the ones Privilege and I were using. If you had not saved your document, you lost everything.

The computer lab was part of the extensive university network managed by a central IT team. The director granted us minimal administrative rights, which frustrated us. One day we had a technical issue we couldn't resolve because of our limited access rights. Our classmate Charles Sandura came to the rescue; he was attached to the central IT team. We envied his position — he had access to a super-user account, the proverbial keys to the kingdom.

We stood over Charles as he logged into the network. As fate would have it, he forgot to move his cursor and carelessly typed a visible password into the username field. Privilege gazed at me, winked, and we both smiled. Charles quickly noted his mistake and jumped onto the delete button but it was too late. We had access to go deep into the network, experiment, and try a few tricks of the day. We retained that power for a long time as that password was never changed. This was my first exposure to cybersecurity.

My economic challenges had not gone away. I could not afford to rent on my own room in Senga, the suburb nearby. Fortunately, I had been the vice-chairperson of the Christian Union and my university networks ran deep. My friend Taponeswa agreed to take me in, to doss in the room he shared with another friend, John Masvingo. This arrangement was known as squatting.

The single beds in the university room were too skinny to accommodate two adults. Taponeswa and I improvised a plan — we slept in the same bed but facing different directions — my head next to his feet and his head next to my feet. I stayed with Taponeswa for several weeks but squatting in the university hostels was eventually outlawed. The university unleashed security guards to enforce the ruling. The guards zealously raided squatters in the middle of the night, going door to door. My luck eventually ran out. I was sternly warned and ordered to vacate the room or face the music. The university also warned resident students to desist from accommodating squatters or be evicted.

This period marked another difficult phase of my life. The Zimbabwean economy was already in freefall. Most of us were surviving on *maputi* and black tea. And now squatting was prohibited.

But as one door closed, by God's grace, another door opened. Kudzai Masunda, a lanky classmate and close friend, pleaded with his family to take me in under their roof. Next stop, I left campus to stay with the Masunda family in Senga. I was apprehensive about everything during the first days, ruminating over my experiences when I stayed with my auntie back in 1994. But my concerns were soon quelled — the Masunda family treated me no less than they did Kudzi. They were already accommodating another classmate, Prince Sibanda, and the family did everything possible to make us feel as if we were their own blood. They showed me extraordinary generosity, an unconditional love I thought I did not deserve. My last eighteen months of university education would have been extremely difficult without their help.

*   *   *

I was determined to maximize the opportunities I had at MSU rather than dwell on my dark Harare experiences. I decided to push myself beyond what Mr Moyo expected of me, volunteering to actively participate in a significant project to design a highly interactive university website. The website would enable students to register and check their results online. I worked under the tutelage of Themba Ndlovu, a handsome computer genius and nerd, who had joined the university as a computer lab technician after graduating from NUST.

Ndlovu used the lab server as his PC because he considered the desktops too weak to handle his resource-hungry applications. After we closed the lab at 5 p.m., Privilege and I congregated behind Ndlovu's large screen and absorbed as much as possible. He solved complex business problems using relational SQL databases, Microsoft FrontPage and Photoshop. I was enthralled by Ndlovu's technical competence.

My website development never advanced to Ndlovu's level but I became good enough to do something with it. Four of us — Ndlovu, Privilege, Tafadzwa Maphosa and I — decided to start a company together and thus alleviate our financial woes. Tafadzwa, whose name means 'we are pleased, was a class behind and later joined Privilege and me at the lab. We referred to him as Zans, short for Zanamwe.

We took over Ndlovu's shelf company. I suggested we rebrand it Global Systems Integrators (GSI) to reflect our vision to take this tiny tech start-up beyond national boundaries. We quickly got down to work, commuting to the city and going door to door with our marketing fliers. Our persistence paid off: we won the contract to develop a corporate website for Zimglass, the nation's sole manufacturer of glass and one of the largest corporations in Gweru. And we secured other smaller-scale contracts: to service computers, troubleshoot software, replace defective hard drives, et cetera.

The Zimglass deal was strategic. It gave us the financial resources to expand our marketing services and covered our daily upkeep. With our confidence flying through the roof, Ndlovu and I hitchhiked to Zvishavane, a mining town 120 kilometres south-east of Gweru. We had arranged a meeting with the IT manager of Shabani and Mashaba

Mines. This company was one of the largest exporters of white asbestos in the world at that time, and owned by Mutumwa Mawere, a business magnate and former World Bank official.

Ndlovu was a handsome fellow and radiated a confidence that belied his accomplishments. We handed our business cards to the IT manager — Ndlovu was the chief executive officer and I was the executive chairman of GSI. The IT manager introduced the mining giant.

'We are one of the largest suppliers of white asbestos in the world. We have large ships carrying our cargo from Durban in South Africa to South Korea and other parts of the world. I am in charge of everything IT across both Shabani and Mashaba Mines. In short, the buck stops with me.'

It was now our turn to sell our services.

'Thank you for having us here. We are co-founders and directors of Global Systems Integrators, the leading tech firm across the Midlands. We have worked with the likes of Zimglass and other entities; our services range from developing corporate websites, e-commerce shopping carts, networking, and computer services.'

Ndlovu pitched an embellished version of GSI. The IT manager enthusiastically bought into our narrative and took us for a personal tour of the server rooms and other computing areas. Beyond our wildest imaginations, we won the contract to service more than two thousand computers. It was maybe one of the largest computer servicing contracts in Zimbabwe at that time.

We firmly shook the IT manager's hand and thanked him for his time. We confidently walked straight into a large car park to give the impression we had driven in one of the Toyota Prados or Mitsubishi Pajeros parked there. Once we were out of sight, we turned towards the main road and jumped onto a commuter omnibus headed to Gweru.

We were thrilled to win such an enormous contract. At the same time, we were deeply uneasy because we had exaggerated our capabilities. We had no workforce or equipment to handle such a complicated scope of work. Ndlovu was the most skilled and experienced of the four of us but he had a full-time day job at the university. We negotiated with Netcom Technologies, a two-man IT start-up owned by Kudzai Masunda and Prince Sibanda, and subcontracted to them at daily rates.

The first Saturday morning, we turned up at Shabani with nothing but a giant computer blower. The IT manager was underwhelmed by the image we projected; he had assembled fifty computers for us to service as a 'proof of concept'.

'Oh, come on, guys, I expected you to bring advanced computer diagnostic kits, but all you show up with is a bloody blower and an empty briefcase!'

I attempted to calm him down. 'We will be fine, sir; most of that knowledge is in our heads.'

But first impressions really matter. He terminated our contract after two weeks. And we were soon to be engaged in petty power struggles that eventually brought GSI to its knees.

The experience I gained from my brief entrepreneurship was never lost. It taught me to always shoot for the stars and go for what others deem unattainable, because in the end, I lost nothing.

CHAPTER 12

Harare

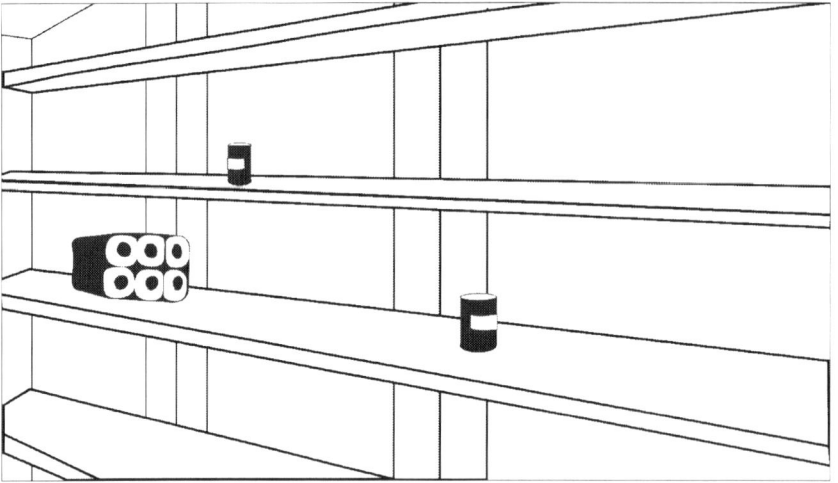

'Our deepest fear is not that we are inadequate. Our deepest fear is that we are powerful beyond measure. It is our light, not our darkness, that most frightens us.' — Marianne Williamson

I was the first one to graduate from university in my family. This was a badge of honour as most of my older siblings had attained diplomas in teaching or other vocational disciplines. But that achievement also carried enormous responsibility and expectation. I received enormous praise; in fact, people back in my village and distant relatives embellished my accomplishments.

Tonderai Chimera was one such friend. He was short and stout, light-skinned, and arguably the fastest doggy-style swimmer of our generation.

'Boys, Phidza is now so educated that he will soon be earning his salary in an open hat!' he claimed, insinuating that my pay would be so huge it wouldn't fit in my pockets.

At Rwizi bus stop, villagers, drinking, shouted *Murungu has arrived!* [The white man has arrived!] — perpetuating the colonial mentality of calling any native perceived to be well-off 'white'. Maodza, a distant uncle, claimed that, because I had studied computers at university, I could count the leaves on a massive tree in a matter of minutes. Immediately after this, he asked me to buy him a beer. Uncle Maodza's compliments were obviously exaggerated but stroked my ego nonetheless.

I completed my final year studies at the end of 2003. A few weeks later, I said goodbye to the Masunda family who had been extraordinarily generous to me for more than one and a half years. I jumped onto a green-and-white Kukura Kurerwa Volvo bus to Harare. I was drawn back to the capital city by the promise of higher-paying graduate opportunities. This was a moment I'd been dreaming of for so many years — to become financially independent and, as a famous Zimbabwean saying goes, *to become a man among men.* My previous stint in Harare had been a very difficult one. Now, armed with a degree and considerable experience, managing computer networks and developing websites, I hoped the script would unfold much differently.

I stayed with Ranganai Zvakafa, my close friend from MSU and fellow Christian Union devotee. Ranga, as I called him, had been hired by Zimbabwe Electricity Supply Authority (ZESA) as a graduate systems administrator. ZESA, a government parastatal, was the country's sole supplier of electricity.

I replayed the old routine, the classic 'spray-and-pray' tactic. I commuted from Budiriro, where Ranga rented a two-roomed boysky, whenever I had the bus fare and scattered my resume everywhere.

I returned to Gweru after a few weeks with the hope of securing a teaching assistant role at MSU. I had put Ranganai's work landline as the contact number on my resume. He called me one afternoon to relay that I had secured an interview with Telefonica. They were an Internet services and IT networking firm located within Pegasus House in downtown Harare. I had to show up at 10 a.m. the next day.

Mrs Mugari, the same compassionate woman who had fed and sheltered me before, gave me some money and I caught the midnight train, arriving in Harare before dawn.

The interview went well and a couple of days later, the recruiter advised that Telefonica was offering me a role as a trainee Internet and networking consultant. I was ecstatic. This was the beginning of a new era in my life, something I had dreamt of for more than two decades. I still had one residual challenge to navigate, however. I barely had any clothes suitable to wear for work. In my excitement, I rushed to Mbare and caught a bus back to my village. Everyone at home was electrified to hear my news. Baba agreed to sell one of his last oxen to facilitate my new opportunity. I returned to Harare, bought shirts, trousers, and a pair of black shoes, and started out on my new journey.

*   *   *

Telefonica was founded in 1997 by three white Zimbabweans, two of whom were previously partners at Deloitte. They instilled high standards of professionalism and excellence. The founders had established a lean and highly successful business, one that was financially prudent. Julie Pearson, my first manager, and one of the kindest Zimbabweans

I have ever known, was moderately stylish. She wore black high heels and coloured, well-fitting corporate suits. She always wore pants; I never saw her in a skirt. The MD, Ben Williamson, on the contrary, wore a charcoal suit and white shirts daily, like forever. Francis Peters, the third director, was a complete nerd who knew the ins and outs of Cisco switches like the back of his hand. He wore baggy clothes and took the lift downstairs every thirty minutes to smoke his cigarette. All three Telefonica directors drove aged but serviceable Mazda 626 sedans. That was in stark contrast to the other, local, spendthrift businesses who co-tenanted Pegasus House. Their parking floors were full of brand new Mercedes S-Class sedans, Mercedes ML SUVs, BMW 5 Series, and high-end Toyota Landcruiser four-wheel drives. It didn't surprise me that most of these frivolous corporations were inevitably wiped out by the economic downturn. Telefonica would keep going strong for decades.

Telefonica deployed me to set up servers and troubleshoot Internet issues at large corporations — such as Delta, Pelhams, Coca-Cola, Rooneys, Zimsun Hotels — as well as in the homes of prominent business people, in Borrowdale Brooke, Chisipite, Highlands and other exclusive suburbs. Sometimes designated drivers picked me up in sparkling Mercedes vehicles to resuscitate Internet connectivity at clients' lavish homes.

As soon as my first pay was in the bank, I rushed to Express Stores, a budget clothing line, to buy my mother a two-piece costume and Baba a black suit.

But the Zimbabwean economic crisis soon exposed the fragility of my dream. My hopes, it seemed, were built on sand. The economy was already in a state of advanced continuous decay by the time I joined Telefonica. The Zimbabwean dollar was no longer of value, depleted by rampant hyperinflation. By the time businesses banked their daily earnings, a substantial amount of the money had already been lost. Zimbabwe's monthly hyperinflation would reach a staggering 79 billion per cent.

The hopes that I had carried for years looked forlorn just when I was ready to soar. I wanted to pay back my parents, give them a feeling of dignity and self-respect, and support my siblings.

Runaway inflation and ensuing economic hardships shuttered hundreds of companies. Large banks and other deposit-taking institutions teetered into insolvency. Century Holdings, which I banked with, filed for liquidation a day after Telefonica deposited my salary. I never retrieved a single dollar.

Mugabe lashed out at businesses that spiked their prices for being complicit with Britain and its allies, who sought to hasten the demise of his regime and, he claimed, reimpose colonial rule. His government responded by unleashing squads of price inspectors who patrolled supermarkets, gas stations and wholesalers, enforcing price reductions and jailing non-compliant businessmen and shop owners. Mobs trailed behind the price inspectors, scrambling to buy clothes, shoes and groceries at unrealistically low prices as soon as the rules were (temporarily) imposed. Many businesses, after suffering insurmountable losses, shut their doors forever.

Predictably, goods disappeared fast from supermarkets as the basic financial laws refused to bend to 'Mugonomics', Mugabe's economic ideals. There was hardly anything on supermarket shelves, except for large packets of *maputi* and rolls of toilet paper. Even if one had money in the bank, the liquidity crunch prevented anyone from accessing the cash.

*   *   *

The air was heavy with the stench of sewerage from burst pipes running continuously down the gutters of Budiriro. Paradoxically, Budiriro translates to 'success'. Personal henchmen installed by Mugabe to run parastatals failed miserably. ZESA, the electricity authority, sinking into chaos, aggressively rationalised supply, a concept known as load shedding. The households that shared the same power grid as the State House (Mugabe's official residence) were the exception, as always. Water supply authorities, equally exhausted, pumped intermittent and soiled water to households, threatening residents with ancient diseases such as cholera and typhoid.

Attempts by the Mugabe regime to re-engage Western countries fell on deaf ears — his administration was regarded as a pariah state. Major economic powers, led by the United States, imposed so-called targeted sanctions against the regime, seeking to accelerate the end of Mugabe's rule. They cited human-rights violations, despotism, and graft. Condoleezza Rice, the US Secretary of State at that time, bundled Zimbabwe together with Belarus, Burma (now Myanmar), Cuba, Iran, North Korea and branded them 'outposts of tyranny'.

Mugabe responded as usual with vitriolic rhetoric, accusing the West of attempting to topple his democratic government because he had redistributed arable land to native peoples. The Western chorus of indignation had little bearing on Mugabe — it was the poor who bore the heaviest brunt of the sanctions. The Western media attacks on Mugabe seemed to elevate his status as a cadre among his strong rural base, not diminish it.

A country once regarded as the breadbasket of Africa, and boasting the continent's highest literacy rate, no longer had the means to feed its people. Zimbabwe's farming industry, previously the mainstay of the economy, crumbled, pushing the country further into a frantic dearth.

During the preceding two decades, immigrants had flocked

from the Democratic Republic of the Congo, Zambia, Malawi and Mozambique. The stampede was now entirely in the opposite direction, as once staunch patriots escaped one of the most precipitate economic collapses in history. My beloved country, once known as the jewel of Africa, was fast turning into a forsaken place.

To further aggravate the situation, the government embarked on an operation to rapidly demolish shantytowns. Referred to as Operation Murambatsvina, which translates to 'rejection of filth', or Operation Tsunami, because of the ferocity of its execution, the arbitrary exercise forced more than seven hundred thousand low-income individuals out of their dwellings. Predictably, homelessness soared. As city life grew increasingly bleak, many retreated to their communal roots. Murambatsvina was, in the words of Anna Kajumulo Tibaijuka, special envoy on human settlements issues for former UN secretary-general, Mr Kofi Annan, 'carried out in an indiscriminate and unjustified manner, with indifference to human suffering, and, in repeated cases, with disregard to several provisions of national and international legal frameworks.'[10]

I was living with Privilege around this time, my friend from MSU. Fortunately, we had already moved from Budiriro before the bulldozers, escorted by armed police, arrived to demolish our old boysky. Milton Park was a relatively posh suburb and the move was strategic. Although the rent was much higher, our room was located just a few kilometres from Harare CBD, so we could just walk the jacaranda-lined streets without worrying about the endless queues at Market Square bus terminus or the bus fare we rarely had.

Civilians everywhere had also reached their breaking points. The main opposition party, Movement for Democratic Change (MDC), galvanised protests to pressure the government for greater civil liberties. Protestors chanted the MDC maxim, 'Chinja maitiro / Guqula izenzo', which translates 'change your ways', in Shona/Ndebele respectively. The Zimbabwe Congress of Trade Unions routinely called for 'stay aways' (or strikes). Yet still, the band played on.

Elections took place about every five years; they were marred by violence and widely considered charades. After disputed election results were announced, the opposition took to the streets again. Soldiers and police officers cracked down and that cycle continued for years. There were long and winding queues at ATMs everywhere. Tired and hungry security officers guarded empty ATMs, black-button sticks dangling in their hands. Drivers waited for hours, even days, in snaking lines at fuel service stations, hoping to buy gasoline when tankers eventually arrived from South Africa. Tempers flared and brawls broke out when queue-jumpers tried to force their way to the front with twenty-litre jerry cans.

Unscrupulous hustlers took advantage as the fuel shortage worsened. In a rather stunning case, police arrested two mortuary workers for allegedly renting out corpses to drivers to enable them to jump the queues. Service stations prioritised individuals with burial orders or those transporting deceased relatives to their graves.

The public transport system inevitably degenerated into deeper chaos. Before we moved to Milton Park, occasionally, I left my old place in Budiriro at 7 a.m. but would not arrive at Telefonica until after 12 p.m. There were not enough buses on the road to ferry commuters. Minibuses, referred to as kombis, exploited the dire situation. They inflated the fares and subdivided trips from Budiriro to the city into three separate journeys, demanding the same fare for each of the shortened legs. I got off at Glenview 8, jumped back on the same kombi, got off again at Southerton, then jumped back on the same kombi again to the city.

The government played down the fuel crisis, arguing that the long queues were testament to the fact there was fuel; otherwise, why would anyone queue? Dangerously, Mugabe challenged his detractors to lie flat on Samora Machel Avenue, one of Harare's busiest roads, and see how long it would take before they were run over by cars. No one took this up of course.

The majority of the Zimbabwean middle class were forced to adapt to the unrelenting economic woes. They were accustomed to driving in big cars, dropping their kids off at elite schools, shopping at Sam Levy's Village, and hosting braais on their green-grass backyards. Their moderate wealth vanished without warning, like warm moist air. Most had no option but to swallow their pride, transfer their kids to public schools, and join the long queues for cooking oil, beans, or maize meals from charity organizations.

The centuries-old demarcations defined by skin colour began to fade. White Zimbabweans resorted to sadza to survive, previously unconceivable as this was regarded as the staple diet of only poor rural folks. They shoved their way into kombis from Copacabana, Fourth Street or Charge Office, going to Highlands, Newlands, Chisipite and other posh suburbs. They endured the long queues to buy rationed bread and struggled to live from month to month just like their native counterparts. Others sold generations-old family estates and fled to the United Kingdom, Australia, New Zealand and other First World countries.

Children were dropping out of school at alarming rates. Street kids with distended bellies hounded patrons at fast-food outlets, begging for food. Desperate to get by, teenage girls resorted to prostitution.

As the situation heated up, the government passed draconian laws, such as the Public Order and Security Act. POSA outlawed demonstrations without prior authorisation; predictably, the police never approved demonstrations. This catch-22 pitted peaceful protestors against heavy-handed riot police officers and sometimes the army. On numerous occasions, authorities evoked POSA to arbitrarily detain and torture suspected opposition supporters or activists 'whose heads had grown too big'.

These repressions invoked contempt from citizens. Demonstrations flared up, with protestors looting shops or destroying private property. Police officers responded by firing tear gas, and sometimes, live ammunition. Millions who had sought refuge in the diaspora started applying for citizenship or permanent residence overseas. Their collective dreams of one day returning to Zimbabwe — to live comfortably in the houses they had built in budding suburbs like Westgate Red Roofs, Zimre Park and Mount Pleasant Heights — were now in tatters. Mugabe had gripped power since independence in 1980; speculation that he was now too frail proved sensational. The media reinforced that narrative with 'breaking news' of Mugabe's demise, only for him to reappear smiling on TV. He would cling on for another fifteen years.

To make ends meet, civil servants demanded bribes or barely showed up for work, pursuing side hustles. Immigration officers openly commanded kickbacks or sexual favours to process imports, grant visas or issue passports. The government's indifference to high-level graft scared foreign investors away, further worsening an already desperate situation. Police mounted roadblocks everywhere to extort innocent drivers, penalising them for absurd transgressions, such as the absence of a fire extinguisher in the vehicle. Corruption quickly spread to the private sector, with executives raiding corporate resources for personal gain.

Graduates were turning into black-market hustlers, profiting from short-term currency arbitrage deals, a practice called 'burning cash'. Tellers, exploiting the liquidity crunch, started earning more than bankers, demanding desperate customers to deposit ridiculously higher and higher amounts into ghost bank accounts, in exchange for cash. Educated people turned into bus rank marshals, rowdy individuals who created a business out of nothing, bullying commuters into minibuses, and getting paid a fee from each trip.

The powerful still managed to buy themselves out of several predicaments. But there wasn't much to look forward to for ordinary people. Life in Harare epitomised Zimbabweans' legendary resilience, for which we are often praised. But that virtue of personal resilience was not going to pay my rent or take care of my ageing parents. I had already pushed through more than two decades of poverty. Yet still, I found it intolerable.

To quote Myles Munroe, the Bahamian minister, 'You can never change what you tolerate.'

*　　*　　*

I had to leave the country. Zimbabwe, which I loved, which previously held so much promise, had become the graveyard of my dreams. To sit still and hope for political change would be a fool's game. I took heed of Rheinhold Niebuhr's words and prayed for *the serenity to accept the things I could not change, courage to change the things I could, and wisdom to know the difference.* I knew the difference — it was impossible to achieve my potential in such a constrained environment. Also, I didn't have the power to alter Zimbabwe's political path, but I could take deliberate action and disentangle myself from the deteriorating situation.

In the words of William L. Watkinson, 'It is far better to light the candle than to curse the darkness.' I had to act.

I worried about the state of affairs in the country but my primary responsibility was to my family. I would have gone mad had I stayed

— leaving became an act of survival for me. Trying to fix anything outside my control would only leave me severely frustrated.

But I wasn't naive — I knew that migrating to the developed world would be slow and fraught with challenges. I had no relatives or close friends in the diaspora to sponsor me for a visa. I had already applied for countless jobs overseas and received zero response. Zero. Still, I knew that no one, except myself, was going to dig me out of the current mess.

I concluded that working for a 'Big Four' consulting firm was the most plausible way to fast-track my move abroad. Each of these firms — PricewaterhouseCoopers, Deloitte, Ernst & Young, and KPMG — had a presence across hundreds of countries and routinely placed their staff on long-term international assignments. They were the envy of many. However, the Big Four had an ingrained practice of hiring trainees from elite schools — such as St George's, St John's (the one whose boys wore Green Blazers, not St Johns Chikwaka), Peterhouse, Jameson, Watershed College — and graduates from over-seas and South African universities. In short, not me and people like me. My chances as a savannah boy with a degree from a relatively unknown university were slim. Not to mention the olive-green suit I wore to work.

Being an underdog was never a reason to quit, however. I had no business worrying about entrenched bias or my inherent disadvantage — both of which I couldn't alter. I had two strengths to build on. First, I possessed a strong determination and will to succeed. Nothing at that time could dissuade me from my mission. I had learned about the power of ambition and definite purpose during my secondary school years and that experience continued to serve me well. Second, my work experience at Telefonica had equipped me with fundamental IT skills. I chose to focus on and sharpen those strengths.

After carefully assessing options, I decided to sit for the Certified Information Systems Auditor (CISA) exam. This is a prestigious certification offered by ISACA, the largest IT governance professional association in the world, with membership across two hundred countries. There were not many CISAs in Zimbabwe at that time. So passing this exam would materially differentiate me from my peers.

As ever, there was an obstacle between my ambition and reality. My salary was about one hundred US dollars, a pittance in comparison to the five hundred US dollars I required to sit for the CISA exam. Yet still, I wasn't fazed. Strategies are of little use unless a bold and vigorous action accompanies them. I saturated my mind with this goal — it became an unshakable commitment.

I took a side gig and started developing websites during my free time, using the Photoshop and Microsoft FrontPage skills I had mastered during my industrial attachment. I teamed up with Marshall, a friend who joined Telefonica as an intern on the same day as myself. He was a Harare native and intuitive entrepreneur; he hustled several leads and persuaded prospective clients that they needed a digital footprint. Once Marshall closed the deal, I rolled up my sleeves and got down to the design work. Once the new website popped up on the Internet, Marshall raised the invoice and pestered the client until the money hit the bank. We shared the profits evenly. I converted my share into US dollars as soon as possible, before it was burnt by hyperinflation.

I raised the required amount and paid for the CISA exam. I had several other normal needs at the time but I had to risk it all to start anew — defer instant gratification in service to my dream. Some of my friends wanted to get rich or famous but I had to get real. If I made weak decisions, I would be stuck in difficult circumstances for a long time. I couldn't have both.

Some of my friends were importing used Japanese cars, known as 'ex-Japs', and brandishing sexy Motorola phones, called Motorazers, in front of girls. Some furnished their apartments with sleek television sets and leather couches. I was twenty-five and admittedly also yearned for these frivolities. But for me, only one race mattered: me versus me. It was important to ignore these externalities and run my own race.

My fixation on leaving Zimbabwe redirected me from the immediate and unessential. I carried my CISA manual everywhere. I studied it on the kombi, as I commuted to and from work. I stopped wandering aimlessly or window-shopping suits at Truworths — I could never afford them anyway. I tackled my goal with a near-obsessive level of intent.

But it was hard to focus on a goal as long term as leaving the country, something that would take years, at a time when my parents in the village were in need, when the landlord was hassling me for overdue rent, when I had no clue how I would get to work the next day. Nevertheless I trusted that if I stuck to that long-term plan, those hardships would eventually come to pass. Achieving big goals demand huge sacrifices and firm impulse control.

* * *

I was discontent and yearned for change. I was determined never to live like this again. It's been said that you will know the limit of your strength when you fight for what you are afraid to lose. I wasn't ready to fail CISA. I knew that, in a best-case scenario, my situation would take years to alter and wasn't keen to make this worse than it already was.

Constant power blackouts made it challenging to study at home. I girded myself using my previous struggles overcome for inspiration. I squeezed study into intermittent breaks during work. I also joined a small study group that met after work and on weekends to go through hundreds of practice questions.

I sat for the CISA exam in June 2005 and blitzed it. After waiting patiently for several weeks, the critical email hit my Yahoo mailbox. I double-clicked on it and slowly dared to look, engulfed with anxiety. When I saw the word 'Congratulations', I vaulted from my seat to the amazement of workmates at Telefonica. They quickly joined me to celebrate my life-changing achievement. The financial sacrifices, the relentless toil, the total commitment had culminated in one of the most significant triumphs of my career to date — and when the odds were stacked against me.

It was a turning point. Passing that exam soon opened up interview opportunities at Deloitte and PwC. When Deloitte called me for the first interview, I borrowed a black suit from my friend Oscar. I did not want to jeopardise this chance of a lifetime by rocking up in my olive-green double-breasted suit. After three interviews, Deloitte offered me an IT audit role, which I quickly accepted. The role paid substantially less than Telefonica but I didn't care. My workmates at Telefonica asked me how much more Deloitte would be paying me and I simply refused to disclose. I had already made sacrifices, so what was one more, as long as my mission was on track.

My experience at Deloitte was deeply meaningful and enriching. My manager, Tristen Thomas, an IT audit and data analytics genius, valued my technical skills, and shortly threw me into the deep end. He assigned me several out-of-town assignments — travelling to Bulawayo, Plumtree, Triangle — to assess technology and business controls. I was empowered to make crucial decisions. I enjoyed being on the road; I never had to worry about food as we lived in hotels or company guest houses with designated chefs. Additionally, I enjoyed the autonomy, as the audit managers I travelled with didn't have any jurisdiction over me — I was my own boss when out of town.

*   *   *

Deloitte was located at 1 Kenilworth Road, in the high-income suburb of Newlands, four kilometres east of Harare CBD. The company offered a complimentary bus service to and from the city. I arrived in the CBD around 7 a.m. each day, an hour before the first bus trip, and proceeded straight to the New Life Church on Sam Nujoma Avenue for my morning prayers. For an hour, I petitioned God for my parents, my siblings and my ambitions.

One morning, as I strolled into the expansive prayer room, I locked eyes with a young lady whose tantalizing beauty stopped me in my tracks. She was tall and walking slowly in her black stilettos in the opposite direction. She was curvy, tan-skinned, and had a black weave that extended to her shoulders. It was love at first sight — from that first stare, she captured my heart. Even from a distance, I could see her personality radiated with serenity. She left the prayer room but I remained stuck 'in the flesh'.

We glanced at each other over the coming weeks. I naively waited 'for the right opportunity' to say hi but it never materialised. Several more weeks later, I got the break I wanted, in the queue at the Food Chain supermarket on Angwa Street. Coincidentally, the young lady I so much admired also stood in the queue, in front of me. I broke the ice. She introduced herself as Fadzi and she worked at Stanbic Bank; she was very pleasant and admitted she had seen me too at New Life. Tragically, I didn't have a cell phone to save her number, so I just said, 'So lovely meeting you', before leaving. Whenever we then bumped into each other, I greeted her and we briefly chatted but never took it any further.

Meanwhile, back at Deloitte, I was assigned as part of a team to audit the Reserve Bank of Zimbabwe. I travelled to Masasa to assess the technology controls at Fidelity Printers, a cash printing and gold refinery company wholly owned by the bank. Bizarrely, Fidelity was one of the major clients of ERP Systems, the business that fired me during my industrial attachment year, who told me, *you might be useful somewhere else.*

It transpired that ERP Systems was solely focused on software functionality but lacked the capacity or will to build a secure system. The MD's words became a self-fulfilling prophecy. I executed my assignment with the highest levels of professionalism, calling ERP Systems to validate my assertions. My report highlighted several severe flaws, and by the time of the next audit, Fidelity Printers had already embarked on a project to replace ERP Systems.

My sister Viola, the second born in our family, was now teaching in rural Hurungwe together with her husband, Fani Nyakudya. Sadly, she contracted an inexplicable illness and her health deteriorated sharply. The Zimbabwean public health system was a shambles and compounding our distress, none of us had the money for a private hospital. Her husband was a primary school teacher like her. I could barely raise the bus fare to visit them in Chitungwiza, where they were staying at that time. I was so close to Viola and lacking the means to do something for her, to rescue her from her anguish, is the worst feeling I have ever had.

Unexpectedly, Deloitte requested me to travel to Lilongwe and Blantyre as part of a team to audit the Reserve Bank of Malawi. This was the break my family needed. Deloitte would pay me almost one hundred US dollars in daily allowance. For the three weeks, I would raise enough to send Viola to a private practice and salvage her deteriorating health. This was my first time on a plane and my first trip out of Zimbabwe. In my rush to secure a passport and book flights, et cetera, I forgot to take my dosage of chloroquine. The world's deadliest animal was to strike — I was bitten by a mosquito. My body temperature soared, my knees shook; I felt powerless, taken over by indescribable nausea, muscle pain and blistering headache. Deloitte Malawi medevacked me to a private clinic, where I was diagnosed with malaria.

I was close to being discharged when my manager walked in and advised that Viola had passed away. The profound pain, the grief, that ripped through my soul has never been surpassed, to this day. It felt devastatingly final; I could not believe I could never see my beloved sister again. None of the tribulations I had previously suffered prepared me for the unbearable loss. Viola was my sister, my mentor and a dear friend. She had been prematurely robbed from us by a completely preventable death — if she had been given two more weeks, I am sure my cumulative allowance could have saved her life.

I flew back home the next day. I visited her grave to pay my last respects, in the company of my good friends, Prince Sibanda and Ranganai Zvakafa, and my friend and workmate from Deloitte, Masimba Munemo. Viola's grave lies beside VaMushonga's, my grandmother's.

About fifteen months after joining Deloitte, I was back on the Internet applying for overseas roles again. My confidence was boosted by my Deloitte experience and CISA qualification. In less than a month, I had secured interviews with PricewaterhouseCoopers (PwC), with three PwC offices — Sydney, London and Auckland. PwC's offices were autonomous so these interviews were effectively with three different (but interdependent) employers.

In mid-2007, the Sydney PwC office offered me a role as a senior IT audit consultant, and I politely declined to proceed with the other two interviews.

CHAPTER 13

Sydney

Four years since embarking on my mission, I departed from O. R. Tambo International Airport in Johannesburg and flew 11,044 kilometres to 'the land down under'. As I walked down the aisle of the packed 747, it suddenly dawned on me that my world was about to change drastically. Almost everyone was white.

My journey across the Indian Ocean had begun after years of dreaming and acting. I had learned that changing my situation didn't require magical acts of inspiration, as was commonly believed. Instead, it came from discipline, intention and willingness to endure extended periods of discomfort — all towards a higher goal. I had the power to dig myself out of seemingly any impossible situation.

Having no one to rescue me when at my most desperate was a gift. It forced me to dig deeper within myself, to excavate a new level of belief, instead of waiting for some external saviour. We are limited by our thoughts; as the African proverb says, 'When there is no enemy within, the enemy outside can do you no harm'.

I saw the world radically differently than I did five years prior. I realised I had the power to shape my destiny rather than falsely believe my circumstances were fated. Some of my friends in Harare were busy complaining about how hard things were at the same time that I was developing websites and raising money for my CISA exam. When I flew out in September 2007, some were still praying for miracles. They forgot that hope without decisive actions only leads to frustration.

After fourteen gruelling hours, I landed in the Harbour City to start my new dream. I had one bag of clothes and three hundred US dollars in my pocket. I had borrowed one thousand US dollars from Elvis Katiyo, a friend from Deloitte who had also just joined PwC (London). But I had needed to spend most of it on pressing family matters before my departure from Harare.

I followed the other passengers through endless corridors until I arrived at the security clearance section of Sydney Airport. Australian and New Zealand citizens and residents breezed through their designated gates. Whereas I joined a painfully slow queue of fellow foreigners. A bad-ass-looking border patrol officer walked up and down the line with a black sniffer dog going at everyone, tail wagging. When I reached the checkpoint, the immigration officer gave me an intense stare, extending his hand to grab my green Zimbabwean passport.

'What brings you to Australia, sir?'

'I am here on a working visa; I will soon be joining PricewaterhouseCoopers,' I replied.

The immigration officer looked enquiringly from my passport photo to my face several times without saying a word, as if saying, *Is this really you?* He flipped through my barely stamped passport until he spotted my 457 four-year working visa, before asking several, what seemed to me irrelevant, questions. I almost cracked when he asked me if I had more than ten thousand Australian dollars cash with me.

I was then shepherded to the next checkpoint where a female customs officer politely asked me to take off my shoes and place them in a plastic container. She disappeared with them for a moment and gave them a thorough clean to remove any lingering Zimbabwean soil. I was through — passing the endless checkpoints and exhaustive questioning. I spotted a suited up old white bloke holding a placard inscribed, 'Mr Zongo, QF64, Johannesburg'. After a brief formal introduction, he chauffeured me to the Crown Pacific apartments on Kent Street, where PwC had booked two weeks of complimentary accommodation for me.

On Monday morning, I dressed up in my slightly oversized black pinstripe Armani suit, which I had bought for forty US dollars at Truworths in Harare. I wore it with pride as I jumped onto the escalator in Darling Towers — which boasts views over Sydney's Darling Harbour — to commence my new role as a senior consultant at PwC. Almost everyone I saw was either white or Asian.

PwC assigned me a buddy, a fellow senior consultant, to help me through the intricacies of work and Australian culture. After a series of work inductions, my Aussie buddy generously offered to take me for lunch. His offer was timely — the three hundred dollars I had arrived with in Sydney was depleting faster than I liked. In Harare, I could buy sadza and stew for lunch for as little as one US dollar. Sydney, however, was an expensive city: lunch cost an average of fifteen dollars. We visited a popular joint a few hundred metres from the office and ordered giant sandwiches stuffed with lettuce, fresh tomato, mayonnaise and skinless chicken breast. The meat was filling but tasteless. After eating and chatting for an hour, my buddy asked for the bill.

'Now, Phillimon, let's pay for our sandwiches,' my buddy said, intensely, as he totted up his portion of the bill.

I slowly pulled out a twenty-dollar note, enough to cover my sandwich and a glass of Coca-Cola. *Why the hell did he invite me for lunch and request me to pay for it?* I silently pondered. I was doing my best to mask my disgust. Back home, if you invited someone for lunch or dinner, you paid. However, while this episode temporarily blew my budget, it was also an important teaching moment that saved me from being regarded as a cheapskate later on. This was the Australian way — the faster I embraced it, the better for me.

While this 'each man for himself, God for us all' characteristic of my new world felt bizarre at first, I quickly became comfortable with it. Simply dividing the bill by the number of guests didn't make sense in most cases. How on earth was I expected to fork out the same amount as some fine-diner — who orders a dozen oysters, wagyu steak and several glasses of Veuve Clicquot — when I ordered chicken parmigiana, chips, salad, plus a glass of Coke Zero?

My new work environment, where just about everybody else was either white or Asian, felt so different. There were no other African-looking people in sight. That was, until later that same afternoon, when I was busy uploading receipts to reclaim my immigration expenses. A slow and deep voice bellowed over my shoulders, *Bambo!*

The mention of the Shona word, which means emperor, almost ejected me from my seat. *Who the hell utters such a hardcore savannah word inside one of Sydney's highest skyscrapers?* I wondered in shock.

I spun around and locked eyes with a twenty-something-year-old African man. He was chuckling hard, clearly impressed by his well-executed prank. I also cracked a smile. It was Jinda Samanyika, known to his inner circles by the nom de guerre Garwe (Shona for crocodile) because 'he takes no prisoners'. Jinda had joined PwC Sydney about three months before me, from Dubai. Jinda means 'prince'. Jinda and I soon developed an unbreakable bond, thanks to our common rural roots.

*   *   *

Jinda and I also shared a common interest in fashion. After work, we went around the shopping malls in downtown Sydney looking for nice clothes. We spotted an Armani shop one Thursday late-night shopping. Without much hesitation, we walked in, hands deep in our pockets. I was, appropriately, wearing my favourite pinstripe Armani suit.

Everything looked very different to the Truworths men's store where I had bought my Armani. A well-dressed, tall white gentlemen in an exquisite bespoke black suit, sharply juxtaposed by his pure-white gloves, ushered us through the glass door. I could not understand how a security guard could afford such elegant apparel. He gently closed the door behind us and reverted to his rigid stance. Except for us, the store was almost empty.

I did not feel comfortable: the secret-service-looking dude kept staring as we randomly browsed from shelf to shelf. I picked out an impeccably crafted, dark two-piece suit with subtle stripes. *These are the suits Big Four consultants like myself wear*, I pondered in excitement. Then I saw the price, hidden behind several overlapping tags. I just opened my mouth wide like a thirsty baby dove — the suit cost a staggering four thousand Australian dollars. *Bloody hell! This could buy twenty head of cattle back home!* I mused in silence. I turned to Jinda, who was busy sifting through T-shirts and hoodies.

'Garwe! Garwe! Guess how much this suit cost?' I expected Jinda to be more worldly because he had lived in Dubai before.

'Umm, this one, Phidza, looks pricey, maybe two hundred dollars.' When I showed him the price tag, we furtively giggled and snuck out of the premises.

I was upset by how, in hindsight, a self-proclaimed exclusive Harare boutique had duped me into believing my Armani suit was for real. I was way less sophisticated than I thought.

My two weeks' accommodation at the Crown Pacific was fast running out so I logged on to an online accommodation website to look for my own rental place. A few minutes into my search, I stumbled across a fully furnished, renovated two-bedroom apartment in Double Bay. Boasting stunning Sydney harbour views, quiet sandy beaches, and trendy cafes, Double Bay is one of Sydney's most exclusive burbs.

The apartment was remarkably cheap — approximately half the average rental price for the area. I was thrilled by the prospect of moving into a bigger place, located in an opulent suburb, and for much less than I had budgeted for. This had to be the one! I emailed the advertiser, who promptly responded. He introduced himself as a benevolent 'man of God' doing missionary work in West Africa. Let's call him David. All David was looking for was a responsible steward to take care of his apartment while he was chasing 'lost African sheep'.

When I asked to inspect the apartment, things took a more devious turn. This so-called man of God advised me that he had left Sydney hastily and took the keys with him to West Africa. To view the apartment, I needed to send four hundred US dollars to him as an initial deposit and to cover DHL fees. The money had to be wired to him via Western Union. It became clear that this transaction resembled a notorious advance-fee fraud, the Nigerian '419 scam', a swindle that predates the Internet. My inner voice whispered to me, *This is crazy — please don't do this!*

Jinda cautioned me against rushing in and committing to an apartment, suggesting that I stay temporarily with him and his housemate, Joe Mapurisa. Joe was a senior auditor at Deloitte and I knew him very well: we had worked together at Deloitte Harare for almost two years. It made sense — my first pay cheque from PwC had not yet hit the bank.

I moved in with Jinda and Joe. They had a two-bedroom apartment in Homebush, a middle-income suburb in the Inner West of Sydney, about a thirty-minute commute by train to the city. Homebush is a multicultural place, with Indians, Chinese, South Koreans and Sri Lankans being the most dominant ethnicities.

Jinda and Joe were both extremely generous but the two had glaringly different personalities. Jinda was the Zimbabwean version of Dennis Rodman: he worked hard during the week, but from Friday evening, he let everything go and switched to party mode. He arranged impromptu parties with relative ease. Zimbos flocked from all corners of Sydney — and as far as Newcastle, in NSW, a two-hour drive — to attend Jinda's parties. I disliked clubbing but enjoyed meeting the new people who visited to pay homage to Jinda. During some weekends, Jinda and I drove to see the magical limestone Jenolan Caves in the iconic Blue Mountains and took the scenic route, the Grand Pacific Drive, to the coastal city of Wollongong.

We lazed around Sydney's stunning beaches — Bondi, Manly, Maroubra — during the blazing-hot summers. I was in awe as daring surfers took on the big ocean waves; it was thrilling to watch. It seemed like nothing was off-limits for these Aussies. Jinda and I swam in the shallows, fully aware of our limits.

*   *   *

After all this time, my mind was still on Fadzi, but I had lost contact since leaving Zimbabwe. I devised a plan to track her down. I called my friend Oscar back home, the same man whose black suit I wore to my Deloitte interview.

'Listen, man, I need you to help me track down a girl I met at New Life. I don't have a mobile number or landline. Her name is Fadzi and she works at Stanbic Bank in the CBD, but I am unsure which branch.'

Oscar did what Oscar had always done, rising to the occasion when I needed him. Armed with only two pertinent data points — Fadzi, who goes to New Life and works for Stanbic Bank — he placed calls across several Stanbic branches and found her. When Oscar explained his mission to her, Fadzi joined the dots and passed on her number.

Fadzi and I quickly fell in love, and talked for hours every day, sometimes only ending our call when the mobile phone battery died. At the age of twenty-six, Fadzi became my first girlfriend. I explained how my out-of-town work for Deloitte, and other excuses, had delayed the obvious.

A few months later, Jinda and I flew back to Zimbabwe for the Christmas holidays. Fadzi and I travelled to Mhondoro to meet my parents and my siblings. My parents were extremely relieved that finally I had fallen in love and were ecstatic to meet 'Madhlamini', as my mum referred to Fadzi, by her totem. We travelled on to Gweru, where I introduced her to my kind pastors, Mr and Mrs Mugari. And during my last week, Fadzi introduced me to her mum — a deeply spiritual, progressive and generous woman. (Her father had passed years before, alas.) It was a whirlwind tour before Jinda and I flew back to Sydney.

In the ensuing months, I made several calls to Fadzi and my parents, and organised *lobola,* bride price. My older brother Osward, my sister Maidei, accompanied by my confidants, Prince Sibanda and Ranganai Zvakafa, travelled to Fadzi's uncle's homestead in Chinhoyi and paid *lobola*. I was overjoyed once I got news back that all had gone as planned.

'How come you were single yesterday, and today, during an audit assignment, you are now suddenly married?' one of my workmates quizzed with disbelief.

'We do it differently in Africa, mate!', I responded before explaining the whole *lobola* thing.

Subsequently, PwC sponsored Fadzi's visa and flights and she flew to live with me in Australia. I bid farewell to Jinda and Joe who had been great comrades. Fadzi and I moved into a place in Darlinghurst, a bustling inner-city eastern suburb of Sydney. My new residence was located ten minutes from the CBD and fifteen minutes from the office.

CHAPTER 14

The Struggle to Belong

Settling in Australia was an unexpected battle for me, a time of constant mental turmoil. Back in Zimbabwe, I had developed deep friendships at work. I preferred my weekdays to the weekends because at work I was surrounded by buddies and we were a tight group. Our small IT audit function at Deloitte Harare was in spirit a manifestation of Ubuntu: colleagues and bosses acknowledged my work and regularly sought my perspective.

We embraced togetherness and responsibility towards one another, sharing the little food that we had. My workmates and I exchanged heavy banter with no hard feelings. We were always hungry but would still laugh despite our travails. Managers with company cars picked and dropped employees in the city when the company bus was not in service. Our bonds were bound by daily expressions of comradeship, kindness and love. My time at Deloitte, before migrating to Australia, remains one of the happiest periods of my professional life.

A group of IT friends used to congregate after work in front of Barclays Bank, on the corner of First Street and Jason Moyo Avenue. We called it *panzvimbo*, meaning 'the place'. We sat there until dark, talking about girls we admired but felt were out of our reach. We shared our hopes and aspirations before disbanding to various bus terminals. Those guys became family to me and I naively thought these bonds would last forever.

Even now, whenever I see an African-looking person in downtown Sydney, we exchange 'the African nod' in acknowledgement of each other. This surprises my work colleagues who sometimes think I must have a personal relationship with every African-looking stranger. I wasn't mentally prepared to lose my familial and friendship bonds in Zimbabwe, and dealing with the solitude that ensued after migrating to Australia. I grew lonely and restless and badly missed those relationships. I found myself stuck in between two worlds and now belonging to none.

Back home, my professional opinions had material impacts on financial audits; I felt like the Lionel Messi of Zimbabwean IT audits. But not anymore. In my new environment, I was a mere statistic, a mediocre performer relegated to support those earmarked for partnerships. Now I felt like that football substitute, the one the coach always instructs to warm up along the touchline but who has no hope of ever getting prime game time.

Back home, technical skills guaranteed unobstructed paths to senior roles. The IT CISA qualification I acquired, rare at that time, had set my early career on fire. A year into my Deloitte role, I had also sat for the Certified Information Security Manager (CISM) exam and passed it. I foolishly assumed those qualifications were lifelong career insurance. I needed to adapt my tactics to suit the new environment, but I resisted change and failed to acknowledge that skills mastered today may not be good enough for tomorrow. Incrementally, I became a shadow of my former self and that hurt badly.

Professional dynamics in Australia were starkly different. Success did not just depend on hard work or technical proficiency, but on one's soft skills, proximity to influential players, significant client relationships, ability to manoeuvre politically and the depth of one's networks. With none of these, I felt like a caged wild animal, a bird with clipped wings.

Who you knew mattered more than what you knew. I started feeling like I had little to contribute and my work felt more and more meaningless. I lacked the self-awareness and humility to acknowledge that my core areas of competence, built around technical proficiency, were now not the be-all and end-all. I was comfortable and did not expect change would be necessary. I defined my own parameters of success and stubbornly stuck with those beliefs despite the change of environment. I foolishly thought that what worked yesterday, in Zimbabwe, had to work forever — but the time that my once-revered certification paid off was gone. I was caught off-guard and every conversation I had with friends who were also nurturing that weak mindset only buttressed my assumptions about the inequities of Australian corporate life. This is what psychologists call confirmation bias.

We talked about race-based glass ceilings, entrenched prejudices, and disadvantages we agreed we had no power to change. We blamed everything and everyone but ourselves. We came up with excuses to rationalise our stagnation. Nothing was wrong with us: the system had let *us* down by failing to adapt to our expectations. Complaining is like a parasite: it poisons its host and infects those around it. Fadzi, meanwhile, was going through her own struggles, attempting to balance her demanding work and undergraduate studies — all while trying to settle into a completely new environment. I will, however, leave it to her to tell her own story and personal experiences.

*   *   *

Herein lies the paradox. Could anyone who escaped such poverty, who four years prior felt the thrill of economic emancipation, sink so deeply into despair? I earned seventy-five times more than I did in Zimbabwe but I had dismally failed to anticipate a flip side. I was caught napping and unprepared.

I rejected change and sought to fight the system, rather than open my mind, learn and adapt to my new reality. The system, much more durable and entrenched, put me in my place. I expected technical mastery to bring fulfilment at work so *who moved my cheese?* Technical skills still mattered, but just not that much anymore. I found my work, previously of so much significance to me, now profoundly meaningless. The impact on me was internalised despair and withdrawal. This period represented a new low point, a gross disappointment, a time of great distress and turmoil.

I was always stressed and felt detached from my work. Predictably, my performance tanked. I used the majority of my sick leave days. The dichotomy of my ambition and my prolonged career stagnation led to intense disorientation. I was like a car running on low fuel: I could go a few more miles but if I didn't take corrective measures, I would soon screech to a halt in the middle of nowhere. I wore nice fitted suits but I was dying inside — I lost my smile.

Our mental wellbeing is intrinsically linked to the quality of our relationships. Work colleagues laughed at jokes I didn't understand. Or if I understood the jokes, I didn't find them funny. *What kind of music do kangaroos listen to?* Hip-hop. *What's left after your local Woolworths has burned down?* Coles. Initially, I faked it, laughing along for fear I would be labelled as failing to fit in.

I joined work functions that I didn't enjoy and endured hours and hours of workmates talking a rugby lingo — scrum halves, charge downs, drop goals — I neither understood nor wanted to learn. I knew of the Zimbabwean Sables and the South African Springboks but everything else was foreign to me.

I was perplexed about the extent of swearing within the workplace. Back home, if Baba hurled 'fokufu', someone had better run to the woods. Australians, though, overused the f-word to an extent it became meaningless. They hurled the f-word to express their disgust, astonishment or even more surprisingly, their delight.

My struggle to remember people's names also frustrated me. There were just too many Craigs, Peters, Michaels, Richards, Matts, Lucys, Chloes, and Lizs. Back home, one would have to be pretty dumb to forget distinctive names, such as Remembrance, Forget, Memory, Granite, Fact-noise, Choice, Have-a-look, Limited, Hardlife, Laughter, Try-thanks, Psychology, Immigration, Victim, Doubt, Kissmore, and Drinkwater.

Some of these names were too real unfortunately. My friend Forget couldn't retain any knowledge, and Hardlife's grey, cracked feet reflected his lifelong hardships. I was also fascinated by Sinzimoni, so named because his mum had been in labour 'since morning'. Others have stuck with me, like No-Name-Why, Maybe-Tomorrow, Does-Matter, Stages-of-War, Mistake, Italian, Cosmetic, Sim-card, and Duty-First (the son of a police officer).

Clients couldn't understand my accent, when I called to clarify requirements, and I couldn't understand theirs. That built up the pressure. I found it difficult to connect at a deeper level with teammates. I withdrew, declining invitations to team functions, tired of talking about the weather, or being asked if I preferred cats or dogs. I fell deeper into solitude and things started falling apart for me. I joined colleagues for coffee runs but I loathed its bitter taste. I turned to hot chocolate but the same colleagues cautioned the excessive sugar would kill me. Aargh! I started having a lot of negative thoughts and doubting my potential.

Further to this, I bumped into Zimbabweans who claimed, strangely, they could barely speak in Shona because they had lived in Australia too long. When I pushed back — *forgetting one's mother tongue after ten years, when one arrived in Australia in their early twenties, was nonsensical* — they quickly pivoted, arguing that in Zimbabwe they belonged to 'private school settings'. When I spoke in Shona, some fellow Zimbabweans always responded in English. Talking to fellow Zimbabweans in English all the time made me feel like our identity was slipping through our fingers. These non-Shona-speaking Zimbabweans talked about how they missed their balis, and endless gwans about pies or dajes they liked to their bruhs, exes, lighties or other self-proclaimed big dawgs.

My friends found solace at the Africa Club, a joint that played African music located in Surry Hills, a suburb on the periphery of the CBD. But because I disliked clubbing, I stayed at home and retired to bed early. Occasionally we visited Lucky Tsotsi, a restaurant located along busy Oxford Street in Darlinghurst, that resembled a South African shebeen. The vibe was nostalgic but I found the food to be average, especially the soup, which tasted just like a bowl of tomato ketchup. I became harder and harder to please.

Besides, whenever I had saved a bit of money, inevitably someone would fall sick back home, obligating me to dip into it to pay 'black tax'. Everyone, from an entourage of Harare friends to an uncle whom I had not seen in more than a decade, expected me to solve a laundry list of problems. Some relatives and friends took my kindness for weakness. They faked sickness and other calamities then asked for money. Western Union attendants ended up knowing me by name. I dreaded picking up any calls prefixed '+263', knowing they would almost always be about money. Increasingly I was helping others put on their oxygen masks before I put on my own — I was inevitably suffocating, financially and psychologically.

I started businesses to reduce the amount of money I remitted home. I imported a minibus from Japan but the venture predictably bankrupted as relatives squabbled for control. Later on, I purchased an investment property, but that quickly turned into an alligator. The bank expected the monthly principal and interest payments on time but my Zimbabwean tenant defaulted as the economy worsened. I sunk deeper into a mental and financial swamp.

*　　*　　*

Did I ever experience racist prejudices? Certainly! I would be deeply irresponsible to deny such ugly realities. I often found myself responding to absurd questions: 'Do you know John from Africa? He is a very nice guy!' I just couldn't understand how a management consultant could ask such a dumb question. A taxi driver asked me where I was from. 'Homebush,' I politely responded as I buckled my seat belt. 'No, I mean where are you really from?' When I told him, the old white fella was quick to rush to ridiculous conclusions:

'Are you one of the refugees? You must be feeling lucky to wake up in Australia than to wake up in Zimbabwe right now.'

People, oblivious to my background, questioned, 'If Zimbabwe is not as hot as Australia, how come you are so dark?' Another workmate argued, 'I didn't think being so dark you would feel cold; I assumed your dark skin would absorb enough heat to emit during colder times?' When I used the word 'capability', a colleague was surprised at how I could have such a strong vocabulary, 'How come your English is so good; do they teach English down there?'

Old ladies still hastily clutch their handbags as I walk up the train aisle, even though I am wearing a nicely fitting M.J. Bale suit. The seat next to me is often the last to be occupied on the train, with several people opting to stand in the aisle. When Jinda and I drove to Bathurst, in regional New South Wales, to attend the V8 Supercar races, strangers shouted abuse. 'Nice car, guys!' We responded politely before the old white guy went on to hail, 'Where did you steal it?'

In Penrith, a suburb in Greater Western Sydney, a stranger left a wedding procession and walked straight up to me, as I was sitting in my car, to quiz, 'Is that your car, mate?' I asked why he wanted to know. 'Because it's an Audi, mate, it's quite expensive.' A related incident happened in Newport, a leafy suburb in Sydney's Northern Beaches. I was enjoying lunch at a waterfront restaurant with some Zimbabwean friends. A twenty-something-year-old looking blonde lady walked towards our table, stood a few metres away and shouted, 'Excuse me! Are you guys the bomboclaats?', before giggling away.

Recruiters confided with me and several of my audit friends that certain hiring managers had been upfront with them, that they were looking for 'an Australian' to fill a particular advertised role, so we better not waste our time.

My experiences are not unique. A good friend of mine, a fine Nigerian Australian, was frustrated after sending hundreds of applications with zero response. I will call him Ikechukwu Olabisi.

Ikechukwu felt something must be fundamentally wrong. He held multiple global IT certifications and had more than five solid years in network administration. He tried a new trick, changing the name on his resume to 'Jonathan Smith', educated at the University of Tasmania (replacing the University of Ibadan). Everything else remained the same. In no time, Ikechukwu received multiple invitations for the initial telephone interview. 'Oh, you have such a beautiful accent!' one recruiter dissembled, clearly shocked that Jonathan Smith spoke in a strong Igbo accent. When the same recruiter requested a follow-up, face-to-face or video interview, Ikechukwu politely declined, knowing how this would end.

Whenever an African Australian commits a misdeed, the entire community cops torrents of racist vitriol on social media. Statements like *Deport them to where they come from* or *These people will never change; it's in their DNA*, are meant to induce shame. They malign and ostracise the entire African-Australian community. The same applies to the intentional fearmongering and shameful generalisation of 'African gang problem' by the media and the public questioning on social media why African immigrants are even allowed in this country. This invariably implicates all people who look like me in violent crime. I go ballistic when fellow golfers ask, 'What the heck is going on with the gangs in Melbourne, mate?' It's ridiculous to expect me to be answerable to any misconduct, real or perceived, committed by any person who looks like me.

All this uninformed hatred ignores the enormous contributions made by hardworking African Australians to this great country. In 2016, 51.6 per cent of Zimbabwean Australians in the state of New South Wales (where I live) fell into the high-income household bracket, and only 2.4 per cent fell in low-income households. In comparison with 30.5 per cent and 11.2 per cent respectively for the same categories across the entire state. This reflects the hard work my fellow countryman put into positively contributing to our new home.

Racism is toxic and insidious and we must all do our best to fight and defeat it wherever it raises its ugly head. But I am also conscious of never allowing racism to overshadow the great opportunities Australia has given to me — to discover my potential and compete on a global stage.

*   *   *

My arrival in Australia in September 2007 signalled a new season, a time of hope, and great delight. My salary had risen by orders of magnitude, but deep inside, the promise of a happier life felt so far away. The burden of detaching myself from the past, the constant battle to belong — and my baseless but deep-rooted belief that the odds of succeeding here, as a young African man, were wafer-thin — was all too crushing.

I also critically lacked social signalling: relatable images of African Australians doing what I deeply yearned to do were very limited. Within PwC, the highest-ranking African Australian was a manager. It felt like an African Australian would make it to partnership level soon after pigs started flying. I can say from experience that it's hard to become something you can't see.

I decided to completely ditch my technology risk career for investment and finance. But to do so, I had to navigate several big obstacles. My existing skill set was not really transferable to the investment sector so I would be starting from scratch. I didn't possess an MBA or any of the qualifications often expected. And maybe the most significant obstacle was that I barely knew anyone in the investment management industry at that time — my networks were constrained.

To boost my prospects, I went in pursuit of the chartered financial analyst (CFA) qualification, a globally recognised professional certification. I knew that passing exams was no panacea: breaking into a new industry without requisite experience would still be difficult. But the CFA would give me a stronger grasp of investment management concepts and connect me with some industry insiders. And importantly, it would prove my ambition to potential employers.

The CFA is challenging. Going through the expansive content including the hundreds of insane mathematical formulae requires rigour and intense focus, let alone passing the six-hour exams. I caffeinated myself with countless cappuccinos and Red Bulls. I went straight to the library after gruelling days at PwC. I locked myself in the study on summer weekends while others sunbaked and drank margaritas. I had to push myself harder than an 'average' CFA student because I had no background in finance or accounting.

I passed Level 1 on my first attempt. After twelve more months of study, I sat for the Level 2 exam, and then waited. Weeks later, an email from the CFA Institute informed me I had failed the exam. I was devastated, given the time, energy and money I had invested in this mission.

I recouped my strength of purpose and registered for Level 2 again. After months of intensified effort, I retook the exam but failed it again — my mark was worse than my first attempt, compounding my agony. I had immersed myself in this goal for three straight years and invested thousands of dollars in exam fees and self-study materials.

Mid 2011, I entered my manager's office to discuss my performance. After a bit of small talk, my manager cut straight to the chase: 'You are a very skilled IT auditor, Phil. Your value to your audit teams is unquestionable. If you start working on leadership and business development skills, I am sure you will be a manager in eighteen months.'

I stared at my manager with blazing intensity. Yes, I had heard right. It was eighteen months, not the following month (as I thought). It wasn't even six months. I had already been in that role for three years. Most of my peers had risen to manager roles in just two years.

The combination of all my frustrations finally tipped me over the edge. In December 2011, I resigned from my role at PwC, terminated our lease and sold our furniture. Fadzi and I flew back to Harare with no intentions of coming back to Australia. I decided to return to the terrain I was familiar with, believing that my chances of rising to the top were tied to my geography. A few months prior to my decisive move, I had initiated a conversation with a senior manager in Ernst & Young (EY) in Zimbabwe, who hinted at strong prospects of EY hiring me as a senior manager.

CHAPTER 15

A Renewed Mindset

'A ship in harbor is safe, but that is not what ships are built for.' —
John A Shedd

Thank goodness, my negotiations with EY Zimbabwe fell through.
After a few months, Fadzi and I returned to Sydney. We stayed
with friends in the suburb of Hurstville, in southern Sydney, and after
several weeks, I landed a new job as an information security associate
with Dimension Data, a global technology consulting firm.

Fadzi and I were blessed by the birth of a gorgeous baby girl the
following year. We named her Nyasha, Shona for grace, reflecting on

how far God's grace had taken us in our lives. She was born at St George Hospital. Witnessing my daughter's birth, hearing her first cry to kick-start her lungs, was one of the happiest days of my life. My mother-in-law, Salome Dhlamini, had flown from Zimbabwe a few weeks before the birth to help and guide us. When the news of Nyasha's birth reached the savannah, my parents were both ecstatic and deeply relieved. They never bought into the idea that we had intentionally delayed having kids for five years.

Hitting rock bottom career-wise provided an excellent opportunity to rethink my goals. In the words of Tim Harford, the English economist, I was able to think outside the box because my box was full of holes. My situation was untenable — if I continued to live a mediocre life, with the knowledge that it could be much more, I was going to lose my mind.

In the summer of 2015, I finally gathered the courage to ditch a meaningless life of indifference and pursue things that set my heart on fire: ambitious goals that I was scared of doing yet were in my heart of hearts. For meaningful change, I needed a structural overhaul of my thought process — I no longer had time for a piecemeal approach to my life. I was now working as a technology risk manager for AMP, one of Australia's largest insurance and wealth management firms. I was sick of conformity and tired of sticking with the devil I knew. I determined never to live an ordinary life again or be resigned to the excuses that had always held me back. I resolved to cut loose any fixed mindset or victim mentality — to start living a fearless life.

I knew of no one who had gone as far as I envisioned by playing safe. I didn't care what people thought anymore — I had to risk being disliked for the sake of my ambition. I was thirty-five years old and wiser. This was an opportunity to learn from my mistakes and press the restart button. I had before cushioned myself from risk at the expense of my growth.

I had to adapt to rather than resist my changed environment. I wanted to pursue my new goals with intensity and the same passion that had carried me through previous challenges. Life is too short to take it easy. I had a less desirable alternative — I *could* choose to amplify the negative encounters of the past. Those challenges were real but I had no business contesting toxic attitudes ingrained in other people, people I barely knew. Rather, I decided to focus on the infinite opportunities presented by my new environment, in Australia.

This was a turning point: acknowledging that I could never become my best while I was now physically in Australia but my mind was still stuck in Zimbabwe. To become my best, I had to extricate myself from the past and be fully present with the task at hand. I pressed Control-Shift-Delete and terminated any plan B. With a safety net, I would be going at things half-hearted, not fully committing my time, money, and mental energy.

I no longer had the time or tolerance for ideas on running satellite businesses in Zimbabwe. I had tried that before and got really badly burnt. Worse still, these side ventures had come at an immense cost to my professional development. Australia was my new reality and I had the power to achieve the life I wanted. This was my new life — I had to embrace it and adjust. Life wasn't going to start when I returned to Zimbabwe upon retirement; it was already happening right in front of me.

During my first four years at AMP, I worked as a technology risk manager. I was motivated by my role in that period. I felt much closer to the business and technology function than my previous IT audit roles, which were more detached and often backward-looking. However, the technology risk role began to feel unfulfilling again after that. I was a jack-of-all-trades but a master of none. I was spreading myself across everything as thinly as Vegemite on toast. I realised then that of all the technology risk domains, cybersecurity was starting to dominate boardrooms and zooming to the top of corporate risk profiles at an astounding pace. It became clear for me, that to position myself for the future, I had to carve a niche and become very good at one thing.

*   *   *

In 2014, I decided to switch careers and go into cybersecurity. I resigned from technology risk and assumed a role as a cyber security analyst. This change was uncomfortable but something had to give. Without sacrificing my ego in this way, I would never have accelerated my career to the extent I did.

I sat down and wrote out a highly ambitious goal towards the end of 2014. I wanted to compete at a global stage, to develop deep expertise that would make me the obvious choice, and thrust me onto the front line in the fight against the menace of cybercrime. I wanted to stand out from the competition and become something like the Kipchoge of cybersecurity.

Some associates advised me to take small incremental steps to protect myself from total embarrassment should I fail in my attempt. This only reminded me of Muhammad Ali's famous words::

'Impossible is just a big word thrown around by small men who find it easier to live in the world they've been given than to explore the power they have to change it. Impossible is not a fact. It's an opinion.'

Life is about taking risks. I was working as a technology risk manager for a large financial services institution; I was presenting to senior executives and writing board papers. Deep down, however, I knew I was tinkering around the edges of my potential. I was in a comfortable place but nothing was growing there. I summoned one of my previous victories for inspiration: I had successfully orchestrated my migration from Zimbabwe against the odds. With that renewed mindset, and a great sense of focus, I started to see opportunities previously invisible to me, bounded by my belief system.

I moved in quickly on my inner circles, cutting off associations with cynics — those consumed with self-doubt who seemed to know every reason why Africans couldn't thrive in Australia. Instead, I surrounded myself with dreamers and doers, those who saw the potential within me even if I hadn't fully grasped it myself. I detached myself from people who exhibited bottled-up mindsets. When I failed, I determined to self-examine deeply, learn from my mistakes, and refine my craft, not blame convenient circumstances.

I consciously avoided anyone who talked about glass ceilings. I had the power to create the life I envisioned for myself. I acknowledged that the IT world had changed dramatically. To boost my trajectory, I needed to start thinking beyond just cybersecurity, and work on a broader skill set: my aptitude to communicate with impact, to influence corporate power brokers and decision makers, to read my own emotions and those of others, to think strategically and solve significant problems, to make decisions under pressure. There were too few places at the top for too many hopefuls; I wanted to make myself the obvious choice. To do so, I had to revamp my mindset and sharpen myself like the tip of a spear.

I no longer had time to rely on fate. The corporate world was slowly getting intentional about diversity, but I loathed the idea of ascending as a token of racial diversity. I wanted to progress on my own terms and let my work speak for itself.

All this required a deep level of self-awareness. Up until then, I had constructed my identity solely around my technical skills, but my new world exposed the frailty of this. I was operating in a new environment, one that placed a huge weighting on 'soft' rather than 'hard' skills. Soft skills were not taught at university, so I established six core principles to underpin my mission.

First. I would not give up easily or even contemplate the possibility of surrendering. My previous experiences had taught me that nothing significant comes easy: quality takes time. No longer could I be knocked down by a single punch, as Nduna had done all those years ago in the savannah. When life gets hard, as it certainly will, giving up is the easiest option. But habitually capitulating at obstacles is a terrible thing. It weakens the mind, for we are what we repeat. Every human being has a breaking point, but I was determined to push as far as I could without forfeiting my mission. Long-term success hinges on grit: the ability to persevere when opportunity looks lost, when those around you have written you off.

Second. No longer would I cast blame on people and circumstances. I was taking complete ownership of my goals. If I screwed up, only the man in the mirror would be to blame: not my wife, my boss, my kids or anyone else. The surest way to achieve nothing is to lay blame on other people. To quit because of the excuses that had previously held me back would be shameful. I knew this time, I had this, and no one could ever dissuade me from my mission. I identified several challenges and rebranded them excuses, because that's what they were. That revelation was profoundly powerful: it helped me rise above and use brute force to get through discouraging moments.

Third. I wouldn't cover my ass anymore, or stick my head in the sand. I would live boldly, throw dogma out the window, and choose to do hard things. A comfort zone is the graveyard of potential. I decided to focus on skills that are rare, valuable, hard to master — aptitudes that differentiate me from the masses. If everyone else was doing it, it didn't stimulate me. The field of cybersecurity was very crowded in the middle; like Mo Farrah, the legendary British long-distance runner, I wanted to burst away from the competition. I would rather face the temporary agony of failure than be consumed by the eternal poison of regret.

Fourth. I would attack my goals with a near-obsessive level of intent, to strive to become the best that I can ever be, while refusing to be restrained by the myth of perfection. I had to attack my goals with undivided attention, the zest of youth, explore new territories with the fearlessness of the honey badger. I would rather do nothing at all than do something half-heartedly. Mediocrity and conformity had sucked the life out of me, but never again.

Fifth. I had to choose my goals wisely. I have always, from an early age, attacked my goals with intensity. The hard work did open up opportunities I had never dreamt of, but I was wiser now and knew that not all pain was gain: hard work alone had its limits. To take my career to the next level, I needed to start hustling *smarter* and harder. This means having extreme clarity about my vision. Without a clear-cut mission, I had been sidetracked by other people's objectives. This time, my vision would dictate my actions. Clarity of focus helped weed out the urgent but non-essential, and fostered the discipline to stick with the important and essential, with a long-term compounding effect on my professional growth. Once I knew what I wanted, I disproportionately allocated my time to one or two non-negotiable habits until they became as natural as breathing. These are routines I stick to religiously, even when I feel disinclined, skill sets that take time to master and most people aren't willing to pursue. When it comes to these habits, I do not negotiate with myself.

Spreading myself thinly across several endeavours had cost me many precious years. It was better to go deep into one or two complementary areas, skills that would sharpen my competitive edge, than be a jack-of-all-trades. This automatically deselected a lot of crap from my life. I barely had the time to scroll through social media or WhatsApp groups.

Sixth, and maybe the most important. I developed routines to harden my mind. I knew that I was the embodiment of my thought patterns. I could not change the outside without transforming my mind. As the African proverb goes, *If there is no enemy within, the enemy outside can do no harm.* I deliberately reinforced my can-do attitude by reading books on mindset. Four books were particularly influential: *Mindset* by Dr Carol Dweck, *Atomic Habits* by James Clear, *Can't Hurt Me* by David Goggins, and *As a Man Thinketh* by James Allen.

CHAPTER 16

Writing Journey

I shifted into execution mode in early 2015, knowing that faith without deeds is dead. Theodore Roosevelt's words had a profound influence on me during that time:

> It is not the critic who counts; not the man who points out how the strong man stumbles, or where the doer of deeds could have done them better. The credit belongs to the man who is actually in the arena, whose face is marred by dust and sweat and blood; who strives valiantly; who errs, who comes short again and again, because there is no effort without error and shortcoming;

but who does actually strive to do the deeds; who knows great enthusiasms, the great devotions; who spends himself in a worthy cause; who at the best knows in the end the triumph of high achievement, and who at the worst, if he fails, at least fails while daring greatly, so that his place shall never be with those cold and timid souls who neither know victory nor defeat.

I searched for business writing courses online but I didn't like most of what I saw. I found the programs too expensive or extremely academic. I feared they would bore me out of my skull. But, as I said, I would not make any financial excuses. I decided to self-study, reading seven books in three months: *On Writing Well* by William Zinsser, *The Glamour of Grammar* by Roy Peter Clark, *Writing Well for Business Success* by Sandra E Lamb, *On Writing* by Stephen King, *The Elements of Style* by William Strunk Jr, *Writing Tools* by Roy Peter Clark, *Bird by Bird* by Anne Lammot, and *HBR Guide to Better Business Writing* by Bryan A. Garner.

I studied these books thoughtfully and scribbled everywhere. I resisted the constant urge to rush into execution mode. These classics taught me the elementary rules of usage, principles of composition, and matters of form; how to write with brevity, clarity and humanity. This self-improvement and daily refinement laid strong foundations for my writing journey.

But no matter how much you practice, you will never truly develop expertise until you step into the arena and do the work. So, after three months of self-study, I shifted gears and put pen to paper. Again, I didn't want to write what everyone else was writing. I decided to focus on simplifying complex and important technology matters to help business executives and boards make smart and informed decisions when embracing innovative technologies.

My first article centred on cloud computing. This was low-hanging fruit because I had just led the risk management stream for a complex, multimillion-dollar cloud transformation program at AMP. The use of the public cloud was a relatively novel concept in the Australian financial services industry at that time. The start of my writing journey was discouraging: the dreaded writers' block haunted me. My drafts were underdone, rambling and desperately weak, but my passion to succeed sustained me through those difficult moments. After weeks of toil, I had at last landed on a three-page final draft titled 'Managing Cloud Risk: Top Considerations for Business Leaders'. I am grateful to my friends whose feedback helped improve the flow and clarity of my article: Innocent Ndoda and Kathleen Lo.

I took a leap of faith and emailed my draft to ISACA (the largest IT governance professional association in the world). This was an ambitious move because I had never published before. But I had nothing to lose — if ISACA rejected my article, I would simply share it on LinkedIn and on blogs.

A few weeks passed before the ISACA editorial team in the US emailed me back. My article had passed the peer review process and would be published in their next international journal. I was thrilled to bits. It's been said that the most meaningful journeys in life are not measured in miles, but in moments. That news transported me back to the magical summer day in 1997 when I collected my O-level results from Rio and ran non-stop across the savannah back to my village.

For years I had read ISACA's long-form articles with admiration. It was a dream result therefore. I was now one of their published authors and my thought leadership piece would be available to approximately half a million professionals to read, including senior executives. I was starting to discover new abilities, previously masked because of inaction. What was the trick? I had found the courage to act in the face of uncertainty. I had chosen a risky path and dumped the old, the safe and the familiar.

The layers of limiting beliefs continued to peel away; I started to believe in bigger things. I began to trust the foundations I had built and the process I had created around them. There was no need to change the equation: all I needed to do was to show up daily and keep exercising my writing muscle.

My career took a sharp, positive turn. ISACA asked me to write blog posts and appear on their podcast. Serendipitously, in November 2016, their Sydney chapter hosted a special conference to commemorate its fortieth anniversary. (The local organisation was founded in 1976 and today serves more than fifteen hundred risk professionals.) I received the inaugural 'Best Ever Governance Professional of the Year' award at a glamorous black-tie event held in Darling Harbour, Sydney. It was immensely humbling to have my work recognised in front of respected delegates. I was an immigrant who arrived in Sydney with three hundred dollars in his pocket and had almost quit Australia for good in December 2011. I was the only African Australian at the event. I couldn't hold back my tears as I remembered with the fondest of memories the many people who had sweated for me over the preceding three and a half decades of my life.

I wanted to share my story and encourage others facing the same obstacles that I had been fortunate enough to overcome: the young barefoot dreamers in the remotest parts of the world, the immigrant struggling to fit in, and so many others living through near-impossible situations. I wanted to be real and tell my story in its most authentic form. Ecstatic, I wrote a post to share on LinkedIn. My post included the following words:

'I got my first pair of shoes when I was twelve and moved out to rent at fourteen. The place was tiny and dingy; no electricity, water, windows, with a makeshift unlockable door. But that's what my father could afford. Most Friday evenings, I would run home, twenty-three kilometres away, and run back Monday mornings. Despite countless setbacks, I never made excuses or felt sorry for myself.'

As I was about to click the post button, doubt crept in. I deleted my post six times before I finally gathered enough courage. I was hesitant to post it because, as we grew up, poverty was shameful. We tried so hard, with zero success, to mask it. In the township, only a tiny fraction of my friends knew of my shabby place. Girls, even those who bathed in rivers, didn't want to be seen with poor boys like me. Everyone, from school to church, respected the rich man. The poor man, as my father put it, had no voice.

Poverty can degrade us, confine us, or often force us to settle for much less than our God-given potential would allow. Growing up, I always had to actively repel the negative stereotypes associated with rural folks: unpolished, ignorant, timid or severely lacking 'standard' etiquettes. Left to fester, these labels can cut deep into our souls, precipitate insidious self-hate, force us to throw away our own identities, lead us to pretend to be who we are not, and cast dark shadows of self-doubt.

Despite my fears, I finally gathered the nerve to follow through with my LinkedIn post. I couldn't have predicted what followed.

My first three LinkedIn posts had generated four likes. Two of those likes were my own. After such a horror start, this post, my fourth, went viral — rapidly generating more than a hundred thousand views, almost six thousand likes, and thousands of messages. The story I had deleted half a dozen times, fearing it would reignite dark memories or repel people from me, had actually endeared me to thousands of people across the world, who responded with insanely positive messages. Here are some of them:

▸ 'What a journey! It brings a lump to my throat when I read this post. God has given each one of us a talent, and it is our duty to explore it. Great post and perseverance for those who have faith and hope. All the best.' — Entrepreneur, Australia

▸ 'The most inspirational article I have ever read on LinkedIn! It should be also read by schoolchildren; it will certainly motivate them to do well. Thanks a lot for sharing your story; your courage and determination are simply wonderful.' — Senior Business Development Manager, United Kingdom

▸ 'My brother, you will undoubtedly inspire generations to come with your story. I hope to write my own. God bless you.' — Program Supervisor, Canada

▸ 'Goodness, what an inspiring read, Phillimon. Congratulations.' — Account Director, Australia

▸ 'You are so inspiring to us all. You have a wonderful gift of writing. Thank you for sharing this story. I will be sharing your story with a few young people I know!!! May God bless you!!' — Medical Technologist, USA

▸ 'This is one of the most inspiring stories I have heard in a very long time. Thank you for sharing.' — Cyber Security Executive, Canada.

This outpouring of warmth and affection made me realise how much my triumph against the odds meant to people all over the world. I exchanged several messages with the CEO of a billion-dollar

European chemical manufacturing firm; he told me that he had sat down with his son and his friends to read my post and share the lessons from it.

'Many people don't know how far they can go if they just believe and keep acting and believing. I am pretty sure it will be very widely spread; I hope it will go viral. It would honour your effort and the depth of your belief in yourself,' he exhorted.

One lady from Ouagadougou, Burkina Faso, promised to buy me shoes, to make up for the twelve years I had spent barefoot. I had no idea the same poverty that made us a laughing stock when growing up would connect me with so many amazing people, the vast majority of whom were strangers. I used to see poverty as something to be ashamed of and there were reasons for that. People blamed the poor themselves for their poverty, thinking something must be wrong with them. They said poor people must be lazy, stupid or simply cursed.

I couldn't hold back my tears again as I scrolled through the thousands of positive messages from people delighted in my turnaround story. My testimony of lived struggles encouraged many people who were going through difficulties, no matter what their race or geography. A story that began in shame had transformed into a tale of resilience, determination and passion. It had inspired those who were on the verge of defeat to fight on, which brought immense meaning to my life. I had also unlocked tremendous strength, through authenticity. I would never again waste time and energy pretending to be anyone other than who I am, the same flawed savannah boy constantly aiming for the stars.

My story also enlightened many about the privileges they had long taken for granted. Most importantly, my account enabled those who grew up in unfortunate situations to throw off pretence, to be authentic and celebrate, rather than hide, their narratives. No one can change how they started out in life, but we all have infinite power to alter how we finish up. I fell deeply in love with my narrative — I was proud, not ashamed, of how I started and how far I had come. I had previously wasted time trying to fit in.

*   *   *

It was September 2016, and I was busy writing a risk report at work in the city, when I got a call from my mother-in-law. She had travelled from Zimbabwe to Australia for the second time to help us out. Fadzi had gone into labour and was on her way to Sutherland Hospital — I quickly jumped into a taxi. Our son was born a few hours later. Fadzi named him Mukundi, Shona for victor. I gave him Christian as his second name. Mukundi, blessed with his mother's natural tan, was one of the most handsome baby boys I had ever seen. His every feature looked proportionate and chiselled. Nyasha, three years old and a bit by then, melted as she held her younger brother in her little arms.

I have seen people lose their focus, slow down or simply get complacent when they succeed. As my writing career took off, I was conscious of this trap. I refused to compare myself with anyone or settle for a low bar; my recognition by the Sydney IT governance community provoked a different response. It inspired in me a new level of self-belief and curiosity, *How much further could I go if I pushed myself a bit more?*

I moved forward and started writing another thought leadership piece. I decided to write on the double-edged-sword nature of artificial intelligence, a fast-emerging consequential technology at that time. Backed up by rigorous case studies and research, I titled the four-page article 'The Automation Conundrum'. After several iterations, including peer review, I emailed it to the ISACA editorial team who agreed to publish it, in the next issue of their international journal.

I was blown away when, in May 2017, I opened an email from the ISACA CEO to inform me that my piece had been voted article of the year by the global ISACA awards committee. Established in 1971, the Michael Cangemi Best Book/Article Award is among ISACA's highest honours. It recognises individuals for major contributions to publications in the field of information systems audit, control and/or security. To win the Sydney award was one thing. But *this* was surreal — to win an award at a global level, against hundreds of articles and books.

A week before flying out to Chicago for the ISACA awards, and still basking in the glory, I turned thirty-six years old. I booked myself into a golf competition at Beverley Park Golf Club, a public course ten minutes' drive from my place in Hurstville. I was doubly excited: it was my birthday and the following week, I would be travelling to the US to receive my ISACA award. Life couldn't feel much better.

I played in a four-ball with three friendly retired Aussie gentlemen. They were all fascinated by my story. I was in a good mood as reflected by my scorecard. I bombed my tee shots down the fairway, hit amazing recovery shots and drained long putts. But as we stepped onto the 14th tee, something just snapped. I saw a missed call from work and excused myself to return the call. I was quickly informed that, as a result of a company-wide restructure, my role as a cybersecurity consultant had been made redundant.

Those words reignited memories of my last savannah bout, when Nduna had shattered my jaw. Moments before, I had felt like a master of the universe; all of a sudden, I did not. My mojo tanked: my brain went foggy and my golf swing deserted me. Worse yet, I could sense the three old fellas questioning my story. *This could only be a fib; how could someone win a global award and suddenly their services were no longer required, in an environment where there was a severe shortage in cybersecurity skills?*

I have learned that each of us will most certainly face trying moments. It's not a matter of if, but when. Things happen to people all the time. This had just happened to me; I just had to find ways to navigate through it. But how we respond matters profoundly. Some feel besieged or crushed by the situation; some find themselves in perpetual denial. And some are able to redirect that fury towards transformation and growth. Behind every perceived failure often lies a major breakthrough.

In Shona we have a proverb that goes, *akava datya ariyambutsa*. It means whoever kicks a frog, inadvertently helps it overcome barriers and leap to the other side. This temporary setback was God's way to push me out of my comfort zone towards my next challenge. During the next week, I landed two interviews with reputable Australian organisations and secured both roles. I accepted an offer as head of IT risk and cyber security for a reputable wealth management firm. This role was two levels higher than the position I had been pushed out of the previous week. My decision to deliberately pursue skills that differentiated me had accelerated my path to a leadership role much faster than anticipated.

In June 2017, Fadzi and I flew to the US for the first time. We landed at Tom Bradley International Terminal in Los Angeles and caught a connecting flight to O'Hare International Airport in Chicago. A sharply dressed white gentleman escorted us to a sparkling black Mercedes and whisked us downtown to The Langham, an exquisite five-star hotel with superb views of the Chicago River and Lake Michigan.

The next day we jumped onto a cruise boat. We sat outside, basking in the glorious Chicago summer sun, with a gentle breeze to keep us cool. It was an excellent vantage point from which to view the stunning

Chicago skyline, one of the world's best. I was really impressed by Chicago's sights: the neo-Gothic Tribune Tower, the second tallest building in the Western Hemisphere; the Willis Tower, 110 stories tall; and the Wrigley Building, the glowing white beacon considered a symbol of Chicago's supremacy in architecture and commerce. After disembarking from the cruise, I strolled along the Magnificent Mile, a portion of Michigan Avenue that stretches between Lake Shore Drive and the Chicago River. Everything about this ritzy shopping district — upmarket restaurants, five-star hotels and high-end designer shops — displayed American affluence. My walk was the starkest contrast to the decades I had strolled barefoot across the savannah grasslands, and the impoverished streets of Dzivarasekwa in Harare.

Going all that way and not eating the famed Chicago-style deep-dish pizza, would not only have been foolish, but irresponsible; this has been a staple of 'Windy City' culture since the 1940s. It would be the equivalent of travelling to the savannah and not eating a well-simmered portion of sadza with your bare hands.

The order took forever but my mouth went watery when the waiter eventually served us. Seven centimetres deep, and piping hot, the pizza looked like a giant pie. It was stuffed with layers of meat and vegetables and mozzarella cheese like nothing I had ever seen; it epitomised Chicago for me. It's supposed to be eaten with a knife and fork, but after a bit of struggle, my savannah instincts kicked in and I gripped it with my hands.

On the eve of the awards ceremony, the ISACA International Board of Directors and executive team hosted us for a dinner at Smith & Wollensky, an American steakhouse overlooking the river; other ISACA dignitaries and award recipients attended the private event. It was one of my most humbling experiences, to rub shoulders and share the same table with highly regarded global technology risk leaders.

There were executives who had held high-ranking positions at *The Wall Street Journal*, Oracle Corporation, Bloomberg L.P., and the United States Congress. That night left an unforgettable mark on my memory.

The master of ceremony requested each award recipient to share a few words. I was the last one to speak. I stuck with my narrative, telling the delegates how twenty-three years prior to that historic day I was a barefoot boy steering Baba's cattle across the savannah grasslands. I stressed how I hated this tedious chore, but couldn't avoid it because I was the youngest boy. I recalled how Baba, a barely educated but deeply wise man, had constantly reminded me how education was my only way to eventually break the bonds of poverty that had held my family down for centuries.

His words were nothing short of prophetic: after a long and winding journey from the savannah, I had finally walked the Magnificent Mile and received one of ISACA's highest awards, for exemplary contributions to the field of technology risk and security publication. I was thrilled to be a recipient of one of seven global awards, representing my adopted country of Australia and my home country of Zimbabwe.

I was touched immeasurably when the entire room of executives and their spouses rose to their feet and clapped and clapped. Everything felt like a magic show. I could not believe how my story of pain, patience and perseverance had endeared me to these global executives. I resumed my seat, and as I refocussed, the ISACA global head of communications approached the table and whispered to me:

'Inspiring journey, my friend; I have already instructed my team to reach out to you after this. We would like to feature your story on our global website.'

The next morning I dressed in my sharp-blue classic M.J. Bale Australian-merino-wool suit, and showed up for the awards ceremony, hosted in one of the Langham's function rooms. The event was grace-ful, smooth and swift, a display of the highest level of professionalism. I received my award from the ISACA CEO and chairman of the board, posed for official photos and flew out of Chicago that afternoon. I will never forget the Windy City.

On the flight home, over the sky-blue Pacific Ocean, I broke down in tears and worshipped. It dawned heavily on me how far God's grace had taken me — along with the generosity of others and my self-worth, my continual rejection of the negative stereotypes attached to savannah kids.

CHAPTER 17

Overcoming Imposter Syndrome

In 2017, as my writing was started to gain industry traction, I was invited to speak at a major cybersecurity conference in Sydney. In fact, the organisers had invited my boss to speak, but he put my name forward, citing other priorities. The organisers rejected the counter-proposal stating unequivocally they preferred heads of departments because their conference attracted hundreds of senior executives from large financial services organisations. I was employed at that time as a cyber security consultant at AMP. But when my manager emailed my credentials — industry awards and pieces of thought leadership I had published — the organisers soon agreed to make an exception.

I felt uneasy about presenting to a large audience of highly accomplished business and technology professionals. To be honest, it terrified me more than my childhood fear of *Tokoloshes* (goblins). I imagined a host of misfortunes. What if my brain froze and I lost my entire train of thought in sheer panic? What if I said the wrong thing and embarrassed my employer who had vouched for my competence? What if delegates just started walking out one by one during my presentation? What if I woke up to an embarrassing news headline, 'An African man pees in his pants during a major cybersecurity conference'?

The initial rejection by conference organisers also activated my nasty 'imposter syndrome'. *Am I technical enough? Do I have any executive presence? Is this all smoke and mirrors?* Several negative thoughts raced through my mind. Compounding my fears, I wasn't aware at that time of anyone else who looked like me presenting at large Australian technology conferences. I was usually the only African-looking delegate at these events so featuring as a speaker for the first time was way outside my comfort zone. It's impossible to become what you don't believe, and it's very difficult to believe what you can't see.

But fear was not necessarily a bad thing, as long as it didn't block me from taking that important first step. Every audacious goal I have achieved terrified me at the start. I know that, while I might not have the required skills in the beginning, as long as I attack that goal with undivided focus and a positive mindset, I will eventually become that person.

I knew that if I declined the opportunity to present at the conference, I would regret it for a long time. It was better to embarrass myself while trying than poison myself with the pain of regret. Acknowledging that no matter how much I prepared I could still stumble, took tremendous pressure off myself.

To differentiate myself, in a crowded and increasingly competitive field, I had to master the art of storytelling. I had worked extremely hard to gain industry recognition; succumbing to this fear of public speaking was a sure way to undermine all of that. Accepting the invitation, in spite of my fear, marked a point of no return: there was no way to back out without damaging my employer's reputation. I quickly redirected my energies towards preparation. I read widely about the subject. I scoured through dozens of case studies and white papers from reputable organisations like McKinsey, Bain Consulting and Microsoft. I blogged about the subject on LinkedIn and refined my thought process using the feedback from other experts. The process of researching, writing and active collaboration also boosted my self-confidence.

I explored as many tools as possible to turn my fear of public speaking around. I immersed myself in TED Talks and watched several YouTube keynote presentations. I read books such as *Ted Talks: The Official TED Guide to Public Speaking* by Chris Anderson and *The Art of Public Speaking* by Dale Carnegie. These books carried a consistent message — almost everyone has experienced the fear of public speaking. My anxieties were commonplace, not exceptional.

As my belief grew, I explored additional techniques. I created my slides, barricaded myself in my room and recorded myself over and over again. I deleted the recordings until I was happy with the end product. I listened to my audio files on the train to work, on the treadmill and during other breaks. I repeated this process religiously over several weeks.

I registered for meet-ups and other conferences to observe speakers from the audience. I noted what worked and adjusted my slides accordingly. These sessions were also a big revelation for me — I recognised that most speakers were mediocre. They inflicted the proverbial 'death by PowerPoint' and were often badly prepared. Some couldn't respond to simple questions from enthusiastic delegates, hiding behind the tactic, 'I will take your details and come back to you.'

Other speakers delivered mind-numbing presentations, full of technical jargon that was beyond the comprehension of the average business professional. Others went through text-heavy slides, tediously going through dull and old compliance standards. Some delegates, bored stiff, dozed off in their seats.

My confidence continued to grow. I realised there was a huge gap in the market, and with undivided focus and perseverance, I could compete against and do better than this ordinary level of performance.

Fast forward, three weeks after the conference I was thrilled to learn that my sessions were the highest rated. My think tank sessions had received a rating of 4.3 out of 5.0, against an average speaker rating of 3.7 out of 5.0.

Right then, I could hardly remember why this had seemed so scary. It was an important mental breakthrough. The email liberated me from the fear that had paralysed me for years. From that moment, I would never look at public speaking the same way. Getting past that obstacle opened a door and my imagination ran wild. It induced higher levels of passion, self-belief and expectation.

This was the start of a new journey. I have since presented to thousands of professionals globally and been the keynote speaker at several high-profile conferences attended by business executives. I have declined dozens more invitations either because they didn't align with my mission or because I was time-poor. Among the most memorable are the two events I keynoted in Melbourne and Sydney alongside Mr Don Codling, the former head of FBI Cyber Crime, and one of the most respected global cybersecurity voices. Iconic technology firms now pay me to speak at global events. I have also given interviews with journalists from several media outlets, such as the *New Zealand*

Herald Business, iT Wire and *CSO Online* magazines, on strategic topics such as the rise of malicious artificial intelligence, cyber resilience and board engagement.

My life has consistently taught me that stepping out of the place I have felt comfortable always reveals abilities I never knew I had.

*   *   *

The same year, I determined to pursue another ambitious goal — to write a book that would strip away the complexity and ambiguity of the cybersecurity subject and communicate practical guidance to business professionals. Again, I would pour my body and soul into this endeavour.

The hardest part, as always, was to start and persist through the initial mental hurdles. As one writer said, 'The hard part, as in swimming, is to take the plunge. The water looks so cold. Can it be warmed up? I think it can.'

I knew from the outset that writing a book would be a protracted grind, but as I have learnt over decades, if you start any mission with a clear sense of the risks and the rewards that lie ahead, you are more likely to succeed. Producing something deep that stands apart from normal life demands persistence, patience and undivided focus. I went through several discouraging moments, but my why was too strong to give up. I knew that the hard work would eventually pay off.

I read several more books on business writing and scoured hundreds of references. For almost two years, I read every issue of the *Harvard Business Review,* and articles from other publications whose style I admired, such as *The New York Times, The New Yorker* and *The Economist.* The more I read and wrote, the more my confidence grew; I experienced prolonged periods of inspiration when ideas and words oozed effortlessly.

I finally fell in love with writing. At first, writing had felt mundane and forced, but not anymore. I read and wrote daily. I no longer had time to entertain escapism — to become a good writer, I had to embrace the arduous parts of the craft. There was no way to game the system and will my goals into existence. The more I refined my writing skills, the more I started to enjoy the process.

'For me not to write,' in the words of Ray Bradbury in *Zen in the Art of Writing*, 'was to die.'

I wrote on my smartphone on my way to work. Ideas started racing through my mind. What previously felt forced had turned into a creative art.

It didn't matter if I wrote one thousand or one hundred words. Writing, just like reading, had become a non-negotiable habit that had to be practised daily. There was no excuse, no higher professional priority. Some of my colleagues started providing unsolicited advice. They encouraged me to wait until I was a 'recognised expert' in the field before writing a book. Some said I was better off writing a book on fiction first as technical books were subject to intense scrutiny and ruthless reviews by 'real' experts. They seemed to have every reason why I would fail. I refused to let any of this stuff enter my mind or allow a negative person to moderate my ambition. If I wasn't worried myself, why were they? I had already lost my need for external approval. I had written a number of articles and blogs, but never a book before. I recalled Mahatma Gandi's words:

'If I have the belief that I can do it, I shall surely acquire the capacity to do it even if I may not have it at the beginning.'

After eighteen months of writing every day, I published *The Five Anchors of Cyber Resilience* in July 2018.

It was standing room only at my book launch. More than 160 professionals, including my editor Bernadette Foley and her team, my best friends, senior business and technology executives from some of Sydney's largest enterprises, showed up at the Hilton Hotel in Sydney's CBD to celebrate. My wife, Fadzi, had constantly tolerated my wild ambitions; she and my daughter, Nyasha, were also in attendance. I shared my story with everyone there, chronicling how a shortage of books in the savannah had sparked a life-long quest for self-improvement, and how those adversities continued to inspire me to maximise the boundless opportunities that I now have. I was humbled to see dozens of fellow African Australians — representing my home country of Zimbabwe, as well as Uganda, Kenya, South Africa and Nigeria.

Within a week, *The Five Anchors of Cyber Resilience* rose to become an Amazon Best Seller and remained there for several months. At one time, my book hit the top ten across all book categories in Australia. Okta, one of the largest cybersecurity firms in the world, bought a hundred copies and supplied them to delegates during one of their largest events in Sydney. My book also got the attention of journalists.

iT Wire, Australia's most-read independent technology news source, wrote:

> It [*The Five Anchors*] is strongly recommended as mandatory reading for any senior corporate manager or board member to assist in an understanding of the broader issues and also to frame the questions to be asked (of the experts within the organisation) and the problems that need to be addressed. It will also give management a framework for optimizing the use of their resources. *Five Anchors* should also be mandatory reading for CISOs [chief information security officers] to better prepare them for potentially difficult discussions that will be instigated by board members who have taken the time to read and digest this book!

Australian Cyber Security Magazine agreed:

> The book is superbly written and crafted, thereby sufficiently enticing and insightful, written with enterprise executive and board front of mind. With publications like these, there really is no excuse for a company director not to be cyber-informed and cyber aware.

The Five Anchors went on to dominate Google's search results for 'cyber resilience book' and remains on Google's first page to this day in 2021, signifying a major achievement for my book.

The Five Anchors of Cyber Resilience was also featured as recommended reading in the first issue of *InfoSecurity Professional,* the global magazine published by (ISC)². (ISC)² is one of the world's largest IT security organisations and certifiers. The magazine stated:

> Author Phillimon Zongo, an award-winning cybersecurity expert, focuses on the need for resilience and offers advice on how organizations can recover from a breach. Zongo looks at security as a strategy, not a tool or technique, and zeroes in on five key elements.

In September 2021, beyond my wildest expectations, *The Five Anchors of Cyber Resilience* made it to the Top Five Best Cyber Books at the UK National Cyber Awards. The prestigious event, which featured top brands like Hewlett Packard (HP), Barclays Bank, Citibank and HSBC Bank, among other finalists, was sponsored by the UK National Police Chiefs Council and the Chartered Institute of Information Security.

While I would have loved to win, I was extremely proud to have my work recognised on such a global stage. Gordon Corera, Security

Correspondent at BBC News, won the Best Book Award for his book: *Intercept: The Secret History of Computers and Spies*. I felt immensely proud to see large portraits of my book beamed at the International Cyber Book Fair, held at the Novotel London West after the awards ceremony.

*   *   *

There are five key things I have learned from my larger journey.

One. You will never know how far you could have gone unless you act. As Chris Anderson, curator of TED, wrote, 'Ideas that could solve our toughest problems remain invisible because the brilliant people in whose minds they reside lack the confidence to, or the know-how to, share those ideas effectively.'

Two. We can all rise above predefined narratives, so long as we believe and act, and not obsess about short-term rewards. It doesn't matter where we come from; we can all rewrite our stories. To do so, we need to muster the discipline of finishing whatever we begin.

Three. Achieving one's goals has little to do with innate abilities or fate — it is a product of resolve, passion and undivided focus. We are only restricted by our own limited belief systems.

Four. All of us will certainly go through adversity. Whether we surrender or prevail, however, comes down to perception. Do we perceive events as hurtful or as key opportunities to learn and grow? For me, undesirable moments such as those in my upbringing, have become what some call 'the blessing of hardship'. They instilled in me an intense distaste for the status quo. It's in the nature of storms to rage; it's how we respond that matters. Harnessed correctly, setbacks can propel us forward with force, but if we are not careful, they will force us back.

Five. It's tempting to directly pursue financial gain, but lasting change comes when we are driven by the mastery of a skill or a sense of a higher calling.

My achievements caught the attention of Zimbabweans everywhere; I received congratulations from all parts of the world. The Zim Awards committee wrote in November 2018 to advise that they intended to honour my exemplary work with the 2018 Zim-Australian Outstanding Achievement Award. This is an accolade that represents exceptional excellence and achievement that far exceeds the norm. Later that month, I rose to the podium and humbly accepted this award at a lavish ceremony hosted by the committee at the Marriott Hotel in Melbourne.

As part of my two-minute acceptance speech, I chronicled for delegates how I had arrived in the great country of Australia with only three hundred dollars in my pocket. I was filled with hope and enthusiasm; I was going straight into one of the largest global consulting firms. But for nine years, I was confined within the corridors of mediocrity. I explained how ceasing to cast blame, on people and circumstances, and taking extreme ownership of my goals had radically transformed my career path. I invoked Theodore Roosevelt's enduring speech, 'The Man in the Arena' — and expressed my deepest pride in every Zimbabwean Australian hustling through obstacles to positively contribute to the place we now call home.

Once again, I shared that little speech on social media, and had no idea it would inspire so many people all over the word, regardless of their race or creed. The hundreds of touching messages gave deep meaning to my work and illuminated the grace of God. I include a few to share here.

▶ 'I was blessed to hear this speech and witness this moment. And yes I was with my 13-year-old daughter. It was priceless for her to be there on this amazing evening.'

▸ 'Well done, I too hope to be a fraction of where you are in the coming years.'

▸ 'Your posts, Phillimon Zongo, are a source of inspiration for Africans who struggle with dust and mediocrity, thank you for your share and god bless you.'

▸ 'I follow your progress religiously, homeboy, because you are beyond inspirational. It's people like you who give us Zimbabweans and black people hope that given the platform we can always excel and compete with the best.'

▸ 'Phil. What an inspiration. Humble and down to earth and committed to excellence. You are a great model of a fine citizen of Zimbabwe. I'm proud to be one of your many friends. Stay blessed, my brother.'

The cake has been iced, and iced again, more recently. In 2018, I was honoured to receive an Outstanding Performance recognition at the Celebrate African Australians (New South Wales) awards in Sydney. And in 2019, I was awarded the Outstanding Achievement in Business Award by Appreciate Africa Asia. The awards ceremony was in Beijing, and although I couldn't travel to China due to business commitments, I was thankful to have my work — helping businesses, large and small, accelerate their cyber resilience postures — recognised once again on a global stage.

CHAPTER 18

Looking Ahead

'The most powerful leadership tool you have is your own example.' —
John Wooden

None of these personal achievements would mean anything if I
didn't go down the ladder and lift others, those going through the
same struggles I was fortunate enough to overcome. The only difference between kids enrolling at Harvard University and those perpetually stuck in the savannah grasslands is opportunity, not lack of

ambition or cognitive powers. I am here today because someone took a chance on my potential. I held on to that chance like a dog holds on to a bone. I am mindful of the thousands of gifted and ambitious kids from my community still trapped in these centuries-old hardships, without access to education, for example. I refuse to sit back and hope that strangers from afar will eventually emerge to give these talented savannah kids some hope.

Two and a half decades ago, I determined never to wait and hope that my challenges would vanish miraculously. My decision was well informed: the situation in my home country has further deteriorated. In 2019, 60 per cent of children in primary school were sent home for failure to pay fees, according to the Zimbabwe Vulnerability Assessment Committee.[11] Without access to education, the hope of escaping poverty in the savannah is almost zero.

I decided to lead with action. In 2011, with the help of Fadzi, I founded a not-for-profit organisation called Education for Rural Africa to raise money for school fees and to assist capable but disadvantaged kids at Rio. We aimed to follow in the footsteps of Kristin Diehl, the kind-hearted German woman whose scholarship transformed my own life. For decades, Kristin gave her heart and soul to our community, giving hundreds of savannah kids opportunities to pursue their dreams; building and equipping classrooms. She helped us rise from the dust and compete on the global stage.

Close friends graced our first fundraising dinner, which we hosted at a steakhouse in Darling Harbour. We raised enough money that night to pay the school fees at Rio for a dozen kids for the entire year. I shared snippets of my journey with a benevolent Australian couple whom I met at church. The plight of savannah children immediately touched them; the couple graciously doubled our efforts, helping us pay fees for twenty-three more kids.

Fadzi and I flew to Zimbabwe in December 2012 to meet Kristin and her Dutch friend, Helga. They were in the country to commission one of Kristin's last projects — a new arts centre to give equal opportunity to creative savannah kids. Those who lack academic smarts are often put to waste because of limited facilities for the arts and a general disregard of anything unacademic. I was over the moon to meet my ultimate heroine, the selfless woman who had made unimaginable sacrifices for hundreds of savannah kids over almost three decades.

Together with Hugh Mbayiwa — a famous artist and Rio alumni, who helps coordinate our charity work on the ground — we met with Kristin and Helga at an upscale restaurant in Harare. The location of that restaurant — along Enterprise Road in Highlands, a couple of kilometres away from 1 Kenilworth Road, where I started my IT audit career with Deloitte — was quite sentimental. My feelings meeting Kristin again are something I will never be able to entirely explain and do justice. We sat there for hours, as I chronicled my journey since leaving Rio two decades prior. Kristin inquired about my family and our lives in Australia, as well as my ambitions.

'I cannot express eloquently enough how proud I am of you, Phillimon. Zimbabweans have always impressed me with how they always look back to help their extended families. But I am more pleased by your attitude, because you have decided to help kids who are not related to you in any form or shape,' Kristin remarked.

Several years later, I learnt with sorrow and disbelief that a mysterious fire in the middle of the night had ravaged the arts centre at Rio. Everything was destroyed. The cause of the catastrophic fire was never ascertained; some suspected an electrical fault, while some pointed to possible arson. I had no means to rebuild the arts centre but was ready to do what I could to help recreate Kristin's vision. I hosted a charity golf event with Kudzi Tagwireyi, a friend I had met at

PwC, and we raised the funds to buy cement used for the foundations of the new structure.

We have been involved in several other initiatives at Rio, raising funds to help repair dilapidated infrastructure, and buy textbooks and other equipment. My heart remains deeply rooted in this cause and I plan to scale up this charity work as my business grows.

*   *   *

In 2019, I flew back to Zimbabwe and revisited Rio again. I met with the headmaster, teachers and parent representatives and explored various ways we can help the school with its formidable challenges. I visited the arts centre construction site, which we were helping rebuild. After formalities, the headmaster assembled the students in the cool shade of the msasa trees. I carefully climbed onto a wobbly brown wooden chair and addressed hundreds of teenagers. I spoke from my heart — telling them that if I could run from Rwizi to Rio, live alongside hookers, and rise past obstacles to eventually win global awards and run a successful business in Australia — they could too. To do so, however, each of them needed to be extremely intentional about their goals and be willing to make responsible choices. Life is straightforward: it is a series of choices and consequences.

My speech generated a lot of attention, stirred deep emotion and ignited hope among the hundreds of teenagers. For the five minutes, no one moved an inch, coughed or sneezed; all you could hear was my voice and a cooing grey dove in one of the giant trees. The teenagers stared at me like villagers transfixed by a solar eclipse. My words resonated so strongly with them because my story was similar to theirs. I wasn't a politician detached from reality, who had travelled from Harare in a 4WD Toyota Landcruiser to donate some cheap foodstuff with journalists in tow. As I climbed down from my makeshift stand, the youngsters clapped enthusiastically at my speech.

We were getting ready to leave when one of the teachers threw his arms around me and shouted, 'Do you remember me, Mr Zongo?' A bit embarrassed, I slowly shook my head and smiled.

'I am Tinevimbo Zaranyika, one of the kids you paid fees for many years ago. I am now a third-year teaching student at Harare Polytechnic, and am back here doing my teaching attachment.'

Tinevimbo's story ignited Nelson Mandela's words: 'Education is the most powerful weapon you can use to change the world.' I was deeply aware that more remained to be done. At that time, more than sixty children were dropping out of Rio every year. And taking into consideration that Rio kids were some of the relatively more 'well-to-do', the situation in village schools across the savannah was even bleaker. Tinevimbo's heartfelt gratitude encouraged me to fight on. It proved the transformative power of our efforts.

A year later, in 2020, I logged on to my Facebook Messenger. Buried in dozens of unread messages sat this, from Tariro, one of the savannah kids we sponsored with Tinevimbo Zaranyika:

Dear Mr Zongo,

My name is Tariro; I was one of the beneficiaries of your bursary scheme at Rio Tinto High. I just want to say thank you sooooo (sic) much for making my dream come true. I managed to finish my high school and recently graduated with a Bachelor of Law degree at the University of Zimbabwe. May you continue with these acts of kindness, and may the Dear Lord richly bless you. Thank you so much.

I quickly sent Tariro a Facebook connection request, and the next day, we exchanged WhatsApp contacts. Tariro's name means 'hope'. When I called her, I was dumbstruck. Upon passing her O-level exams at Rio, she proceeded to do her A-level studies in Mutare, a city in the mountains on the border with Mozambique. She smashed her A levels, scoring straight distinctions, or fifteen points, the best possible score one can get in Zimbabwe from three A-level subjects. The University of Zimbabwe accepted Tariro's application to study law.

A few months before our emotional call, Tariro had graduated and enrolled in her articles of clerkship with the leading legal firms in Harare. I was impressed by Tariro's rare combination of extreme gratitude, unwavering determination, and above all, her long-term ambition to return to the savannah and rescue other girls stuck in near-impossible situations.

When I think of the things I am most proud of, Tariro's story is up there. Tariro's success is undoubtedly a result of many factors. Chief among these are the selfless support and mentorship she received from her wonderful parents, and her courage to dismantle the negative stereotypes and misunderstandings about village girls. I am, however, proud to have played a small part in Tariro's journey.

From Rio school, I travelled to Gweru where I had been invited to deliver MSU's first-ever information systems public lecture. As I drove through the old suburb of Senga, I remembered how sixteen years before, together with four hundred other pioneers, I had arrived at MSU with my old blanket and a few items of clothing. But *that* sweat had now turned into sweet. I was back at my alma mater with multiple accomplishments behind me: international awards, a best-selling book, and my own consulting business in Australia.

The university welcomed me like a prince. I met with the dean of Commerce, who was also one of the founding lecturers at MSU. We shared so many beautiful memories. I then met Dr D. Z. Moyo, acting vice chancellor, a distinguished scientist and another founding lecturer. She thanked me for raising the MSU flag high on a global stage. I also listened with great fascination and delight as she chronicled how she had shattered glass ceilings to become MSU's first-ever female pro-vice-chancellor. I was delighted to learn MSU had pushed boundaries. In just nineteen years since its establishment, it has become the largest university in Zimbabwe, boasting more than twenty-one thousand students across four locations.

As planned, we proceeded to the great hall, where I shared my story of grace, grit and gratitude; telling my audience that through drive, persistence and responsible choices, they too can become anything they can visualise. My nieces Mercy and Cheryl, my nephew Takudzwa, my sister Maidei, all sat in the front row. My pastor Crispen Mugari and his benevolent wife, Sylvia, who had given me the money to buy a train ticket so I could attend my job interview at Telefonica, also sat beside my relatives. The crowd was every bit as enthusiastic and inspired as the Rio teenagers two days before.

From Gweru I drove straight to the savannah to celebrate my mother's birthday and my homecoming. I stopped in Mubayira for a couple of hours to pick up groceries. I learnt with sadness that the store owner, Sekuru Samanyemba, had long since passed on, and Gogo Samanyemba had retreated back to her father's village. Lizzy had migrated to Gokwe, a township far away, where she died. I could not establish the fate of Masibanda and Sekuru Gava.

My family, local teachers, fellow villagers and strangers gathered in the late afternoon to welcome me. When the word spread that 'Phillimon of Australia' was back, villagers flocked from all corners of the savannah, knowing there would be plenty of free chicken and booze.

Baba told the story of how he had sold his cattle, goats, and Juri, his famous dog, to afford his kids access to better education. In contrast, most of his savannah friends were short-sighted, dropping their kids from school so they could till the cornfields. He spoke with deep regret about how he had let me live in that distressed boysky alongside prostitutes.

'But I am so glad today that Phillimon, my bigger brother, was invited to a very big and faraway country called America because he came out number one, as he did at Gavaza and Rio. He takes after me, because I have always had a powerful *medulla oblangatta*.'

The old man concluded his long and rambling speech. My mother frowned — she has always claimed we inherited our smarts from her, not him!

Baba's speech moved me — he had undoubtedly been the most influential figure in my life. His matchless patience, foresight and appreciation of education (despite being barely educated himself) left an indelible mark on my life.

It was beautiful not only to celebrate my success but also to acknowledge several of my siblings who, even though their journeys were different to mine, had exploited the tiniest opportunities to rewrite their savannah narratives. Society had labelled my brother Lancelot as dim and that became a self-fulfilling prophecy. Lancelot came last in his class and repeated the same grades multiple times. But he remained brave to the end, and eventually shook off that label. Lancelot finally passed five O levels after three sittings and returned to teach in the same class he had come last in as a student. I sponsored him to attend an agricultural college in Mutare, and through hard work and determination, he graduated second in his entire class.

My young sister Letwin also proved unconquerable. She dropped out of primary school for a couple of years due to ill health but came back stronger. She pushed through lifelong health issues to graduate with a nursing diploma and now works in the same surgeries that saved her life. My little sister Salome, on the other hand, survived the harshest savannah conditions, herding cattle alongside boys to pass her O levels after several sittings. She eventually joined MSU via a mature student program, and became the second-ever university graduate in our family, finishing with an upper-second-class bachelor's degree in agriculture.

The story would be incomplete without talking about my older sister Rosemary, who, on paper, is my twin. When she graduated from the village secondary school, she struggled to secure any meaningful jobs. But Rosemary never made excuses; she trained and graduated as a prison guard. She kept an eye on some of the most hardened criminals at Chikurubi Maximum Prison, armed with an AK-47. That's a tough job for a woman in Zimbabwe by any measure. She hustled through a myriad of challenges, raising four kids and studying dental nursing in her free time. After more than a decade, she was able to rescue herself from that exacting job at the prison. She now plies her trade as a freelance dental nurse in several high-end Harare surgeries.

My sister Maidei, with whom I stayed after my stint at Samanyemba's, can never be forgotten. She took on multiple jobs when her husband passed away ten years ago to afford her two boys — the well-mannered, Takudzwa and Tadiwa — access to quality education. The same applies to my brother Osward and my sister Cecilia, who have survived remarkable hardships to earn dignified lives and fend for their kids. Sadly, my beloved sister Viola was not there but I was glad to see her two, Cheryl and Anotidaishe, had grown into accomplished kids. (The following year, it would feel immensely fulfilling for me to sponsor Cheryl's university education.)

Lancelot was distributing free beers from my silver Toyota Corolla rental. As the festivities climaxed, he handed a 'Super', a two-litre sorghum beer, to my father. Baba was busy inhaling his *bute* and had my *Five Anchors* book (which he could barely read) balanced in his lap. He lashed out at my brother and dispatched the Super to some thirsty villagers sitting nearby.

'Fokufu! I sent my children to school; I don't drink *masese* anymore! Bring me Lion or Castle lager!' The old man cracked up the entire gathering.

I learnt from villagers that Malume, the instigator of my last and most inflicting savannah bout, whose leg had been amputated at a young age, had gone on to become a school teacher in spite of his physical handicap. His brother Nduna, the boy who shattered my jaw during the fight, had also defied the odds and was now a police officer. I didn't get to meet them during my homecoming but their stories inspired me nonetheless.

* * *

During my time with PwC, I had the privilege of meeting Maria Simpsons, an adventurous white American expatriate. Maria was actively involved with Aid for Africa Down Under (AFADU), an Australian not-for-profit organisation that runs an orphanage in Chikombedzi, communal lands situated approximately five hundred kilometres south of Harare. AFADU's orphanage, Lihranzo, supports about fifty orphan children at a time, giving them access to education, medical care, food, and shelter.

AFADU's work reignited my narrative. Fadzi and I immediately joined AFADU's sponsorship program and have supported these self-less volunteers for almost a decade. In 2018, I was thrilled to learn that one of the kids we sponsored, Fibion Sibanda, had graduated from university with a bachelor's degree in education. He had just assumed a role as a local high school teacher, giving him an excellent opportunity to mentor more kids whose lives have been transformed by AFADU's work.

One of the best parts of my journey has been helping people of all races dream beyond their self-imposed mental limitations, to see what's possible. In 2017, I met a Zimbabwean man at a social gathering in Sydney. I enquired about his family, dreams and aspirations. He spoke of his twenty-year-old son, who was studying finance at a leading Australian university. 'That's quite impressive,' I responded. Angrily, the man quickly shot back:

'My son is a stubborn fool. We have told him to dump that course and study something else. These courses are for Australians; no bank will ever hire him. He will learn the hard way.'

This profoundly ignorant pronouncement felt like a stab wound deep in my chest. Nothing could be further from the truth! I was already working as head of cyber security for a leading wealth management firm. Several of my close friends were chief financial officers for large corporations.

'As a man thinketh … so is he.' We are the physical manifestation of our thought patterns. To box our ambitions based on how we look, and pass on such a toxic mentality to the next generation, would be our most profound tragedy. My biggest challenge when I embarked on my journey was the lack of social signalling — the limited number of people who looked like me who were doing things I aspired to do. I had read inspirational books about American corporate heavyweights, but I found their stories unrelatable; their backgrounds and struggles were starkly different from mine.

The Zimbabwean man, who was doing his best to attach to his son some gravely misplaced stereotypes, had just provided a compelling 'why' answer for my mentoring journey. Over the last few years, I have actively mentored dozens of professionals from different walks of life.

I have had the privilege of helping hundreds of global professionals revitalise their careers, write books, present at conferences, and break into cybersecurity. One young African-Australian professional wrote to me, 'Your work is very inspiring! I started looking into cybersecurity after my friend told me about your work.' I am grateful to God to have used my once-ordinary story to help others push beyond their perceived limits. I shed tears when I read one of the notes I received, from my good friend Mavis Thole in 2018, who wrote:

'Dear sir, I just read about your work and accomplishments, and I had to write to you. Your story not only touched me and inspired me because you are a fellow Zimbabwean, but I saw myself in your experiences. This day I make a promise to myself and God as I took the courage to write to you, that I will strive to make the best of my potential and the opportunity that has been granted me in Germany. Keep up the good work. You are you touching lives.'

Mavis meant everything she wrote. We connected, and I shared my experiences via Zoom. Like me, some Westerner had also taken a bet on Mavis at an early age, sponsoring her education. She eventually escaped so many trials in her home city of Bulawayo and landed in Germany. Following our conversation, and of course her determination, Mavis managed to pivot her career towards her passion, and wrote to tell me she had been promoted. My experiences mentoring others bring recall the words of Saint Francis of Assisi: 'Happiness is found in helping others. For it is in giving that we receive.' My experiences mentoring others bring recall the words of Saint Francis of Assisi: 'Happiness is found in helping others. For it is in giving that we receive.'

I had no idea that my story, which started with so much suffering, would connect me with so many amazing people — my own narrative pales in comparison with some of those. I had the honour to meet one of those fantastic human beings, Francis Deng, during my trip to Melbourne in 2019. As we sipped our cappuccinos beside the majestic Yarra River, Francis's story blew my mind. He is one of the so-called 'Lost Boys of Sudan', innocent kids uprooted from their families through the brutality of war and forced to fight as child soldiers.

Francis radiated extreme humility, clarity of purpose and an in-depth perspective about life. Now that he lives in an environment that gives him a fair go, Francis, like me, never takes anything for granted. He expressed how he felt grateful for living in a refugee camp in Kenya for ten years after being rescued as a child soldier. Rather than complain about filthy conditions, often going with less than one meal per day, Francis appreciated the safety and sporadic education opportunities the camp afforded him. Some of the youngsters weren't so lucky: those who lost their lives to violence, hunger, exhaustion and suchlike atrocities.

It didn't surprise me his attitude of gratitude continued to serve Francis well. He graduated with a Bachelor of Commerce degree from one of Australia's leading universities and was working as an advisor for one of Australia's largest banks. As if that wasn't enough, Francis had also published his captivating memoir, *A Child Escapes: A Boy Soldier's Journey from Civil War to Civil Pride*. On the back of that, he was now invited to events to inspire others to become the best version of themselves. Francis's gratefulness was an essential reminder that someone else could die for what we sometimes despise.

*   *   *

In 2019, I joined up with two highly decorated and battle-hardened cybersecurity executives and we founded the Cyber Leadership

Institute (CLI). The first was Jan Schreuder, a cybersecurity veteran with over thirty-five years' experience, including twenty-five years at a Big Four consulting firm where he held various leadership roles. During my time at PwC, Jan was already an experienced partner, so I felt highly privileged to partner with him a decade later when building our new enterprise. The other founder was Darren Argyle, the group chief information security risk officer (CISRO) for Standard Chartered Bank. Darren was also rated Top 100 Global CISOs and cybersecurity influencers by respected *SC Magazine* in 2017 and 2018.

We envisioned a world-class institution that would rapidly develop a strong tribe of global cyber leaders who actively collaborate to tackle what is arguably the greatest challenge of our generation — the menace of cybercrime. Our vision was very bold from the start: to equip at least ten thousand cyber leaders and business executives with practical leadership skills by the year 2025.

What we achieved in our first three years of operations exceeded even our own expectations. The CLI has managed to cut through geographies, cultures, genders and generations — positively impacting cyber leaders across dozens of countries. By the team of this writing, the CLI has trained cyber security and business executives from more than forty countries. Some of our graduates and premium members hold senior positions at some of the world's most iconic brands like Nike, World Economic Forum, HSBC, MTN, USA Airforce, Telstra, Standard Chartered, Salesforce and Amazon Web Services.

I was deeply humbled in August 2020 to be nominated by my co-founders to take on the chief executive officer role, when the CLI was starting to gain global traction. I look forward to working with my business partners and our dedicated team to rapidly build a closely bonded global community of cyber leaders who confidently lead their organisations towards cyber resilience.

My business partners and I are deeply aware that our industry has structural and deep-seated gender inequalities that need to be dismantled. According to a report by (ISC)^2, women represent a low 24 per cent of the cybersecurity workforce globally. As a minority myself, I have first-hand knowledge about structural and historical imbalances. I actively reject being drawn into protracted and worthless arguments about why women are to blame for their under-representation. The best form of leadership is action, so, together with my amazing co-founders, we decided to actively use our privileged position to do our best to correct this imbalance.

We decided from inception to go beyond LinkedIn blogs and arguments and help women who aspired for top leadership positions in a practical way. We have issued dozens of scholarships for women cyber leaders to participate in our leadership programs. By the time of this writing, 35 per cent of all CLI graduates are women, but more remains to be done.

One of my proudest moments came in December 2020 during our inaugural awards ceremony. We honoured individuals from our global community who had demonstrated exceptional leadership. The Cyber Leadership Program Skills Embodiment Award went to Diana Waithanji. I was deeply moved by Diana's inspiring story; she is the youngest CLI graduate, twenty-four years old at the time of her award. Growing up in Nyandarua County, Kenya, Diana had no access to the Internet, and like rural kids all across Africa, constantly faced formidable obstacles. I saw much of myself in her story. In high school, Diana was concerned about the tiny proportion of girls taking on sciences. At the young age of twenty-one years old, she decided to lead. She founded STEM Wahandisi La Femme, an initiative that mentors young girls in grassroots Kenya, encouraging them to take up engineering and tech courses.

This admirable leadership earned Diana a scholarship in our Cyber Leadership Program (CLP), where she collaborated with a global team of experienced cyber leaders. The strategic communication skills Diana mastered during the CLP helped her beat competition and gain entry to a highly coveted African-German tech fellowship program. She was one of the 40 young African change makers selected out of 9 100 applicants. Diana joined the cybersecurity team at SAP in Germany in 2021, one of the world's largest tech firms. Her incredible story of grit, passion and selflessness is a clear testament that there is no correlation between age and leadership. We are humbled to have had played a small part in helping Diana accelerate her career path.

A CLI graduate boasts on average ten to fifteen years on the front lines of cyber resilience. The aggregated experience gives our close-knit community incredible depth. But for our sustainability, we also have to actively engage and listen to upcoming cyber leaders like Diana Waithanji, who are not scared of thinking differently and shaking things up.

*　　*　　*

Towards the end of 2019, I planned for my fortieth birthday celebrations. On the morning of 15 May 2020, I would fly out to Dubai and wander across the Arabian Desert. From there, I would fly out to London and host our first-ever Cyber Leadership Conference in Europe. Then I would catch the train to Paris and indulge in some shopping. I would head over from France to Ancona, a bustling port on the eastern coast of Italy facing the Adriatic Sea. There I was scheduled to meet Marion Bertram at Kristin Diehl's house. To meet Marion for the first time, together with Kristin, would have been one of the best days of my life. It's a day I have dreamed of daily for two and a half decades; there was no better date than my fortieth and with that I booked the tickets. But as the day drew closer, the COVID-19 pandemic intensified through Europe, forcing us to defer everything indefinitely. Both Kristin and Marion deeply regretted the drastic change of plans, but there was nothing we could do other than send each other kindest wishes.

In 2019, I was so proud to see my daughter, Nyasha, overtaken by excitement, join the 'big people school' here in Sydney, Australia. Nyasha's journey sparked memories of thirty-one years before, that amazing day when I stepped into my own savannah primary school. I had no lunch box, no school uniform, no books, no shoes. It was just me, parents who always inspired possibility, and a teacher who tolerated zero nonsense. I can't wait for my son, Mukundi, the five-star general, to walk the same path.

Of all my struggles and accomplishments, that caps them all — seeing my kids go forward without any of the limits I wrestled with for three decades, growing into the healthy, confident, humble and kind people they were meant to become. They start their journeys in an unconstrained environment, with choices as many as grains of sand. As I look back, I see the generosity of so many people who made unthinkable sacrifices for me. But above all, I am grateful to God for raising a poor savannah boy from the dust.

Savannah Poem

Dear savannah
A land mighty and gentle in same measure.
The years I steered my father's cattle across your grasslands,
Transformed me, and marked me deeply.
The dreary and moody cumulonimbus, the king of the clouds
That towered high like giant dark mushrooms,

Unleashing raging storms,
Pounded me into submission.
You taught me to rise up from defeat,
Like Mosi-Oa-Tunya
The mighty smoke that thunders
To remain unyielding in the face of obstacles.
All the bouts imposed against my will,
The black wasps that injected venom deep into my scalp,
The livid bees that defended their liquid gold with their lives
Exposed the tenacity I never thought myself to possess.
Your daily exertions hardened my resolve,
Schooled me to be a man.
To push through pain and fight to the bitter end.
Your long, exacting, and tedious days,
Imparted enduring patience.
I learnt to play the long game,
Because you gave no mulligans.
You schooled me to pave my own path through the thickets.
As I scavenged for mobola plums, snot apples and other organic treats,
That you so generously gave,
As I quenched my thirst from the cisterns that oozed perpetually
from Mother Earth.
When my cows drifted and grazed crops
Justice was swift and bitter,
Instilling the habit to own up when I mess up.
That nasty game of fongo
Induced durable street smarts,
Because if I snoozed, I got cracked.
Whenever I felt like quitting
You reminded me again and again,

That I could handle the grind one more time.
Through you, I discovered that the pain of regret,
Is way more bitter than the agony of failure.
You taught me that I can be what I can't see.
You thrilled me and terrified at the same time.
The first day I stumbled into your grasslands,
I was as fragile as a baby gazelle.
But I left tougher than the Tasmanian devil.
I'll forever be grateful to you for the gift of obstacles,
The long and winding journey of grit, grace, and gratitude.

ACKNOWLEDGMENTS

I offer my deepest gratitude to the following incredible people, without whom this book would not have been possible.

My amazing wife Fadzi and our two kids — Nyasha Valerie and Mukundi Christian — thank you for your unconditional love and support. I could not have achieved this without your sacrifices.

Thank you to my visionary parents, Philip and Helena Zongo, for your unthinkable sacrifices and unwavering belief in the power of education to defeat poverty and despair.

I am eternally grateful to two amazing Germans, Marion Bertram and Kristin Diehl, for giving me one of life's most precious gifts — a rare chance to pursue my boundless potential through education which they selflessly sponsored.

Next, I would like to thank my siblings — Osward, Viola (of blessed memory), Cecilia, Maidei, Lancelot, Rosemary, Letwina and Salome — thank you for your unwavering support and love.

A special thank you to my amazing friend Ivi Olszewska for believing in my story and never leaving my corner throughout this protracted grind.

My warm thanks to my editors Bernadette Foley, Paul Anderson, and Emma Moylan. Thank you for steadfastly guiding me through several drafts with incredible patience and empathy.

I am greatly indebted to my incredible friends Judah Chikomba, Taff Karimanzira, Richard Long, Kemi Daji, Sam Spry, Nandi Spry,

Kuda Kwatara, Innocent Ndoda, Brighton Mukuvari, Pfungwa Murombo, and Tamara Koch. I am grateful for your unwavering encouragement that pushed me through the difficult moments and your friendship that kept me grounded.

A heartfelt thank you to my dear friends who volunteered their time to peer review my early drafts: Andrea Penze, Kathleen Lo, Privilege Simango, Tapiwa Mupereki, Al Xiao, Prince Sibanda, and Joseph Chidwala. Your insights were pivotal in the formation of my memoir.

My brother and friend Claudius Sithole, thank you for your unconditional friendship and support. I am blessed to have a friend like you.

I would like to thank my business partners, Jan Schreuder and Darren Argyle, for your camaraderie and the fantastic entrepreneur-ship ride.

Thank you also to my LinkedIn connections for your overwhelming response to my shared blogs and for encouraging me to go beyond them and write this memoir.

And finally, my deepest thanks to you, dear reader, for choosing to read my memoir and sharing my journey of grit, grace and gratitude.

ABOUT THE AUTHOR

Phillimon Zongo is the chief executive officer of the Cyber Leadership Institute, an enterprise that has trained cyber and business leaders from more than 40 countries. Zongo has received numerous accolades for exemplary leadership, including:

- 2017 winner of the ISACA Global Best Article Award, one of ISACA's highest international honours that recognises individuals who have made major contributions to the fields of IT governance and cyber security.

- 2020 Global Top 100 Most Influential People of African Descent (MIPAD) — Fourth Industrial Revolution Category. MIPAD is a unique global list that identifies high achievers of African descent globally in support of the International Decade for People of African Descent (2015-2024).

- Author of The Five Anchors of Cyber Resilience, named top five cyber security books at the 2021 UK National Cyber Awards.

- Winner of the 2018 Zim Awards Outstanding Achievement (Australia), 2018 Australian African Professional Excellence Award, and Pride of Africa Asia Outstanding in Business Award (China) — recognitions for achievements that far exceed the norm

ENDNOTES

1   Totem Network Africa. 11 October 2018. 'Nhari IneNdoro /UneNdoro Origins'. Available online: https://totemnetwork.blogspot.com/2018/10/nhari-inendoro-origins.html

2   The Patriot. 2 May 2019. 'Chaminuka: Prophet of Zimbabwe, prince of peace'. Available online: https://www.thepatriot.co.zw/old_posts/chaminuka-prophet-of-zimbabwe-prince-of-peace/

3   Paul Berliner. June 1993. The Soul of Mbira: 'Music and Traditions of the Shona People of Zimbabwe', Chicago University Press. Available online: https://books.google.com.au/books?id=ag_85hJI9aMC&sitesec=buy&source=gbs_vpt_read

4   Misheck Samanyanga. 7 December 2019. 'Mutasa kingdom (district)', Zim Tribes. Available online: https://www.blog.zimtribes.com/mutasa-kingdom-district/

5   Michigan State University. 'A Description of the Ceremony of Kurova Guva'. Available Online: http://pdfproc.lib.msu.edu/?file=/DMC/African%20Journals/pdfs/Journal%20of%20the%20University%20of%20Zimbabwe/vol2n1/juz002001008.pdf

6   Simba Mazoyo. 30 December 2016. 'The words we corrupted into Shona', Nehanda Radio. Available online: https://nehandaradio.com/2016/12/30/words-corrupted-shona/

7   AfrikaIsWoke.com. 'Pacesetter Novels: An African Literary Classic'. Available Online: https://www.afrikaiswoke.com/pacesetter-novels-african-literary-classic/

8   Jairos Saunyama. 24 April 2018. 'The legend of 'Dhiziri paChinhoyi' revisited', Newsday. Available Online: https://www.newsday.co.zw/2018/04/the-legend-of-dhiziri-pachinhoyi-revisited/

9   Vlad Sokhin. 'The Secret Cult of Nyau Dancers', Maptia. Available Online: https://maptia.com/vlad_sokhin/stories/the-secret-cult-of-nyau-dancers

10 Anna Kajumulo Tibaijuka. 18 July 2005. 'Report of the Fact-Finding Mission to Zimbabwe to assess the Scope and Impact of Operation Murambatsvina by the UN Special Envoy on Human Settlements Issues in Zimbabwe', United Nations. Available Online: http://hrlibrary.umn.edu/research/ZIM%20UN%20 Special%20Env%20Report.pdf

11 BBC. 9 March 2020. 'Zimbabwe crisis: Parents of school dropouts face jail'. Available Online: https://www.bbc.com/news/world-africa-51803825

Printed in Great Britain
by Amazon

74857523R00154